Couples Therapy

COUPLES THERAPY
A Nontraditional Approach

DANIEL B. WILE
California State University, Hayward
University of California, Berkeley

A WILEY-INTERSCIENCE PUBLICATION

JOHN WILEY & SONS
New York • Chichester • Brisbane • Toronto • Singapore

This publication is designed to provide accurate and
authoritative information in regard to the subject
matter covered. It is sold with the understanding that
the publisher is not engaged in rendering legal, accounting,
or other professional service. If legal advice or other
expert assistance is required, the services of a competent
professional person should be sought. *From a Declaration
of Principles jointly adopted by a Committee of the
American Bar Association and a Committee of Publishers.*

Library of Congress Cataloging in Publication Data:

Wile, Daniel B.
    Couples therapy, a nontraditional approach.

    "A Wiley-Interscience publication."
    Includes bibliographical references and index.
    1. Marital psychotherapy. I Title. [DNLM:
1. Marital therapy. WM 55 W676c]

RC488. 5.W55   616.89'159   81-4958
ISBN 0-471-07811-5   AACR2

Printed in the United States of America

10 9 8 7 6 5 4

To Joanne, my principal collaborator,
professional and otherwise

Foreword

This is a book about collaborating. Therapists collaborate with couples and partners collaborate with one another. This may seem naive to most therapists. Although partners usually have every intention of collaborating with one another and with the therapist, most therapists do not count this conscious intention for much, seeing partners as untrustworthy allies who are just as ready to sabotage the therapy and one another as to collaborate.

Of course, all couples therapists believe that some degree of collaboration is essential but are afraid of being drawn into the couple's manipulations and into a tangle of accusations and rationalizations. As Dan Wile shows, what unites the three major approaches to couples therapy (psychoanalytic, behavioral, systems) is a belief in the necessity to cut through the web of the troubled relationship by relying heavily on the uses of authority. These therapists are like hardworking labor–management arbitrators: arguing, cajoling, threatening, and confronting. The systems therapist wages a kind of guerrilla war against the couple (or against the couple "system") that makes it difficult for the partners to continue to wage their own battle with one another. The behavior therapist authoritatively imposes a new relationship on the couple in which conflict is ruled out. The analytic couples therapist may insistently confront partners with their commitment to the continuation of conflict, that is, may insist on having them recognize their wishes to sabotage the relationship and the therapy. In this perspective, to collaborate with the partners is to be caught in the web of their troubled relationship.

In his critique of the three major approaches, Dr. Wile observes that the couples therapist typically avoids conversational give-and-take, believing that such discussion would be subtly subverted, since behind the seemingly tangled web is the fine hand of an unconscious (or "covert") design. This vision is directly traceable to the principle of unconscious purposivism, a now widespread legacy of psychoanalysis. Psychoanalysis has taught us to be suspicious of conscious intentions and to look for the unconscious purposes that contradict them. The student with work inhibitions, seemingly desperate about not graduating, really wants to flunk out. The speaker who panics at losing his voice is secretly pleased at not having to make his speech. The frigid woman who appears to feel guilty and depressed about not responding sexually really does not want to enjoy sex. People who beseech the therapist to help them not overeat really want to be fat. And, of course, couples in conflict who act as if they are desperate to solve their problems have no real intention of giving up their punitive or exploitive ways.

Such suspiciousness about what the patient says and does rules out collaboration in psychoanalysis, despite talk of the need to establish a "working alliance." The analyst cannot help treating the patient as an adversary, as someone possessed by an unconscious "will" that never sleeps, ever ready to take advantage of the slightest misstep to undermine and thwart the aims of the analysis. As a result, analytic treatment is famous for its prickly silences and truculent pronouncements. Most analysts have managed to hold fast to this position, inured to a workday in which they are regularly accused of being cold and inhuman. Whatever a "working alliance" might turn out to look like in such a context, the opportunities for analyst and patient to work shoulder-to-shoulder against a common foe are severely limited by the principle of unconscious purposivism.

This principle has proved to be the most enduring element of psychoanalytic thinking, appealing even to those therapists who reject all the other elements of that model. A Gestalt group would give no more credence to the student with study blocks, the frigid woman, and the overeater than would an analyst. The group is likely to take any smile of embarrassment as evidence of a secret enjoyment of the symptom and a readiness to sabotage the group's efforts to help. The same style of interpretation characterizes Synanon games and other encounter therapies. It is also exemplified by est exhortations, TA's exposes of unconscious game playing, the insistence on the fact of unconscious choice by existential therapists, and unconscious power plays by systems therapists. Typically, the client must be confronted, shaken up, made to confess. Although it has not been said in so many words, collaboration is thought of as a refuge for unsophisticated or irresponsible therapists.

Since many therapists now reject psychoanalytic thinking, what makes the belief in unconscious purposivism so widespread and so compelling? Relationships can be so tenaciously and consistently depriving and frustrating that it is hard to believe that they have no purpose in being this way. The partners *must* be getting something out of it. Why else would they keep it up? Their conflicts must be perpetuated by unconscious wishes or, by another name, covert patterns of reinforcement. Even systems theorists argue that systems are the product of unconscious wishes (power plays).

This makes it easy to explain what keeps the system going. The couple wants it that way. If, with Dr. Wile, we assume that couples do *not* want it that way, and that relationships are just as frustrating as they look, then it no longer is easy to explain what keeps the system going. This requires the therapist to approach the partners as expert witnesses on their relationship, a collaboration that serves as a model for the way the partners need to approach one another.

Collaborating is difficult and, at best, time-consuming for the therapist who believes that couples are getting something out of their apparently depriving relationship, since the couple usually is aware only of feeling deprived and desperately wanting a change. When the therapist does take seriously what the couple is aware of, and even helps the partners more fully express it, it becomes harder to believe that they have an investment in continuing the conflict. The clarity and simplicity that the purposivistic explanation offers then looks like the product of circumstantial evidence.

A parallel with the Postal Service might seem to make the point. No one wants the mail to be late or lost, but this is the predictable outcome of a tenacious system. If one were to assume that the underlying purpose of the Postal Service is to frustrate its users, then the Postal Service would look a lot more irrational than it is. Dan Wile asserts that current explanations make couple systems look a lot more irrational than they really are, and that this is what leads couples therapists to oppose these systems with non-rational and noncollaborative methods.

In his review of a host of cases taken from the current literature, Wile shows how what appears to be the result of unconscious design is just the opposite—a system that has spun out of control, satisfying no one. Thought of this way, relationships look much less diabolical, the partners look like more trustworthy therapeutic allies, and, more important, the couple relationship itself can be thought of as a vehicle for change. Wile can even take the position that it is the *function* of relationships to have a therapeutic effect. Although this function is rarely realized in most relationships, the therapist will want to know why, in any given instance, this resource is unavailable.

From this position, not only do troubled relationships look less irrational, they look more *normal*. As long as such relationships are seen as a reflection of unconscious purposes, they appear arbitrary and deviant. Wile represents the position that relationships are not reducible to the idiosyncrasies of the particular couple but are, instead, reflections of the human condition. In this sense, troubled partners are only encountering more directly the issues that underlie everyone's relationships. The task of therapy is then to help them to work on whatever issue on the frontier of intimacy their problem represents.

Bernard Apfelbaum, Ph.D.

Preface

Practitioners entering the field of couples therapy are greeted with a rather pessimistic view of human existence. Intimate relations are conceptualized as pragmatic arrangements between individuals. Partners are urged to renounce their hopes and fantasies and, instead, negotiate and compromise. People are seen as acting out primitive wishes, manipulating and double binding their partners, and preferring their pathological couple systems to more healthy ways of relating. Given this view of couples, it is not surprising that many therapists have adopted an adversary approach, pitting themselves against the couple system and the partners' "infantile" wishes.

The purpose of this book is to present an orientation to couples therapy that, in contrast to the traditional adversary model, makes therapeutic contact on the side of each partner and enables each to feel more entitled to his or her position. I suspect that much of what I say will resonate with other therapists' experiences and beliefs. When I described an early form of my approach, many practitioners expressed relief in finding an orientation that viewed partners and partner interactions in a neutral and nonaccusatory manner.

This approach is founded on a simple shift. Instead of being seen as gratifying regressive impulses and exploiting each other, troubled partners are viewed as deprived, trapped, and isolated. This immediately places the therapist on the side of each individual and legitimizes feelings to which partners might previously have felt unentitled. The result is a couples therapy based on incorporating, rather than renouncing, fantasies, arguments, and problems.

Daniel B. Wile

Oakland, California
July 1981

Acknowledgments

Alan Plum, Ph.D., Betty Wenz, Ph.D., and Bernard Apfelbaum, Ph.D., read the manuscript and made many important suggestions. Joanne Wile, LCSW, contributed to the day-by-day formulation of ideas and served as my major editor.

This book is based in part on two articles, "Is a confrontational tone necessary in conjoint therapy?" *Journal of Marriage and Family Counseling,* 1978, **4**, 3, 11–18, and "An insight approach to marital therapy," *Journal of Marital and Family Therapy,* 1979, **5**, 4, 43–52. Appreciation is expressed to this journal and to the following publishers, authors, and editors for permission to reprint material.

Ables, Billie S., and Brandsma, Jeffrey. *Therapy for couples: A clinician's guide for effective treatment.* San Francisco: Jossey-Bass, 1977.

Anonymous. Toward the differentiation of a self in one's own family. In James L. Framo (Ed.), *Family Interaction: A dialogue between family researchers and family therapists.* Copyright © 1972 by Springer Publishing Company, Inc., New York.

Freud, S. *Introductory lectures on psychoanalysis. Standard edition,* Vol. 16. Translated and edited by James Strachey. Copyright © 1963 by George Allen & Unwin. Copyright © 1966, by W. W. Norton & Company. Copyright © 1965, 1964, 1963 by James Strachey. Copyright 1920, 1935 by Edward L. Bernays.

Jacobson, N. S., and Margolin, G. *Marital therapy: Strategies based on social learning and behavior exchange principles.* New York: Brunner/Mazel, 1979.

Paolino, T. J., and McCrady, B. S. (Eds.). *Marriage and marital therapy: Psychoanalytic, behavioral and systems theory perspectives.* New York: Brunner/Mazel, 1978.

D. B. W.

Contents

1

Background Theory

1

Introduction

This book presents an approach to couples therapy that differs from conventional views in two important ways: (1) it rejects the traditional image of troubled partners as gratifying regressive impulses and seeking exploitive control and views them as deprived of the minimal satisfaction and control necessary to make a relationship livable; (2) instead of helping partners negotiate and compromise, it encourages them to incorporate their conflicts into the relationship.

ARE PARTNERS EXPLOITIVE OR DEPRIVED?

People struggling with relationship problems look and often feel ridiculous. They argue over trifles, exchange barbed endearments, sulk, and rage. The adjectives and phrases with which some therapists describe these individuals reflect the absurd and pathological appearance of their behavior. Partners are viewed as sadomasochistic, symbiotic, exploitive, narcissistic, dependent, immature, controlling, deceitful, toxic, double binding, manipulative, and as colluding, having hidden agendas, being dishonest, or playing games. This book challenges such conceptualizations and offers what in my opinion is a less accusing and more accurate explanation of couples' behavior.

My approach is based on a style of psychodynamic reasoning developed by Bernard Apfelbaum (1977b, 1980a, 1980c). The thesis, in essence, is that troubled individuals, traditionally viewed as gratifying infantile impulses, are actually deprived of what in many cases are ordinary adult satisfactions. This simple shift has dramatic consequences. When examined from this new perspective, traditional couples therapy approaches are found to have serious problems. Interventions that made sense given the therapists' particular framework now appear accusatory, moralistic, invalidating and, in general, counterproductive.

The recognition that partners are deprived immediately places the therapist on the side of each, a favorable position from which to do couples therapy. The interventions this kind of therapist may make—emphasing how each partner is feeling trapped and isolated—will be inherently reassuring to

2

individuals, validating experiences and feelings to which they previously felt unentitled. The result may be an increased appreciation not only for their own positions but for those of their partners. People who feel entitled to their positions will have less need to compulsively renounce or defend them and, as a consequence, may be better able to work out their difficulties.

SOLVING PROBLEMS VERSUS INCORPORATING THEM

The goal of much contemporary couples therapy is to exclude irrationality from relationships and to eliminate problems. Partners are encouraged to renounce their unreasonable demands, uncontrolled fighting, and fantasy based expectations and to negotiate and compromise. This book questions such an approach. Irrational reactions, viewed by some therapists as purely destructive, are seen here as providing important information about the relationship. The irritability, sulking, and romanticized longings of partners are often the only available indicators of an alienation and dissatisfaction from which both may be suffering. The appropriate therapeutic task, accordingly, is to expose these underlying issues. The ultimate goal is a relationship in which partners are able to use their irrational reactions as an interpersonal barometer, an instrument for measuring the present relationship atmosphere.

Lederer and Jackson (1968) are perhaps the best known of the authors who warn about the danger of unrealistic expectations in relationships. The title of their book, *The Mirages of Marriage,* suggests this concern, and they begin by describing several fantasy based misconceptions of marriage to which they attribute major responsibility for contemporary marital unhappiness.

The need to challenge fantasy based expectations and to reorient relationships on more rational grounds appears to be the one issue in the scattered field of couples therapy on which therapists tend to agree. Authors from each of what Gurman (1978) describes as the three major schools of couples therapy make essentially the same point. Jackson (Lederer and Jackson, 1968), an originator of the systems approach, discusses the value of setting relationships upon a *quid pro quo* basis and training partners to bargain. Sager (1976), writing from a psychoanalytic perspective, talks about the need to renounce unconscious fantasy based expectations and the infantile wishes associated with these expectations and to renegotiate the marital contract on a more realistic basis. Stuart (1969) and Weiss (1975), approaching from the behavior therapy orientation, show partners how to positively reinforce each other, satisfying each other's needs in exchange for having their own needs satisfied.

These authors reject a romantic or idealistic view of relationships and instead appeal to the notion of enlightened self-interest. Intimate relations are conceptualized as pragmatic arrangements between individuals. The terminology employed is derived from labor negotiations (bargaining, contracts, negotiation, *quid pro quo*).

There is much to be said for this approach. The excessive expectations, requirements, and claims that partners have with respect to each other, spoken and unspoken, wreak havoc with relationships and it would be to everyone's advantage to have a forum in which these requests could be clearly stated, their realistic or unrealistic nature evaluated, and a compromise achieved.

There are serious defects in this orientation, however. One is the isolating effect it may have on partners. The process of bargaining and negotiation implies an adversary relationship. Each person is pursuing his or her own separate wishes and destiny. Another problem is the dismissal of fantasy. Fantasy, which provides much of the charm in couple interactions, is viewed as incompatible with a workable relationship. A third problem is that the partners' own tendency to make compromises and be reasonable may be causing much of the difficulty. A husband who withholds anger in an attempt to avoid a dispute may merely be setting the stage for an even worse fight when the warded-off anger eventually reappears.

A preferable approach is to incorporate the conflict into the relationship. Constance Apfelbaum talks about helping individuals "inhabit" their problems and fantasies. Partners who have frequent fights often devote themselves to avoiding fights. Their effort, following each battle, is just to be glad it is over and to work hard to prevent another. Such individuals are "trying to not have the relationship they are having" (Apfelbaum, 1980a).

The alternative is for them to acknowledge that "we're a couple that gets into fights" and to become joint experts in studying their fights. They might become skillful in anticipating when a battle will occur, what it will be about, and how it will develop. When the fight is over, they might then be able to get together and review what happened. Instead of dismissing the unfulfilled relationship fantasies that lie at the root of their dispute, they might be able to commiserate with each other about them. What they would be doing, in essence, is incorporating their problems, arguments, and fantasies into the relationship.

2

Depth Analysis
Versus Ego Analysis

Freudian psychoanalysis can be thought of as a kind of primordial ocean out of which differing and even incompatible theories emerge. Freud himself developed several lines of such competing theories. Apfelbaum (1977b, 1980a, 1980c) has distinguished two basic types of psychoanalytic or psychodynamic reasoning, each leading to a distinctive and internally consistent clinical approach. The first, which he calls "depth analysis" or "id analysis," traces psychological symptoms to infantile impulses and developmental defects. This is the more traditional approach and is what we have come to associate with the term psychoanalysis. This form of psychodynamic reasoning is also the basis of most other contemporary psychotherapeutic approaches including, as I show later, family systems theory.

The second form of psychodynamic reasoning, which Apfelbaum calls "ego analysis,"* is less familiar and to my knowledge was not distinguished as a separate approach prior to Apfelbaum's 1977 paper. This orientation does not focus on the regressive gratification and secondary gain (e.g., control over others) that people obtain from their symptoms, but on the obvious deprivation they are experiencing in their lives and the lack of control they have over others.

My approach to couples is based on a rejection of depth analysis and an acceptance of ego analysis. Because of this, careful attention will now be devoted to describing the differences between these two orientations. This chapter begins by presenting five examples, taken from the field of psychotherapy at large, and considers them from both depth analytic and ego analytic perspectives. The second section describes the major factors distinguishing the two approaches. The third section presents a theoretical rationale for the ego analytic orientation.

---

*The term "ego analysis" has the disadvantage of being easily confused with "ego psychology" (i.e., the work of Hartmann, Rappaport, Blanck and Blanck, and others). Apfelbaum, however, is talking about something very different.

FIVE EXAMPLES

The Student

Murray (1964) describes a college student, "extremely shy and unhappy with people," whose response to an unexpected low grade in an important course is to defecate while taking a bath and smear his body, especially his genitals, with feces. Murray, adopting the depth analytic orientation, emphasizes the gratification this patient is obtaining, describing it as a "fulfillment of primitive desires" and as an expression of "unconscious, unresolved anal excitements." He sees this individual as having regressed to a state of "narcissistic entitlement" in which he claims "a right to reject the rest of the world and make it hostile and evil, to end up with the feeling, 'only mine is good and wonderful and I will have nothing else.' "

The ego analytic interpretation is that defecating in the tub and rubbing himself with feces is a graphic expression of this patient's sense of defeat and humiliation at his academic failure. The student is thus seen not as narcissistically contented but as narcissistically distressed.

The Partners

In a recent case conference at an outpatient clinic, a husband was described as making no apparent effort to conceal his extramarital affair while his wife seemed relatively unconcerned about the whole matter. One conference participant suggested that these partners were engaged in a sadomasochistic interaction while another believed that the husband was exhibitionistically flaunting the affair, and the wife was voyeuristically enjoying it. Both therapists felt that these partners were obtaining too much gratification from their interaction to be willing to change. A third participant offered an ego analytic view. She pointed to the fact that these partners had been unable to discuss day-to-day disappointments and resentments throughout the marriage. The husband's affair could be viewed as a consequence of these unexpressed and perhaps unrecognized feelings. Since he had not been able to talk about his marital dissatisfactions he was now acting on them. The overt manner in which he was conducting the affair could be thought of as a desperate and clumsy effort to break through the mutual denial that had characterized their relationship. The betrayed wife was having as much difficulty expressing her feelings now as she appeared to have been having throughout the marriage. She was unable to communicate her sense of helplessness, panic, and rage, and instead was acting on her helplessness, proceeding as if the affair were not happening.

The Aunt

Konrad Lorenz (1966, p. 55) writes about a widowed aunt of his who never kept a maid longer than eight to ten months. The aunt was always delighted with a new servant, praised her to the skies, and swore that she had at last found the right one. In the course of the next few months her judgment cooled, she found small faults, then bigger ones, and toward the end of the stated period she discovered hateful qualities in the poor girl, who was finally discharged without a reference after a violent quarrel. After this explosion the old lady was once more prepared to find a perfect angel in her next employee.

Eric Fromm (1973), in discussing this anecdote, attributed the aunt's behavior to her "narcissistic, exploitative character."

She demanded that a servant should be completely "devoted" to her, have no interests of her own, and gladly accept the role of a creature who is happy to serve her. She approaches each new servant with the phantasy that she is the one who will fulfill her expectations. After a short "honeymoon" during which the aunt's fantasy is still sufficiently effective to blind her to the fact that the servant is not "right"—and perhaps also helped by the fact that the servant in the beginning makes every effort to please her new employer—the aunt wakes up to the recognition that the servant is not willing to live up to the role for which she has been cast . . . she experiences intense disappointment and rage, as any narcissistic-exploitative person does when frustrated. Not being aware that the cause of this rage lies in her impossible demands, she rationalizes her disappointment by accusing the servant. (pp. 22–23)

The ego analytic explanation is that the problem is not the aunt's narcissistic-exploitive character and her impossible demands, but rather her inability to make demands.* The finding of "small faults, then bigger ones" ending with the discovery of "hateful qualities" and a "violent quarrel" is a common occurrence with individuals who have difficulty making complaints. The aunt needed her servants to be perfect and to anticipate her every need because she was unable to tell them what she wanted them to do or confront them for not doing it. Underlying her inability to make demands may be a feeling on her part that she is not worthy of good care.

The Wife

Don Jackson (1959) describes a woman who, in response to her husband's friendly suggestion that they go to a movie, states that "there's nothing

---

*Constance Apfelbaum, who brought the example to my attention, suggested this interpretation.

good playing" and "besides I have a headache." They thus end up watching TV, which is what she wanted to do in the first place.

Jackson describes this woman's response as a "ploy" and as a demonstration of how she has all the power and control in the relationship. Certain psychoanalytically oriented therapists might go on from there to describe this wife as a castrating woman, attributing her behavior to an underlying hatred toward or competition with men associated with unresolved male sibling rivalry, penis envy, or preoedipal rage toward her mother displaced on her husband.

A therapist who approaches this situation from an ego analytic perspective might point out that this woman's alleged "power" is difficult to distinguish from powerlessness. Describing her as controlling and powerful ignores the fact that she had to be cautious and indirect in order to express her wishes. She would have had significantly more power, this line of reasoning goes, if it were possible for her to reply to her husband's invitation by saying simply, "Actually, there's a TV show on tonight that I have been looking forward to all day." Rather than being an uninhibited and calculating tyrant with a pathological need to control everything that goes on in the relationship, this woman may actually be suffering from the reverse: a limitation in her ability to make her wishes known and exert direct control in the relationship.

The Game Player

A premier example of an Eric Berne game and "the original stimulus for the concept of games" (Berne, 1964) is "Why Don't You—Yes But." Here the game player asks for advice and then systematically rejects all suggestions offered. "Yes, that's a good idea," this person says, "but it won't work because of such-and-such" or "I tried it already and it did not help." Berne sees the game player as enjoying the game. The "payoff," he explains, is the satisfaction of rejecting suggestions, demonstrating the inadequacy of others and, in general, refusing to surrender.

A contrasting view is that game players are not at all getting what they want. The advice being offered is often not very good. Furthermore, people who talk about their problems generally do not like to be brushed aside with simple solutions but want others to appreciate the extent and difficulty of the problem. These game players, it thus appears, are relatively ineffective in communicating their needs and motivating others to gratify them. Their "yes buts" may be the best way they have available, given their lack of awareness of what they want or their inability to complain about not getting it, of saying "I want to be listened to rather than given advice" or "Why are you giving me all these useless suggestions?"

THE ESSENCE OF THE DEPTH ANALYTIC-EGO ANALYTIC DISTINCTION

The five examples just discussed come from different areas in the psychotherapeutic establishment. Murray employs a traditional psychoanalytic orientation, Fromm is a major figure in the interpersonal–character–cultural school, Jackson is an originator of the communications and systems approaches to family therapy, and Berne's notion of game playing is a major element in many present day approaches. It seems clear that the issue described here is a pervasive feature in contemporary psychotherapy.

Gratification Versus Deprivation

What is the common element running through these pairs of alternatives? The first interpretation in each case, the depth analytic interpretation, attributes the problem to infantile or destructive impulses. Attention is focused on the student's anal-erotic drives, the partners' sadomasochistic or exhibitionistic-voyeuristic wishes, the aunt's narcissistic-exploitive impulses, the wife's controlling needs, and the game player's oral, manipulative wishes.

The second interpretation in each example, the ego analytic interpretation, considers the apparent impulselike behavior of these individuals to be a superficial manifestation of a more fundamental problem, an underlying inhibition or inability. The student's feces play is seen as the consequence of his inability to experience and verbalize his sense of disappointment and humiliation, the partners' sadomasochism as the result of their inability to discuss their relationship, the aunt's narcissistic-exploitiveness as the consequence of her inability to give orders, the wife's controlling behavior as the result of her inability to state wishes, and the game player's "yes buts" as the consequence of an inability to complain about unwanted or useless advice.

The problem with these individuals is not their impulses but their feeling of unentitlement to their impulses and feelings (Apfelbaum, 1980c). If they had felt entitled, they might have been able to express their feelings in direct and straightforward ways rather than in the inhibited and offensive forms they did.

These alternative types of psychodynamic reasoning lead to dramatically differing pictures of the individual's state of gratification. Therapists who focus on partners' underlying "infantile impulses" are likely to see these individuals as obtaining significant gratification and, in fact, as perhaps obtaining too much gratification to be willing to give them up. The first two participants at the conference ("the partners" example) talked about the unwillingness of these partners to renounce their sadomasochistic or exhibitionistic–voyeuristic gratification, and Murray (1964) and Fromm (1973) wrote about the reluctance of the student and aunt to give up their narcissistic satisfactions.

Therapists who adopt this general view appear to assume that gratification exists behind all human actions. People only do things because they are getting something out of it. If they engage in destructive interactions or remain in unhappy marriages, the reasoning goes, they do so because they are obtaining substantial gratification from it. The notions of secondary gain and Skinnerian conditioning are thus raised to the level of a universal prepotent principle.

Therapists who adopt an ego analytic perspective (e.g., Wachtel, 1977, pp. 56–60) are likely to see individuals not as gratifying regressive impulses but as deprived of what in some sense might be considered ordinary adult satisfactions. (In some cases, in fact, these individuals are seen as deprived of the very gratification in which depth analysts view them as overindulging.) The student is suffering from what he experiences as a serious setback in his personal ambitions and career plans, the partners have been deprived of the minimal sense of contact and intimacy that most couples take for granted, and the wife, aunt, and game player are unable to express wishes, make complaints, and in general to establish the control that anyone might need to make an interaction or relationship tolerable.

If we were to fully appreciate the conditions under which many couples exist, our amazement is likely only to be that people appear to have great tolerance for what may seem unbearable or unlivable circumstances. Ego analysis draws attention to an obvious truth about human life that depth analysis tends to obscure. A certain minimum of satisfaction and safety is required if people are to function in adequate ways. Haley (1959) described the catastrophic conditions in which family members disqualify and disaffirm everything anyone in the family says and does. People who are exposed to such chronic deprivation and repeated violation cannot be expected to behave normally. If they react with dependent, narcissistic, exploitive, manipulative, sadistic, or masochistic behavior, it is not because they are gratifying infantile impulses. They are suffering psychological malnutrition resulting from an inadequate emotional diet.

Control

The term control has come to have a negative connotation. People are not supposed to control, dominate, exploit, or manipulate each other. We are told to accept others and to take responsibility for our own needs. This popular philosophy, although having a certain validity, violates an important human truth. People have just been described as requiring a certain mini-

premise

mum of satisfaction to make a relationship tolerable. They also require a certain minumum of control. Individuals need to have a way of asserting their needs, making complaints, bringing issues of concern to their partners' attention, correcting problems, and in general getting through to and having an effect on their partners if their relationships are to be viable.

While depth analysts would view the wife, aunt, and game player as excessively controlling, demanding, or manipulative, I see them as unable to establish necessary control. This fact is clear in the case of the wife. While the depth analyst might seek an effective way of confronting the wife with her controlling behavior and her domination over her husband, an ego analyst such as Fenichel (1941) would suggest that the problem is her fear of being controlling. She is so concerned about the danger of being selfish and controlling that she holds back rather ordinary statements of wishes (e.g., "I would like to stay home and watch the TV show that I have been looking forward to all day"). The task of therapy, accordingly, is for her to become more aware of her fear of being controlling and more accepting of her wishes. The ultimate result will be a greater sense of freedom in and control of the relationship.

The example of the aunt can be stated in similar terms. While the depth analyst might look for an effective way of confronting her with her narcissistic exploitiveness and her impossible demands, I would point out to her that it is her fear of being too demanding, based perhaps on the concern that she is not worthy of good treatment, and her consequent attempt to suppress or repress all criticisms and complaints that lead to her growing antipathy toward her servants.

The ego analyst, it thus appears, is seeing this wife and aunt as already saying to themselves what the depth analyst wishes to tell them. The wife is worried about being too controlling and the aunt is concerned about being too demanding. The appropriate therapeutic task, from the ego analytic view, is to point out the existence and effect of these self-hating ideas—that is, to counteract these individuals' tendencies to be depth analysts to themselves.

The two types of therapist would also make opposite interventions to Berne's game players. Although depth analysts might describe the games these individuals are playing and, in so doing, confront them with their manipulativeness, I view them as inhibited or deficient in their ability to get what they want from others—that is, as unable to exert sufficient control.

To summarize, depth analysts and ego analysts view troubled partners in sharply contrasting ways. Whereas depth analysts see them as obtaining significant infantile gratification and seeking exploitive control over their partners, I picture them as deprived of the minimal satisfaction and control that anyone would need to make a relationship livable.

THE THEORETICAL UNDERPINNINGS OF EGO ANALYSIS

Since ego analysis has had only a brief history as a distinguishable approach, it has not developed the theoretical superstructure that exists for depth analysis. The following is my attempt to provide it with one.

Psychodynamic Issues

Depth analysis and ego analysis have different psychodynamic explanations for infantile-appearing behavior. The depth analyst's explanation is straightforward. The behavior of disturbed adults appears infantile because it is infantile. The uncontrolled outbursts of accusing partners and the dependent pleading of certain demanding partners are viewed as a residue or reemergence of an underlying anal sadism and oral dependency.

Whereas depth analysis attributes the problem to impulses, ego analysis (e.g., Wachtel, 1977, pp. 43–48) attributes it to defenses. An angry feeling or impulse, experienced and expressed in a direct and straightforward manner, often has a clarifying and beneficial effect. It is only when it is suppressed or repressed that it obtains an infantile quality. As generally happens when anger is warded off, it reappears in regressive forms, as sudden rage, sadistic fantasies, or chronic irritability (Freud's "return of the repressed").

These reemerged or derivative expressions can be divided into two general types: exaggerated expressions and subdued ones. In the first case, suppressed anger breaks through in intense and magnified forms. An example in couples therapy is the outbursts or tantrums of the mutually accusing couple.

In the second case, warded off anger reappears in diffuse forms such as whining, nagging, complaining, or irritability. While certain depth analysts view this behavior as expressions of oral or anal sadism, I see it as inhibited expressions of ordinary anger. Complainers cannot stop complaining because they never get a chance to state their complaints fully. "Nags" are reduced to offering repeated, hesitant, unwanted reminders because they are unable to confront partners with their failure to complete the requested task.

These two categories of derivative expressions provide a useful insight into the concepts underlying "assertive training" (Alberti and Emmons, 1976), a method sometimes used in couples therapy. Such training is based on three notions: assertion, nonassertion, and aggression. Partners who are nonassertive or aggressive are taught how to be assertive. Ego analysis provides a dynamic understanding of these three response types. Assertion is seen as the original healthy form of the impulse. If fear or self-criticism (guilt) prevent people from being assertive, the impulse goes underground and reemerges in sudden blatant expressions (aggression) or subdued inhibited ones (nonassertion). What assertion trainers are seeking to do, in essence, is to teach individuals how to express the original, unmodified form of the impulse.

A personality characteristic quite different from that of anger or assertiveness is dependency. The term is often used in a pejorative sense. Certain depth analysts trace dependent behavior to infantile orality and talk about an individual's greedy insatiability or cannibalistic impulses. I would argue, however, that the direct expression of dependent impulses may have a refreshing and clarifying effect. Problems occur when these impulses are warded off and reemerge in distorted forms, as sudden exaggerated expressions (insistent demands for love and affection) or as subdued inhibited ones (longing, pleading looks). It is these distorted expressions that have given dependency its bad name. People feel coerced and offended by them and become entirely uninterested in providing the wished for comfort or caring.

Structural Issues

The difference between depth analysis and ego analysis can be stated in terms of the structural concepts of id, ego, and superego (using these terms in a rough and loose manner). Depth analysis sees the id (infantile impulses) as the problem and counts on the ego (the voice of reality; defensive measures against these impulses) and the superego (the sense of moral responsibility) to keep the id in line. Ego analysis views the id (original impulses) as benign and attributes the problem to the ego (defenses or reactions against these impulses) and, ultimately, to the superego (guilt). It is people's fear and guilt about ordinary anger or dependency, I would argue, rather than an underlying primitive anger or dependency, that lies at the root of the problem.

Developmental Issues (Not Even Infants Have Infantile Impulses)

The depth analyst notion of infantile impulses is supported by a sophisticated developmental theory (Freud, 1905). Distressed adults do behave as children, as Freud and his followers so convincingly demonstrated, and it seems natural to conclude that these individuals are reexperiencing the impulses they had as children. I do not deny the relationship between childhood and adult psychopathology. Instead, I propose an alternative theory of childhood. Disturbed adults do not have infantile impulses; and infants don't either.

Infants and children are traditionally viewed as motivated by dependent, aggressive, narcissistic, exhibitionistic, and other primitive or infantile impulses. These impulses are seen as dropping out in the course of normal development and being replaced by or subordinated to more mature impulses. Thus, dependence yields to independence and narcissism to object-relatedness. Adult psychopathology is then seen as a regression to infantile psychological functioning and a revival of these infantile impulses.

The ego analyst would point out, however, that most so-called primitive impulses of childhood do not drop out with advancing age. Adults are not less dependent, narcissistic, sadistic, or exhibitionistic than they were as children. What has happened instead is that they have developed better ways of expressing these impulses. While infants are restricted to rather limited forms of dependency gratification, for example, and must seek it from the few not necessarily reliable individuals whom chance has placed around them, adults have generally developed subtle, flexible, and effective means of satisfying these needs. Adults can pursue dependency gratification in a variety of ways, vicariously enjoying the experience of those they are nurturing at some moments and asking for more direct forms of comfort and reassurance at others. They are also freer to choose from whom to seek such satisfaction and, if disappointed, freer to look for it elsewhere.

The shift from childhood to adulthood is traditionally thought to require renunciation of childhood dependency. I would argue, on the other hand, that adulthood provides dependency gratification about which the child can only dream: the chance to have one's wishes and needs fully respected and attended to and the opportunity to be the most important person to the person who is most important to you.

A similar argument can be made for most of the other alleged infantile inpulses. Unlike the young child who is limited to ineffectual physical expressions of anger, the adult can devastate with a word or glance. Whereas the two-year-old is restricted to a global indiscriminate negativism, the adult has developed efficient and multilayered ways of controlling situations. And compared to the five-year-old's crudely insistent, "Look at me! See what I can do!" the adult has established sophisticated, compelling, and powerful ways of attracting attention.

Infants and children are "infantile," it can thus be argued, not because of the savage, animal-like, or uncontrolled nature of their impulses or drives but because of their undeveloped egos—that is, their awkwardness or inefficiency in gratifying what we may now recognize as standard or universal human needs. And it is this awkardness or inefficiency that psychologically disturbed adults appear to be sharing with children. They too seem to be having difficulty expressing and gratifying common human wishes and feelings.

The major proposition of ego analysis is this: it is not people's wishes and feelings that cause problems but how they feel about their feelings and, in particular, their sense of unentitlement to their feelings (Apfelbaum, 1980c). Powerful jealous feelings, considered by some therapists as inherently pathological, are viewed here as a problem only when the individual sees them as frightening, humiliating, unacceptable, or pathological. If the person feels comfortable with or entitled to these feelings, he or she is likely to express them in direct and inoffensive ways (e.g., "I enjoy the way other men are attracted to you, but I am also jealous as hell"). An unanxious and straightforward comment of this sort is likely to have a resolving effect and to be intriguing and flattering to the partner rather than being threatening or offensive.

It is in terms of the psychotherapeutic theory presented in this chapter that I now consider the psychoanalytic, systems, and behavioral orientations to couples therapy and go on to develop an alternative approach.

2

Traditional Approaches To Couples Therapy

3

The Psychoanalytic Approach

The three traditional couples therapy approaches appear seriously deficient when viewed through ego analytic glasses. A critique of the psychoanalytic orientation is offered in this chapter, systems theory in the next, and behavioral marital therapy in Chapter 5.

In the selection of examples, I have chosen from the best known and/or most recently published works. Paolino and McCrady (1978) asked representatives from the major schools to write chapters describing their views. Nadelson wrote the chapter on the psychoanalytic perspective, O'Leary and Turkewitz the behavioral orientation, and Sluzki the systems viewpoint. These authors give rich clinical examples and extensive use is made of them in my critique.

Repeated reference is also made to the work of Sager (1976), perhaps the best known psychoanalytically oriented couples therapist, Jacobson and Margolin (1979), "the preeminent spokespeople for the social learning approach to marital problems" (Patterson, 1979), Jackson, Haley, and Bowen, major figures in the family systems approach, and Ables and Brandsma (1977), who have written the most recent general textbook on couples therapy.

A distinctive feature of psychoanalysis is the appeal to childhood for its major descriptive and explanatory concepts. This chapter discusses how psychoanalytically oriented couples therapists may attribute partner problems to (1) "infantile impulses," (2) childhood conflicts, and (3) failure in separation–individuation.

INFANTILE IMPULSES

Depth analysis appears to be the predominating force in psychoanalytically oriented couples therapy. A prime example is Rubinstein and Timmins' (1978) description of the manner in which depressed people approach their "caretaking" partners. They talk in quiet, low-pitched voices with few inflections, much hesitation, long silences, lack of eye contact, restrained body movements, whining voice quality, and relatively little content in what they are saying.

Rubinstein and Timmins emphasize the gratification and control that depressed individuals are obtaining by behaving in this manner. "Being taken care of" by their partners, these authors claim, "supplies an endless source of narcissistic gratification" to these people. They are extremely angry, demanding, dependent, oral persons who fail to take responsibility for their own actions, engage in a fight for control, use the relationship defensively to prevent personal growth, engage in symbiotic and sadomasochistic interactions, and use guilt provocation to control their partners.

There is a modified form of depth analytic thinking in which partners, although viewed as under the sway of regressive impulses, are not necessarily thought to be gratifying these impulses. This appears to be the position taken by Sager and his colleagues (1971) in their influential paper on the marital contract. After presenting their theory, they demonstrate it with an example of a couple. At the root of this couple's unconscious marital contract, these authors suggest, is the husband's "hostility toward women" and the wife's "insatiable need for acclaim and power" and her "destructive feelings toward" and "intense competition with" her husband. It is not certain, however, that these partners are successfully gratifying these infantile impulses. They seem rather to be seeking to gratify them.

These examples of psychoanalytic reasoning, typical of a major segment of the literature, paint a rather unflattering picture of partners. They are viewed as dependent, narcissistic, sadistic, or immature individuals who are controlling the relationship, exploiting, manipulating, or dominating their partners, and seeking or obtaining significant regressive gratification.

If this is the way people actually are, we, as couples therapists, certainly need to know about it so we can take it into account in our work. My own view is that this is not an accurate picture. The depth analytic view is correct, I am convinced, only in a descriptive or superficial sense. Behind the apparent impulse gratification and manipulation of partners is inhibition, deprivation, and an inability to control.

A therapist with an ego analytic orientation would view Rubinstein and Timmins' depressed patients as seriously deprived and inhibited and as unable to adequately control the situation. Their nonverbal appeals (low pitched voices, hesitation, long silences, lack of eye contact, and so on) would be seen as a consequence of their inability to ask for comfort and nurturance in a straightforward manner, perhaps because they feel they do not deserve it or that their partners would not be willing to give it. The whine in their voices would be viewed as a result of their inability to state resentments directly. These people are obtaining very little of what they, or anybody, would want and are inhibited in their ability to ask for it or complain about not getting it.

Moralism

A practical disadvantage of the depth analytic view is the ease with which it can lead to accusational and moralistic interpretations. Sager's major case example in his 1976 book is that of Susan and Jon Smith, a couple who came to him with a variety of complaints. In the first session, Sager "suggested the sexual area for initial work" and "instructed them to take turns at home playing out each other's sexual desires" (p. 61). This went well the first week, but Susan came in after the second session complaining that Jon was merely complying with Sager's suggestions and "did not feel the proper love for her because he acted lovingly only when he wanted sex." She saw Sager as "her mother pulling the marionette strings and her husband as her weak father" (p. 64).

Sager's response to Susan's complaint was to point out that

> good sex and love were ready for them when they both felt willing *to give as well as receive* and that was not up to me or for me. I interpreted her transferential designation of me as strong mother and showed her how *self-defeating* that was for her in this situation. Sex would have to wait for further attention or would eventually take care of itself when suspiciousness, hostility, and the use of sex in their power struggle were no longer necessary. (p. 64, italics added).

Telling people that they have to learn to give as well as receive is accusing and moralistic (Sager is saying in essence that Jon and Susan *should* be willing to give as well as receive, a familiar moral position). Such an intervention could be made only by a therapist who was attributing the problem to the individuals' regressive strivings. A therapist with an ego analytic orientation would be too aware of the underlying deprivation these partners were experiencing (how neither was getting very much from the relationship) to be viewing them as receiving without giving.

The second part of Sager's comment is an example of how a transference interpretation can become an accusation. Telling Susan that seeing him as pulling the strings is "self-defeating" and a transference reaction (i.e. unjustified) ignores the fact that he (Sager) did instruct them to play out each other's sexual desires. He was, in a sense, pulling the strings. Her complaint, "that her husband was merely following my [Sager's] instructions and did not feel the proper love for her," also seems partially valid. Since both partners were acting on Sager's suggestions, how was either to know what the other was really feeling? Sager's view of Susan as a woman with "underlying feelings of infantile rage" and "murderous impulses" (p. 61) and as engaged in a "power struggle" with her husband (p. 64) appears to have caused him to discount the possibility that her complaints might still be valid.

CHILDHOOD CONFLICTS

A feature of psychoanalytically oriented couples therapy is its attention to childhood experiences. Partner difficulties are often viewed as symptoms of unresolved childhood conflicts (Meissner, 1978; Nadelson, 1978). One common therapeutic approach is to shift attention from the present couple situation to these early experiences (Kadis, 1964; Sager, 1967).

There may be certain practical advantages in making such a shift. Fogarty (1976) suggests, in working with mutually accusing partners, that drawing attention to their experiences in their extended families "cools the system off. Talking about events of their lives that happened before they knew each other depersonalizes the discussion and they can begin to listen to each other" (p. 327).

Nadelson (1978, p.125) and Sager (1967) point out that such interpretations may also be helpful to the opposite type of individuals, those who are blaming themselves for the problem. A wife who feels badly about not being sufficiently affectionate with her husband may be relieved to discover that his complaints about this may have more to do with his early experiences with his mother than they do with his present experiences with her.

The problem with childhood oriented interpretations is their tendency to draw away attention from what I see as the central issue—the fact that the partners are being deprived and are lacking control in their present relationship. Consider the following example presented by Nadelson (1978, pp. 116–117).

Mrs. A, a 28-year-old teacher, married for three years, requested therapy because she felt increasingly less interested in her husband and sexually attracted to other men. She expressed ambivalence about ending the marriage because she objectively felt that her husband was a "good person" with whom she had much to share, and she was uncertain about the reasons for the change in her response to him. She requested individual therapy and did not want her husband included because she felt that he would be hurt and angered if he knew of a recent affair with a mutual friend. She was seen in intensive psychoanalytically oriented psychotherapy twice a week for six months. During this time the role of her unresolved oedipal conflicts in her search for another more sexually attractive man became increasingly apparent.

She began psychoanalysis at this time, focusing on her intense desire to please her father and her competitiveness with her mother. She became aware that she viewed her husband as very different from her father and that this factor had played a significant part in her choice of him. The affair she'd had was with a man who more closely resembled her father in his manner and way of relating to her. The realization of these factors and her ability to work through the oedipal issues resulted in her decision to remain with Mr. A and to make a commitment to the marriage.

Nadelson's explanation seems reasonable. Since Mrs. A was fond of her father, one might think she would look for a husband who was like him. That she did not and, in fact, married a man who was "very different" from her father, suggests that she might have a conflict about it. Nadelson points to her competitiveness with her mother and suggests an oedipal conflict. Since Mrs. A is still basically attached to her father, it is then understandable that she might at times be sorry her husband were not more like him and be attracted to men who were. Since the problem had to do with her unresolved feelings toward her parents, there appeared to be no necessity to involve her husband in the therapy.

Nadelson's account overlooks an important factor, however. If Mrs. A is becoming less interested in her husband and more sexually attracted to other men, this must mean something about her present relationship with her husband in addition to whatever it might mean about her unresolved childhood conflicts. It is even possible to speculate what the problem might be. Mrs. A is keeping the difficulty to herself. She appears not to have told her husband about her loss of interest in him and growing interest in others. We can further guess that Mr. A does not notice that there is a difficulty or, at least, that he is not talking in a direct or effective manner about it. The problem thus appears to be one of a mutual withdrawal. Mrs. A has married this "good person" whom she is afraid of hurting. It stands to reason that their life together might lack intimacy and stimulation and that Mrs. A, and perhaps Mr. A too, might find themselves attracted to others.

Fogarty (1976), Nadelson (1978), and Sager (1967) have described how shifting partners' attention from their present impacted situation to their early family experiences can have a clarifying and reassuring effect. There may also be cases, however, when such shifting has the effect of confusing partners and invalidating their feelings. Let us consider another of Nadelson's case examples.

Dr. and Mrs. P initially presented because of frequent arguments and increasing distance between them. Both partners had been working until the birth of their son two years before. At that time, Mrs. P left work to stay at home. Dr. P increased his work commitments in order to make up for the decreased income, and Mrs. P was left alone with the child for greater lengths of time than she had anticipated. She began to feel that Dr. P did not care about her, she suspected that he was interested in other women, and she felt "stupid and dull." Dr. P denied her accusations, but he did acknowledge that she was not as spontaneous and interesting as she had been when she was working. He complained that all she did when he arrived home was to berate him for his inattention and order him around. He stated that he felt he "just lived" in the house and was like another child (burden) to her.

When they decided on marital therapy, Dr. P complied with Mrs. P's wish to have a woman therapist because she thought that a man would merely side with her husband and see her as responsible for the difficulty because she could not understand the demands of her husband's work.

In the initial phase of therapy, the couple began to look at the evolution of their inability to communicate. After several weeks, they were able to talk with each other without becoming so angry that one or the other would feel impelled to leave the room. However, as the therapy became more intense, Dr. P became seductive with the therapist and developed a full-blown transference neurosis, based on his unresolved oedipal conflicts. Mrs. P became enraged at the therapist whom she accused of having "everything" because the therapist was a professional woman with a family. She felt demeaned by the therapist and accused her of being "as bad as a man." Mrs. P had grown up mistrust-ful of men. She stated that they never gave anything. On the other hand, she feared her powerful mother who had controlled and managed her father and the rest of the family, but who never gave her enough. She projected her anger at her mother onto the therapist.

Because Mrs. P had developed enough of an observing ego early in the treatment, had substantial ego strengths, and had a positive alliance with the therapist, she was able to tolerate the intensity of her anger and recognize it origins in her childhood experiences. She became aware that the therapist and her husband had become parental figures and that she related to them as she had in the past. Dr. P's oedipal conflicts were more difficult to work through. He repeatedly attempted to involve the therapist as a colleague, in order to avoid the intensity of his oedipal anxiety. The therapist and Mrs. P both became maternal objects, and it was essential to help him understand the split he had made. An important insight came to him in one session when he clearly confused the therapist with his mother in a question he asked. (pp. 144–145)

The therapist's response to the event in question (Dr. P's infatuation with her and Mrs. P's angry reaction) is to attribute it to the unresolved oedipal conflicts of both partners. Such an interpretation has the unfortun-ate effect of invalidating the partners' feelings and reactions. Mrs. P's anger, the therapist is suggesting, is a displacement of anger she felt toward her mother and is thus inappropriate to the present situation. It is possible to argue, however, that it is quite appropriate. Mrs. P had given up her job to raise their son and appears to have certain regrets about doing so. It stands to reason that she might feel envious of a woman (the therapist) who has both children and a career. The final straw is when this therapist also ends up obtaining what Mrs. P is desperately seeking—Dr. P's love.

A similar argument can be made concerning Dr. P's infatuation with the therapist. Attributing this to unresolved oedipal conflicts draws attention away from the important fact that Mrs. P, as both partners agree, has become less interesting and less lovable since leaving her job. It is understandable, then, that Dr. P's thoughts might wander to "more interesting" women. It is not just unconscious oedipal conflicts that are being played out in the therapy but the partners' present reality situation. The appropriate therapeutic task, accordingly, would be to use the "transference" situation (the partners' feelings toward the therapist) to explore this present reality. In any event, Dr. P may have been correct to reject the oedipal interpretation of his behavior, and perhaps Mrs. P should have rejected the oedipal interpretation of hers.

SEPARATION-INDIVIDUATION

Another concept that has exerted influence on the development of psychoanalytic couples therapy is Mahler's (1968) notion of separation-individuation. Ables and Brandsma (1977), Nadelson (1978), and Meissner (1978) suggest that it is the failure of one or both partners to have mastered the developmental task of separation-individuation that lies at the root of most couple problems.

It is understandable that these authors might employ Mahler's theory in this manner. Her developmental description (from autism to symbiosis to separation-individuation) has intuitive appeal, is founded on an empirical base (observations of infants), has obtained widespread acceptance in the field of psychoanalysis at large, and has the advantage of being consistent with Freud's developmental theory (i.e., the progression from primary narcissism to object relatedness).

However, there is another and even more important reason for the use of the concept of separation-individuation in couples therapy. The working out of a relationship with one's mother has certain formal similarities with the working out of a relationship with a partner. Both require an ability to establish a level of contact and intimacy while at the same time developing a certain measure of independence.

The notion of separation-individuation may at first appear to be free from the objections I stated for depth analytic concepts. Its emphasis is on the development of an interpersonal ability or ego capacity and not on infantile impulses or gratifications. The notion of regressive impulses lies just beneath the surface, however. People who fail to achieve separation–individuation are seen as functioning at a symbiotic level—that is, as motivated by oral dependent wishes.

The problem with the concept of separation–individuation, which is also true of other depth analytic notions, is that it discredits the individuals' feelings and reactions (by attributing them to developmental defects) and does not consider important current factors. Ables and Brandsma (1977) give the example of "the wife of the graduate student who feels left out and jealous when her husband's time and energy are invested in work outside the home" and attribute the problem to her "failure to resolve early symbiotic ties and the subsequent failure to complete successfully the separation–individuation stage" (p.24).

The first point to make is that the wife may be partially correct. My own experience with such couples (though it is just as often the wife who is going to graduate school) is that the husband frequently is leaving her out, and in a way and to a degree that is not completely explained by his graduate school responsibilities. Both partners may have been suffering from a lack of intimacy and satisfaction in the relationship, that is, both may have been feeling left out. When the husband (or wife) then enters graduate school and becomes even further withdrawn, the situation becomes intolerable. The wife is feeling (and is being) too excluded already to tolerate this added abandonment. From this point of view, the wife's strong reaction can be seen as bringing to the surface an important problem in the relationship (a shared abandonment) from which both are suffering.

A major difficulty with relating envy to early symbiotic ties and failure to separate–individuate is that it is the wife's criticism of herself for being dependent and immature that may be causing much of the problem. In alarm at this view of herself, she suppresses her complaints. As generally happens when complaints are suppressed, they reemerge in "regressive" forms, as whiny demands or hostile outbursts. She, her husband, and the therapist then mistakenly view these distorted expressions as true indications of her basic underlying feelings. The real problem, however, is her sense of unentitlement. If she did feel entitled to her feelings, she might be able to describe them in ways that would be more convincing and less offensive to her husband and herself.

Attributing this woman's jealousy to developmental defects has the unfortunate effect of reaffirming the self-criticism that lies at the root of her problem. In fact, even a neutral comment may be misunderstood. As Apfelbaum has illustrated (Apfelbaum et al., 1980, p. 65), any intervention short of justifying her feeling is likely only to reaffirm her sense of unentitlement.

Psychoanalysis is the source from which couples therapy and all other forms of psychotherapy emerged. It was thus the natural starting point for this review of contemporary couples therapy approaches. I now turn to the other two major orientations—family systems theory and behavioral marital therapy.

4

The Systems Approach

The thesis developed in this chapter is that family systems theory has retained or resurrected in a subtle and modified form what I feel to be the most unfortunate feature of the psychoanalytic approach, its depth analytic orientation.

Family systems theory developed in large part as a direct reaction against the psychiatric labeling of individuals (Jackson, 1967, 1977; Satir, 1970). Attention is instead focused on the couple or family as a whole. Although systems theory has achieved a certain success (it has rescued the family scapegoat or "identified patient"), it appears to have done so at the cost of condemning the family unit. "Instead of identified patients, we now have identified families."*

An effect of family systems theory is the development of a new set of accusations. Partners are described as "double binding," as having "hidden agendas," "colluding" with each other, and attempting to "sabotage" the therapy. This derogatory, reproachful tone is perhaps most clearly expressed in Lederer and Jackson's (1968) *Mirages of Marriage* where the mutually withdrawn couple is labeled the "gruesome twosome" and the mutually accusing couple the "weary wranglers."

It may be incorrect, as Steinglass (1978) and Gurman (1978) point out, to consider family systems theory as one unified approach. There are at least three major clinical versions of family systems theory—Minuchin's, Bowen's, and the Palo Alto school's (Jackson, Haley, Weakland, Watzlawick, and Fisch). Since Minuchin (1974) is concerned predominately with families and not with couples, primary attention is devoted to Bowen and the Palo Alto school. This chapter is divided into three parts: homeostasis (a major organizing concept of systems theory), the Jackson-Haley (Palo Alto) orientation, and the Bowen approach.

HOMEOSTASIS

The generating concept of systems theory is circular causality (Bateson, 1971; Jackson, 1967). The traditional causal model, these authors state, is

*This irony was pointed out to me by Joanne Wile.

linear. One can imagine a straight line extending from the alleged cause of the problem (the neurotic reactions or childhood experiences of one or both partners) to the effect (couple discord). The notion of circular causality changes the picture. Each partner's behavior is now viewed as a reaction or adjustment to the behavior of the other. One partner withdraws because the second nags while the second nags because the first withdraws.

This new form of reasoning has dramatic implications. Since the causal pattern is a circle with all elements occurring in the present, the past becomes less important and perhaps irrelevant. And since each individual's behavior is caused not by his or her personal problems or "neurotic" reactions but by the system, intrapsychic factors also become less important and perhaps irrelevant.

The prime example of circular causality is negative feedback or homeostasis (Jackson, 1957). If there is an organizing principle in family systems theory, this is it. The couple or family, having achieved some sort of equilibrium, is seen as resisting and counteracting all forces that threaten this equilibrium.

The commitment to the homeostatic or negative feedback model has encountered certain criticism (e.g., Speer, 1970; Wertheim, 1973; Olson, Sprenkle, and Russell, 1979). Jackson, the originator of this view, was himself dissatisfied with it and made major modifications, as Greenberg (1977) describes. Nevertheless, homeostasis continues to be viewed as the key pathological element. Practitioners from all the major schools of systems theory start with the assumption that they must find some way of dealing with family homeostasis—that is, the tendency of families to maintain their pathological patterns and resist the therapist's constructive efforts.

The major disadvantage of the concept of homeostasis is its assumption of an adversary relationship between therapist and family. Individual family members are viewed as active proponents of the family system, willing victims of this system, or both. Since the aim of systems oriented therapy is to challenge and change the family system, a task that requires disrupting the family's homeostatic balance, these therapists often see their goals as directly opposed to those of the family (Ferreira, 1963; Haley, 1963b; Jackson and Weakland, 1961; Jungreis, 1965; Minuchin, 1974; Speck, 1965; Zuk, 1968).

The concepts of homeostasis and family systems need not inevitably lead to family–therapist opposition. Family members appear to have mixed feelings about their family system. It seems possible, then, that members might resist the therapist's attempts to change the system at some moments and collaborate with these efforts at others (Freeman, 1976). The impression generally given in the family systems literature, however, is that family members are almost entirely dominated by the system and exert a constant oppositional force against the therapist's attempt to alter it.

A further factor that may contribute to the sense of opposition often experienced by conjoint therapists is the tendency of some to see family members as being duplicitous and manipulative, as using "ploys" (Jackson, 1959) or Eric Berne type games to get what they want.

The systems approach thus appears to lead to a picture of the conjoint therapist struggling gallantly against great odds—against concerted family efforts to maintain homeostatic balance, against powerful family forces sabotaging all attempts to change the family system, and against the subtle maneuvers and deceits employed by family members. It is perhaps this general picture that accounts for the dramatic, forceful, and at times coercive measures taken by some systems oriented therapists. Opposed as they believe they are by recalcitrant family members and by this powerful and uncompromising adversary, the family system, these therapists may feel impelled to use whatever means are at their disposal.

Thus Ackerman (1966) deliberately charms, ridicules, and bullies family members; Haley (1963b) and Watzlawick, Weakland, and Fisch (1974) strategically manipulate them with paradoxical instructions; Jackson and Weakland (1961) tactically place them in therapeutic double binds; Haley (1977) systematically browbeats certain partners who fail to do the tasks he assigns them; Minuchin and his colleagues (1967) "frontally silence" overbearing wives to "rock the system" and show their passive husbands how to stand up to them; Speck (1965) openly engages in "power struggles" with families; Satir (Haley and Hoffman, 1967) forcefully structures the therapeutic session and undercuts all attempts to challenge her control; and Zuk (1968) intentionally sides with one family member against another, challenges the whole family, and does so in inconsistent patterns in order to shake them up, keep them guessing, and "tip the balance in favor of more productive relating." The tactics of family therapists, Haley (1962; 1976, p. 97) comments, are similar to those used by family members in disturbed families. Haley and Hoffman's (1967) presentation and discussion of therapy sessions conducted by seven family therapists provide a vivid picture of therapists struggling against families and Beels and Ferber's (1969) review of the family therapy literature appears in some sense a catalogue of confrontational and manipulative therapeutic measures.

It is perhaps surprising, considering the dramatic nature of these methods, that they have been incorporated into the couples and family therapy traditions with so little discussion and debate.* The assumption underlying their uncritical acceptance appears to be that measures of this sort are somehow necessary and unavoidable. An entrant into the field is often taught this general adversary orientation as if it were the only possible way of doing family and couples therapy.

*The only criticisms of which I am aware are those of Levant (1978) and Boszormenji-Nagy (1979).

My own conjoint therapy experience is at variance with this traditional view. Confrontation and manipulation do not seem to me to be as necessary as these authors suggest. It is my guess, furthermore, that other conjoint therapists may have had similar experiences but have perhaps been limited in their recognition or acknowledgment of this by the absence of an official model or supporting tradition.

THE JACKSON-HALEY APPROACH

Practitioners of the Jackson-Haley school argue that their concern is with the family or couple as a whole (the motivation of the system) and that they make no assumptions or speculations about the motivation of individuals (Jackson, 1967; Haley, 1967, 1970; Sluzki, 1978). My own view is that their approach implies a rather dramatic and distinctive theory of individual motivation.*

Power and Control

The Jackson-Haley approach appears to be based on two related axes— homeostasis and power relations (Haley, 1963b, pp. 160–161). The role of homeostasis has already been discussed. Much of what happens in a family or between partners is thought to be determined by the need to maintain the status quo. But there is a second factor. Haley, to the apparent dismay of Bateson (1976, p. 106), the original intellectual leader of the Palo Alto school, went on from their early collaboration to emphasize the significance of partners' struggle for control. "The major conflicts in a marriage," Haley (1963a, p. 227) wrote, "center in the problem of who is to tell whom what to do under what circumstances."

Jackson (1959), in agreement with Haley, described the early stages of a couple relationship as devoted to the determination of who is to have the power. He refined these notions in his later writing (Jackson, 1965a, 1965b), drawing attention to the implicit "rules" by which partners determine, among other things, who is to have control in which situations and what each is to give or allow in return for what. The term he employed was the "marital *quid pro quo.*"

The twin issues of homeostasis and control show themselves in Jackson and Haley's theory of symptom formation (Haley, 1963b, p. 15). Symptoms may arise, these therapists argue, as a means of maintaining homeostasis. A wife's agoraphobia is an example. Her fear of leaving the house (and con-

*Watzlawick, Beavin, and Jackson (1967, pp. 48-50) have said that it is impossible to not communicate. It may also be impossible to not have a theory of individual motivation.

sequent dependence on her husband) may be the only factor keeping her from divorcing him. Symptoms may also develop, these authors suggest, as a means of gaining control in a relationship. In his chapter, "Symptoms as tactics in human relationships," Haley (1963b) describes how a wife's alcoholism gave her power in her marrriage.

> A patient with an alcoholic wife once said that he was a man who liked to have his own way but his wife always won by getting drunk. His wife, who was present in the therapy session, became indignant and said she won nothing but unhappiness by her involuntary drinking. Yet obviously she did win something by it. In this case she won almost complete control of her relationship with her husband. He could not go where he wanted because she might drink; he could not antagonize her or upset her because she might drink; he could not leave her alone (unless he could encourage her to pass out) because of what she might do when drunk; and he could not make any plans but had to let her initiate whatever happened. In other words, she could bring him to heel merely by picking up a glass. She might suffer distress and humiliation and even provoke her husband to beat her, but *she* provoked those situations and thereby controlled what was to happen. Similarly, her husband could provoke her to drink at any time, either by exhibiting some anxiety himself or forbidding her drinking. Each partner must make a contribution to perpetuating the symptom and each has needs satisfied by it. (pp. 15–16)

Haley and Jackson are viewing "control" in a different manner than I do. This wife is my idea of a person who does not have much control in the relationship. Any woman who has to get herself drunk and perhaps beaten up in order to make her husband responsive to her needs is clearly doing so as a desperate, last-ditch effort because she lacks better methods. A related point can be made about a man whose marital satisfactions appear to be limited to provoking his wife to drink. *Both* partners need greater control in the relationship.

An Implicit Theory of Individual Motivation

Jackson and Haley take the position that homeostasis and power relations are issues having to do with couple or family systems and not with individuals. In the case of homeostasis, in fact, family members are sometimes viewed as sacrificing their individual needs and welfare—that is, their personal wishes or motivations—for the good of the family. The agoraphobic wife is putting aside her own personal wishes (to get a divorce) in order to keep the family together.

Concealed within the notion of family systems, however, is an implied theory of individual motivation and human nature. Family members are viewed as helpless (i.e., controlled by the family system), dependent (i.e., dependent on the family), resistant (i.e., opposed to all threats to the family system), and irrational (i.e., not responding to logic or reason). In addition, they are indirect and deceitful, using games and ploys to pursue their secret purposes. It is clear that Haley views the woman in his example (the alcoholic wife) as underhanded and corrupt.

And what are these secret purposes? The agoraphobic wife and her husband are trying to prevent the breakup of the family. This is a motivation having to do with the family as a whole, a systems theorist might claim, and not with the motivation of either individual. The implicit theory of individual motivation becomes clear, however, when one asks why this husband and wife are interested in maintaining a marriage that is causing one member so much unhappiness. (The wife is clearly dissatisfied with the relationship and wants a divorce.) The wife, we can imagine, is feeling too afraid, ashamed, or guilty to leave her husband while he is feeling too humiliated or desperate to tolerate her departure.

The existence of individual motivation is even more apparent in the second major element of the Jackson-Haley approach, their view of intimate relations as a struggle for control. Haley (1976, p. 78) sees "a power struggle as a product of the needs of a system rather than the needs of a person." This is a difficult view to uphold. As mentioned, Bateson differs strongly from him on this and Keeney (1979, p. 123), among others, believes that Haley has never adequately proven his case. The issues of power and control fall too naturally into the province of individual motivation.

What is the nature of this implied theory of individual motivation? I view it as a variant of depth analysis. It is true that Jackson and Haley do not talk in terms of infantile impulses. However, their approach is consistent with depth analysis in the denigrating or accusatory terms in which people are described. In addition, a central theme in the Jackson-Haley approach, the effort of partners to control the relationship, and the games, ploys, gambits, maneuvers, subterfuges, and manipulations used by these partners to establish this control, has the ring of regressive or immature functioning (Bursten, 1973; Shostrum, 1967).

Jackson and Haley are well known for their belief that interpretation and understanding are ineffectual or even counterproductive in psychotherapy. "Explicitly talking about the control problem can solidify it" (Haley, 1963a, p. 227). If partners or families are to make a constructive change, these authors believe, they must be manipulated into it by being placed in therapeutic double binds or paradoxical situations. Haley and Jackson do not talk about regressive impulses; they simply assume that everyone is functioning in such a manner, that is, below the level of rational discourse and problem solving.

The Noncommunication of Communication Theory

The systems theory of the Palo Alto school is commonly referred to as a communications approach. There is an irony here. As just discussed, these therapists have little confidence in the value of communication as it is ordinarily conceived, as a direct, verbal expression of thoughts, feelings, and wishes. I suggest that systems theorists may be overlooking a powerful form of therapeutic intervention.

The Double Bind

The most dramatic early concept to come out of the Palo Alto school was that of double bind communication (Bateson, Jackson, Haley, and Weakland, 1956). This concept, perhaps more than any other, captures the spirit of the Jackson-Haley approach, the idea that people control relationships by means of subtle, often nonverbal, forms of communication that may be separate from or even directly opposite to the content of what is being said.

The classic case of the double bind is that of the mother who beckons to her child to come kiss her and then stiffens and turns away. The next time she beckons to him, the child (let us make him a boy) is in a no-win situation. If he runs to her, he will be punished (i.e., she will turn away again). If he hesitates, he will be punished (i.e., she will complain "Don't you love me?"). And since he is dependent on his mother, he cannot leave the field. The situation soon becomes more complex than this, as these authors suggest, because the boy's ultimate response is to learn to double bind in return.

For purposes of discussion, however, let us consider the simple case. An obvious solution to the boy's double bind, and to double binds in general, is to make the nonverbal message verbal. The boy, or a therapist speaking for the boy, could point out that he is getting two messages. The major reason that this cannot be done, Bateson and his colleagues (1956) argue, is that this mother could not tolerate this information and would deny, attack, and put increased pathological pressure on her son—that is, she would punish her son for claiming that she is punishing him.

While these authors may be correct, and it may be impossible to approach this mother directly, the difficulty may be the manner in which they were considering approaching her. The Bateson group is employing a largely depth analytic orientation. The problem with this mother, these authors believe, is that she is afraid of intimacy and has hostile feelings toward her child. "The child's very existence has a special meaning to the mother which arouses her anxiety and hostility when she is in danger of intimate contact with the child" (Bateson, Jackson, Haley, and Weakland, 1956).

I would argue, on the other hand, that the problem is not her hostility toward and rejection of her son, but her desperate effort to be nonhostile and nonrejecting. She appears to have accepted the conventional notion that good mothers have only love and patience for their children. Since she is unable to acknowledge and accept the irritation and exasperation that are an inevitable part of child rearing, she may have no choice but to experience and express them in indirect, warded-off forms such as stiffening and turning away. Her double binding behavior is thus a consequence of her attempt to be unconditionally loving.

This mother could not tolerate hearing that she is afraid of intimacy and has hostile feelings toward her son because this would inflame her own worst fears about herself: that she is insufficiently loving and a poor mother. What she needs instead is a sympathetic appreciation of how her wish to be a good mother and her overly stringent view of what this entails is causing much of the problem.

It is adherence to depth analytic thinking that may have prevented the authors of the double bind concept from pursuing the obvious solution to the problem: helping the victim (and also the perpetrator) verbalize the nonverbal message. What Jackson, Haley, and Weakland did instead was to give up on interpretation and to respond to double binds and other pathological behavior of family members with double binds of their own ("therapeutic double binds" or paradoxical assignments).

Paradox

A major method of present-day adherents of the Jackson-Haley approach is the paradoxical intervention. Instead of encouraging the decrease of symptomatic behavior, the therapist prescribes such behavior. When individuals report a decrease in symptomatic behavior, the therapist predicts a relapse. And when people describe an obviously negative characteristic the therapist redefines it as a positive quality (Sluzki, 1978).

The tendency of these therapists to think in terms of paradox and manipulation and to doubt the value of direct discussion and interpretation may cause them to miss important therapeutic opportunities. Sluzki (1978) describes

> a couple whose explicit problem was centered in her stubborn insomnia, recent loss of appetite, and fluctuating weakness and irritability which she related to her insomnia.
>
> In the course of that interview, the therapist stated that the symptoms the woman was presenting were correlates of depression without feelings of sadness. The man reacted immediately by stating, defensively, that she didn't have any reason to be sad. To defuse, the therapist proposed that maybe it had to do with old sadness (nothing to do with the present context) and pre-

scribed that, in the course of the next week, she should behave as though she were very, very sad, especially on those days in which she was least sad, and asked him to help her in that task by letting her express her sadness without trying to counter-argue or shush her. The therapist added that they would probably find the task surprisingly difficult to comply with. She agreed that it was against the grain of her tendencies to show her sad side. The man stated, in turn, that he did not foresee any difficulty in his share, because, "After all, she may be just acting it."

In the next session, they reported that she cried as never before, and that he felt that he was helping her get rid of the pain by just being there, instead of feeling defensive about it. Two stormy sessions followed in which several current frustrations were discussed, and the crisis subsided with a drastic change in the couple's style of coping with conflict. The presenting symptoms were not even mentioned during that period, and when explored, they were reported as having vanished.

The symptom prescription seemed to accomplish the function of facilitating a break in an otherwise repetitive cycle that kept them locked, until then, in their respective roles of sick and sane. (pp. 382-383)

The therapeutic exchange was clearly helpful. The wife's irritability, loss of appetite, and insomnia appeared to be a consequence of her inability to discuss relationship dissatisfactions and frustrations with her husband. The problem was that it was difficult for them to have such discussions. The wife did not feel entitled to be sad or to make complaints, and the husband had difficulty hearing them. The therapist used paradoxical methods to bypass these problems. By prescribing the symptom—that is, by instructing the wife to behave as though she were sad—the therapist had given her the right and even the responsibility to express sadness. And since her sadness was defined as something she was just making up, the husband was less threatened by it. This then allowed them to have the discussions they needed to have.

My own view, however, is that this therapist may have imposed unnecessary limitations upon the therapy. The problem began with the husband's defensive comment that his wife did not have any reason to be sad. The therapist's response was to "defuse" the situation by stating that it might be an old sadness (and thus have nothing to do with the husband). This was the turning point. The practitioner had abandoned direct communication and had shifted to manipulation.

Even if it had been necessary to defuse the situation, the therapist's method, making a clearly false statement, is a questionable way of doing this. My main concern, however, is why the therapist felt the need to defuse. I can imagine two possible reasons. One may have been the therapist's adversary view of the therapist-couple relationship—that is, the belief that one cannot reason with partners, particularly with those who presumably want the identified patient to remain symptomatic. The other may have been this husband's defensiveness. He was clearly alarmed at the possibility that there might be something about him or about their relationship that was depressing her. The therapist may have felt that the husband was too threatened by this idea to be able to deal with it usefully.

My belief is that the husband's defensiveness was an opportunity to be used rather than a danger to be defused. I can imagine saying the following to him: "The idea that your wife might be sad about your life together seems upsetting to you, I take it, or unjustified." My guess is that he would enjoy the chance to answer this question although, if he were feeling particularly defensive, he might prefer to say, "I'm not upset about it. It's just that it's unjustified."

This is then likely to lead to a discussion of his underlying concerns. It may become clear, for example, that he cannot tolerate the idea that his wife is depressed about their marriage because he might then feel that it is entirely his fault. He, like the double binding mother, may have an overly restrictive view of what a marriage (or mother–child) relationship should be. He may believe that partners in a good marriage never have any real complaints or dissatisfactions with each other. The possibility that his wife may have some would then mean that he has been a failure as a husband.

The major problem, in other words, might be this husband's or both partners' philosophy of marriage. What he may need, and what the therapist may provide, is an appreciation of the fact that complaints and dissatisfactions are inevitable in an intimate relationship and that problems arise from partners' inability to talk about them.

The disadvantage with Sluzki's paradoxical intervention is that it did not lead to these important realizations. Although it relieved the wife's immediate symptoms, problems are likely to reemerge once she again suppresses feelings and complaints. The real value of a therapeutic procedure, I believe, is what it teaches partners about their relationship. Since paradoxical methods are based on subterfuge and misdirection, they do not teach very much.

Working Under Difficult Conditions

Words can be a great convenience. Therapists who do not trust direct discussion and who place their reliance on nonverbal or paradoxical measures can be seen to be at a disadvantage. Consider the following nonverbal method recommended by Sluzki (1978, p. 376):

> If A is consistently defined as the "victimizer" (or as the "identified patient") by B, *then:* (a) reduce physical distance with A, and/or (b) mirror A's body position.

The problem, Sluzki explains, is that the couple is trying to establish a coalition between the therapist and one of the partners. The practitioner can counteract this by suggesting nonverbally that he or she is forming a coalition with the other.

Nonverbal methods are unreliable and imprecise. One can never be sure whether they are received in the manner in which they are meant to be received or whether they are received at all. A further difficulty is that nonverbal methods are obscure to the receiver. Even if these measures do have an effect, and precisely the effect the therapist intends, the affected individual is unlikely to be able to detect what is happening. Partner B may vaguely sense that the therapist is taking A's side, but may be unable to pin down the feeling. He or she is thus unable to comment on it or learn very much from it.* B is likely to feel confused and subtly invalidated.

Finally, nonverbal methods of this sort do not seem to me to be necessary. It is possible and more efficient to bring up the issue directly. I might thus say to B, "If I understand, then, your best guess or even deep conviction is that many and perhaps all of the problems in the relationship are the result of the failings in A that you (or both of you) have just been discussing. Do I have that right?" If I have not said this in an accusing way, B will almost always answer with what he or she really believes (as judged from later comment). I might then go on to discuss how B might be hoping that the two of us might help A change in the ways that B has suggested. Coalitions, or the wish to form coalitions, are generally a serious problem only when they are not openly acknowledged.

Since nonverbal methods are indirect and based on manipulation, they are difficult to execute and require careful planning.† A slight miscalculation can completely destroy the desired effect. Therapists who employ verbal methods, however, and who assume some element of collaboration between therapist and partners will be able to check directly on the effect they are having on these individuals (i.e., by talking about it) and will thus be able to make adjustments.

This brings us to the final and perhaps most subtle point. Since systems theorists of the Jackson-Haley school assume an adversary relationship with partners and doubt the possibility of direct communication and collaboration they are in some sense cut off or isolated from these individuals. They are thus unlikely to think of using them as resources. Consider the problem faced by therapists when they are not understanding the couple interaction. Sluzki (1978) suggests the following measures:

---

*This would not be a problem, of course, to a therapist who does not place much value in discussion and understanding.

†The same is true for paradoxical interventions.

If you find yourself not understanding what is going on with the couple, *then* cease paying attention to content, and observe verbal patterns, sequences, gestures and postures, and/or observe your own emotions, attitudes or postures. (p. 389)

If the actual observation of the couple's interaction process fails to give you a meaningful understanding, *then* switch to the exploration of the couple's history. (p. 390)

If even then you find yourself unable to detect meaningful regularities and/or to produce change, then increase the number of participants in the session (introduce offspring or parents or co-therapists). (p. 391)*

These all seem like potentially useful things to do. Noteworthy by its absence, however, is the alternative of consulting with the partners about this puzzlement. Are *they* puzzled? Do they have any ideas why things are not clear? Is this the kind of confusion they themselves have been experiencing for many years? How do you and they wish to proceed on this mutual problem?

THE BOWEN APPROACH

Murray Bowen occupies an important but ambiguous position in the family systems theory establishment. Several authors have questioned the extent to which his orientation is a systems approach or a psychoanalytic approach (Whitaker, 1975; Gurman, 1978). I too have difficulty classifying his orientation, although for somewhat different reasons. Certain aspects of his theory have the manipulativeness and strategic planning of the Jackson-Haley tradition. Whitaker (1972, p. 169), commenting on Bowen's account of how he manipulated a change in his own family (discussed in the next section) said, "I think one of the things you said that nobody has had guts enough to say before is that those people who go into family therapy are really master manipulators." The bulk of Bowen's therapeutic approach, however, assumes an element of rationality in and collaboration between people.

Bowen as Master Manipulator

Bowen exploits an ambiguity (or flexibility) in systems theory to construct an approach that has interesting similarities to certain psychoanalytic ideas. Although systems theory attributes the problems of individuals to their family relationships, it is not always clear whether the family at issue is

*I might also consider decreasing the number of participants.

the nuclear family or the family of origin. Bowen differs from certain other systems theorists in placing an important emphasis on the family of origin. He has even gone so far as to suggest that working out problems with one's family of origin may be a more effective way of resolving marital conflicts than dealing with these marital conflicts directly. There are "strong indications," he writes, "that psychotherapy as we have known it in the past may one day be considered superfluous." Instead of conjoint therapy or traditional individual therapy, he suggests, therapy may consist of people returning to and differentiating themselves from their families of origin (Bowen, 1972, p. 164).

Bowen appears in some ways to have taken psychoanalysis one step further. He does not limit himself to reconstructing the early family life of the individual or dealing with it in the transference but recommends that the person return to this original home, or to the next best thing, the home as it exists now, and attempt to alter the early established pathological patterns.

Framo (1976), who employs a related approach, discusses the purposes and value of his procedure in unabashedly psychoanalytic (object relations) terms.

> The client, by having sessions with his or her family of origin, takes the problems back to where they began, thereby making available a direct route to etiological factors. Dealing with the real, external parental figures is designed to loosen the grip of the internal representatives of these figures and expose them to reality considerations and their live derivatives. Having gone backward in time, the individual can then move forward in dealing with the spouse and children in more appropriate fashion, since their transference meaning has changed. (p. 194)

Among the most important and provocative documents in the family therapy field is Bowen's account of his own attempts to return to and influence his family of origin (Bowen, 1972). Bowen presents this as an example of family psychotherapy with one motivated family member (himself). It is a premier example of the manipulative and strategic aspects of Bowen Theory.

Bowen's primary goal was to "differentiate" himself from his family. Family problems occur, Bowen suggests, when two members gossip about or form an alliance against and behind the back of a third member. Bowen's objective in his trip home was to keep from being drawn into such triangles (to avoid being "triangled" or triangulated) and to interrupt the major destructive triangles that were presently operating among the other family members.

The major triangle into which Bowen had been drawn was with his mother and brother. In her attempts to deal with this brother, Bowen's mother would "triangle in" Bowen. The mother would communicate by some means that Bowen was on her side and the brother would react as if this were a reality.

Bowen would have liked to go directly to his brother and, by talking to him about what was going on, "detriangle" himself. The problem was that this brother, possibly because of his view that Bowen was on their mother's side, was avoiding him. The brother always managed to leave town just when Bowen was due to arrive for a visit. In a concerted effort to meet his brother, Bowen once delayed the announcement of his arrival until the very last moment. Even then his brother found an excuse not to be there. Bowen's plan, then, was to turn the situation around and make his brother want to seek him out. Having done this, it would then be possible to detriangle himself.

Bowen wrote a carefully thought-out letter to this brother to be mailed exactly two weeks before his trip home. He started the letter by saying that he had wanted to talk to him for some time, but, since this brother had always been away when Bowen came to town, he had to resort to putting his ideas in a letter. Bowen then repeated some of the gossip that had been going around the family, stories that were calculated to arouse his brother's anger and make him want to confront Bowen.

As an added element, Bowen then wrote "a full paragraph of 'reversals,' " a technique reminiscent of the paradoxes of the Palo Alto school that, as Bowen states, is a way of "making a point by saying the opposite. . . . Here was my brother," Bowen commented, "who was working a 16-hour day," devoting himself to the family, and by and large doing "a wonderful job." Instead of suggesting that he "slow down and take it easy and not get so overly responsible for everyone, . . . I implored him to be more responsible," suggested that "maybe he had not worked hard enough to take care" of their parents, and advised him to "limber up his back and give it the good old college try." (p. 155)

Bowen's manipulation was a success. He called his mother a week later to discover how his brother had reacted to the letter and found out that he was "furious about 'that' letter, . . . that he was showing it to people, he was going to have it Xeroxed, and that he would take care of me [Bowen] when I arrived." (p. 156)

Bowen was careful to avoid getting anyone in the family on his "side" which, from his point of view, would be forming a triangle (with the rest of the family as the third side), the very thing he wanted to avoid. When his sister caught on to his general plan and wrote, "I am back of you if I can be of help," Bowen undercut this offered alliance by telling her that he "was going to tell the family she had invited me home to help her with her Big Mother role." (p. 157)

The high point in Bowen's account is his description of the meeting he had with his brother and the rest of the family. His goal was to avoid being "fused into the family emotional system." He did this by responding to every accusation with an immediate casual comment. When his brother said he must have been drunk to have written that letter, Bowen replied that he had the advantage of living in a place where alcohol was cheap and offered to get some at good prices for his brother. When the brother threatened a libel suit for a story about him in the letter, Bowen agreed that he should find out who started the story and "prosecute the person to the full extent of the law." When the brother accused Bowen of conspiring with his mother and planning it all on a recent trip, Bowen said, "You are really intuitive about some things! How did you know about that? You're right. That's when she and I planned the whole thing." Bowen's mother quickly interjected, "That's the biggest lie I ever heard! I will never tell you anything else again." (pp. 158–159)

> At the end of the meeting, as my brother and his wife were leaving, his wife said, "I never saw such a family in all my life. I think we should do more talking to each other and less talking *about* each other."

> The end of that Sunday afternoon was one of the most satisfying periods of my entire life. I had actively participated in the most intense family emotion possible and I had stayed completely out of the "ego mass" of my very own family! I had gone through the entire visit without being "triangled" or without being fused into the family emotional system. (p. 159)

It is difficult not to be impressed with this account. The family does exert a strong emotional pull on its members. Bowen's concept of the "undifferentiated family ego mass" makes sense to everyone who has ever had a family. His notion of triangles as the critical functioning element in such an ego mass is also ingenious. Difficulties arise between partners, it could be suggested, when one or both withhold certain important feelings about the other. Bowen can then be thought of as extending this principle one step further and suggesting that additional difficulties may occur when one or both partners withhold certain important feelings about the other and then tell them to someone else (who becomes the third person in the triangle).

Bowen's presentation is a forceful and elegant statement of his theory. Whitaker (1972) commented in reaction that he wished Bowen were his brother.* It is clear from the family members' ultimate response to his visit

*As an added demonstration of his theory, Bowen immediately detriangled Whitaker's attempt to form an alliance with him (i.e., "Bowen, I wish you were my brother!") by saying that he could not be his brother since Nathan Ackerman was already his brother (p. 165).

that they all were glad he *was* their brother (or son, etc.). In a letter written two weeks after the visit, Bowen's mother said, "With all its ups and downs, your last trip home was the greatest ever." (p. 161)

The question remains in my mind, however, why Bowen felt it was necessary to do all this behind everyone's back. It is not clear, for example, why he had to contrive to get his brother to stay in town to see him. Bowen had made a concerted effort to meet with his brother (i.e., by planning a sudden visit). Instead of doing this as a unilateral act, however, I can imagine letting his brother in on the experiment, telling him, for example (by letter or phone), "I notice that you are always out of town when I visit and I have the sense you want to avoid me." If the brother denies this, then Bowen could say, "Well, I am planning a visit, particularly to meet with you, and, if my guess is right, you will find some excuse to be away."

A similar argument can be made about "detriangling." Bowen seems correct that many family problems take the form of concealed grudges, hidden collusions, and gossiping behind someone's back. This could be handled simply by getting the involved people together and talking with them about it or by reporting "secrets" said about a third person to this third person. This is what Bowen did, in a sense, in the dramatic Sunday afternoon meeting, but in what seemed an unnecessarily contrived and roundabout manner. The imagined alliance between Bowen and his mother was brought into the open as well as certain gossipy stories about the brother.

It is not clear, however, why this could not have been discussed in a straightforward manner. Bowen himself says that detriangling can be achieved by direct means and he gives several examples of this. The brother, for instance, complained to Bowen about how their older sister, the identified emotional invalid of the family, seemed to defeat his every effort to help her. Bowen reacted to this triangling attempt of his brother by going to this sister and saying, "Hey Sis, I have been talking to your brother about your problems and he said you refuse to listen to him. What in the world have you been doing to him to make him talk like that?" (p. 160). The sister's response to this, and to additional comments from Bowen about others in the family taking care of her, was to report, sometime later, that "she was perfectly capable of taking care of herself, that she did not know where she had been for the last 40 years, but she had a new outlook and a new lease on life" (p. 161). My own guess is that direct means of this sort could also have been used successfully in the Sunday afternoon meeting.

Not only is it unnecessary to use indirect methods but there can be disadvantages in doing so. One is the lack of precision in the way issues can be discussed. The immediate conflict in this family at the time was the brother's wish to assume financial control of the family business and the mother's partially hidden objection to this and her secret attempt to bring in others (and particularly Bowen) on her side. While Bowen's Sunday afternoon meeting alluded to these factors and, in particular, to the brother's sense that Bowen and his mother were colluding, the major issue was never fully addressed. Exactly why Bowen did not talk directly to his mother and brother about their conflict was never adequately explained.

Bowen as a Proponent of Rationality

Interspersed among the manipulations just described (and the associated assumption that people must be approached indirectly) are concepts that assume the possibility of direct, rational, collaborative contact between people. One example, already mentioned, is direct detriangling—that is, counteracting hidden collusions by bringing them into the open. This approach assumes the therapeutic value of direct discussion. A second example is the emphasis placed on developing "person-to-person relationships" with members of one's family. Bowen talks about the "parental we-ness," the consequence of parents' efforts to present a united front to a child, and of his own effort to break through this with his parents and to establish an individual relationship with each. Here again, value is placed on direct personal contact between people.

Bowen's appeal to rationality is perhaps most clearly seen in the therapeutic method he calls "family psychotherapy with both parents or both spouses." What this turns out to be is couples therapy. The decision to omit children and grandparents from "family psychotherapy" appears to be a consequence of Bowen's theory of triangles. According to Bowen, "The triangle is the basic building block of an emotional system. . . If one can modify the functioning of a single triangle in an emotional system, and the members of that triangle stay in emotional contact with the larger system, the whole system is modified" (Bowen, 1978, p. 245).

Bowen then goes on to say that there are two major ways of modifying the functioning of a triangle. One, as previously described, "is through one family member. If one member of a triangle can change, the triangle will predictably change; and if one triangle can change, an entire extended family can change." The other is "to put two people from a familiar emotional system into contact with a third person who knows and understands triangles, and who does not play into the emotional moves of the familiar twosome." Bowen meets with the "two most responsible members (both spouses)" using himself as the "potential triangle person" (Bowen, 1978, pp. 245-247).

Bowen (1978) discusses his couples therapy approach in terms of four therapist functions. All four attempt to develop the rationality of partners.

The first function, "defining and clarifying the relationship between the spouses" (p. 248), is devoted to developing a rational dialogue. A major problem in relationships is that the attempts of partners to talk to each other are impeded by intense emotionality. Bowen's solution is to reduce this emotionality. He does this by taking control of the interaction, directing questions first to one partner and then the other, and asking each what he or she was thinking while the other was talking.

The second therapist function is "keeping self detriangled from the family emotional system" (p.250). Becoming triangled is Bowen's way of describing overinvolvement by the therapist in the emotional system of the couple. The therapist becomes angered, charmed, or otherwise emotionally engaged by one or both partners and as a result takes sides, becomes confused (cannot find anything to say), or withdraws. The ideal is to interact with the individuals in a direct manner and to stay in close contact with them without becoming overinvolved. There is something intuitively satisfying and appealing in such communication, and partners who are treated in such a manner by the therapist are likely to begin treating each other in the same way.

The third therapist task, "teaching the functioning of emotional systems" (p. 251), involves a direct appeal to the rationality of partners. Bowen, in contradistinction to Jackson and Haley, believes that partners can benefit from understanding their patterns. Part of the therapist's job, accordingly, is to promote such understanding.

The fourth therapist function is "taking 'I position' stands" (p. 252). By taking the "I position," Bowen means calmly stating one's own convictions and beliefs and taking action on these convictions without criticizing the beliefs of others and without becoming involved in emotional debate. If the therapist does this with the spouses, they will start doing it with the therapist, with each other, and with everyone else in their family. Here again the emphasis is on rational discussion.

Teaching a Family Member to Be a Therapist

In the typical application of Bowen's "family therapy with one motivated family member," the therapist serves as coach in the clients' efforts to return to their families of origin. This coach teaches such persons about the characteristics of family systems, helps them delineate their place in their own family systems, and then assists them in developing ways of modifying their emotional reactions in the system (Bowen, 1972, p. 127). Since Bowen devised the technique and used it first in his own family, he had to serve as his own coach.

What I find most striking in Bowen's discussion is the dramatically different tone in the relationship between the coaches and clients and between the clients and their families. Bowen, as coach, uses nonmanipulative means (education, logic, collaboration) to instruct clients how to manipulate or deal with their families.

What Bowen is doing, in a sense, is teaching these individuals to be therapists to their own families and, in particular, therapists of the Jackson-Haley type. Certain of the tactics he recommends seem similar to the paradoxical interventions, therapeutic double binds, and strategic maneuvers of the Jackson-Haley orientation. It is not immediately clear why Bowen does not coach individuals to be therapists of a Bowen type—that is, to be the same sort of therapist to their families that he is to them.

Jackson, Haley, Minuchin, and, to some extent, Bowen view family members as entirely dominated by the family system. If change is to be produced, it must be done by manipulating the family system.* Implicit in this general approach is a depth analytic view of human nature. According to these therapists, everyone is functioning at a primitive level.

---

*These therapists are untroubled by their use of manipulative therapeutic methods because they assume that everything anyone does—talking included—is a manipulation. Bowen, perhaps because of incomplete commitment to systems theory, intermixes manipulative and direct methods.

5

The Behavior Therapy Approach

Behavioral marital therapy appears at first to be completely free from depth analytic concepts. The orientation is based on generally accepted principles of learning and makes few assumptions about human nature. The problem with the approach is its inadequate analysis of the psychological meanings of behavior and its subsequent appeal to training, rule giving, and forced solutions. Behavioral marital therapists have a precise picture of what they consider appropriate couple behavior and can be coercive and occasionally moralistic in their efforts to impose or promote this behavior. The effect can be similar to that produced by depth analytic interventions.*

In this chapter attention is directed to three major elements of behavioral marital therapy: contingency contracting, cognitive restructuring, and communication training.

CONTINGENCY CONTRACTING

The central concept in behavioral marital therapy is positive reinforcement (Stuart, 1969; Rappaport and Harrell, 1972; Weiss, 1978; O'Leary and Turkewitz, 1978; Liberman, 1970; Jacobson, 1977). Weiss, Hops, and Patterson (1973) teach partners to become aware of what "pleases" and "displeases" (i.e., positively reinforces) the other. Therapy is then devoted to increasing their predisposition to provide "pleases" (Weiss, Birchler, and Vincent, 1974). Weiss, Hops, and Patterson (1973) recommend the use of "love days," and Stuart (1976) of "caring days," in which partners are to make special efforts to please each other.

Partners are then instructed to positively reinforce each other for providing "pleases." "Each time the husband helps the wife feed the baby (acceleration of a desirable behavior)," Rappaport and Harrel (1972) recommend, "he should receive verbal praise or a kiss from his spouse (a posi-

---

*Depth analysis establishes idealized and stereotyped behavioral norms or standards and describes as regressive any behavior that falls beneath these standards (Apfelbaum, 1980c). Behavioral marital therapy can be thought of as depth analytic in that it too judges people in terms of idealized and stereotyped norms.

tive reinforcer)." If one partner says "I love you," Stuart (1975, p. 252) writes, the other should make a comment that reinforces the thought (e.g., "Thank you") rather than one that weakens it (e.g., "No, you don't").

This general approach has a certain simplicity and elegance. Positive reinforcement can be viewed as the means of solving the two major relationship problems discussed in Chapter 2: mutual deprivation and inadequate control. If partners are being mutually deprived, it could be argued, why not deal with this directly and teach them how to gratify, please, or positively reinforce each other? And if these individuals are suffering from inadequate, inefficient, or nonoptimal means of establishing control in their relationships, why not teach them the method of controlling behavior often thought to be the most effective—positive reinforcement?

The most eloquent application of positive reinforcement in behavioral marital therapy is the method of contingency contracting. According to one form of this method, each partner is positively reinforced for positively reinforcing the other. In a case quoted by Gurman and Knudson (1978) in their excellent critique of behavioral marital therapy, a husband gets what he wants, a glass of beer, in return for doing what his wife wants, spending 10 minutes playing with the kids before dinner. In another, more striking example also quoted by Gurman and Knudson, a husband gets fellatio five times a week and the wife gets French provincial furniture (Koch and Koch, 1976).

Contingency contracting is criticized here on two grounds: its behavioral bias and its overly restricted view of positive reinforcement.

The Bias Toward Concrete Behavior—A One-Way Theory in a Two-Way World

Behavioral marital therapists typically begin by translating the general concerns of partners into behavioral terms. Partners who are accusing each other of being uncaring, irresponsible, or domineering are asked to give specific examples of events or interactions that demonstrate or typify this view. This can be very useful. The accusing individual may turn out to be primarily upset about a specific issue (e.g., the failure of the partner to help with housework), and asking for concrete examples may help focus on this concern.

Partners also make the opposite error, however. They make specific complaints ("you never take out the garbage") when their real concern is a more general issue, the feeling of being taken for granted or the sense of not being listened to or loved (Strayhorn, 1978). Behavioral marital therapists, with their preference for concrete behavior, are less likely to be helpful with this type of problem. Their approach might be to accept the original definition of the difficulty and to arrange a reciprocal exchange (i.e., the accused partner agrees to take out the garbage three times a week in return for something he or she wants).

The danger of an overly concrete definition of the problem appears inherent in the method of contingency contracting. Consider the exchange of a glass of beer for 10 minutes spent playing with the kids. The wife's concern that her husband spends insufficient time playing with the kids may be a specific statement of her feeling that he seems generally withdrawn from and uninvolved with the family (Gurman and Knudson, 1978, p. 130). She may also be concerned that he no longer seems interested in "playing" with her. The husband's preoccupation with beer, correspondingly, may be an expression of the fact that he is finding his family more of a burden than a source of satisfaction and that the only pleasures he looks forward to at home are noninterpersonal ones. The prescribed behavioral exchange, rather than producing change, can actually preserve the partners' unsatisfactory situation.

The fellatio–French provincial furniture example can be discussed in similar terms. Each partner appears to have given up on any real involvement or intimacy in the relationship. The wife has turned her attention, instead, to the outfitting of her home. If she cannot get satisfaction from the relationship, at least she can get a well-furnished house. The husband may be able to capture a fleeting sense of intimacy by convincing his wife to go through the motions of fellatio. An additional factor could be a desire to make her submit the way he feels he has been made to submit to her in other areas of the marriage. Here, as in the previous example, the major therapeutic task would seem to be not to institute an exchange but to draw attention to these underlying meanings and issues and, in general, to show how both partners are being deprived.

An Overly Restricted View of Positive Reinforcement

Behavioral marital therapy, it has been suggested, is based on positive reinforcement and, in particular, on facilitating the reciprocity of positive reinforcement between partners. My objection, from one point of view, is not that these therapists have overly extended the use and importance of the concept of positive reinforcement but rather that they may not have employed it quite fully enough.

This point can be made by considering the following two examples. In one, a husband agrees to do the dishes three times a week (which is what the wife wants) in return for sex twice a week (which is what he wants). In the other, presented by O'Leary and Turkewitz (1978, p. 280), a husband agrees to spend one evening or afternoon engaging in an activity with the whole family while the wife agrees to greet her husband when he comes home from work and show interest (i.e., ask questions) about his day.

The question I would ask is why these partners are not already engaging in these behaviors. How come the first wife is not interested in sex and how come the first husband does not enjoy helping his wife around the house? Similarly, why does the second husband not look forward to spending time with his family and why is the second wife not eager to find out what happened to him during the day?

The answer, behavior therapists would say, is that the individuals are not being reinforced for these responses. While I would agree, I disagree with the manner in which these practitioners conceptualize this lack of reinforcement. Behavioral marital therapists seem to assume a rather loose and general relationship between the reinforcing stimulus and the operant response.* At least this is what can be surmised from their therapeutic interventions. The assumption appears to be that having the dishes washed by her husband will eventually motivate the wife to want sex, and having sex will eventually motivate the husband to want to wash the dishes. In a similar manner, having her husband spend time with the family will motivate the second wife to express interest in her husband, and having his wife express interest in him will motivate him to spend time with the family.

I recommend a much tighter and more precise analysis of operant response and contingent reinforcement. O'Leary and Turkewitz (1978, p. 279), in a passage quite uncharacteristic of behavioral marital therapy, have suggested the kind of analysis I have in mind. They believe that changes in sexual behavior should not be included as part of a written contract or behavioral exchange. Rather than encouraging a wife to engage in sexual relations when she may not wish to do so, they recommend taking one step back and finding out why she does not desire sex. Attention is then directed to what in the relationship (e.g., lack of affection on the part of her husband) is interfering with her sexual interest.

My own suggestion is for behavioral marital therapists to apply this reasoning to every case. Agreeing to sex relations when you do not want them is an extreme example. But doesn't the same general principle apply in agreeing to greet one's husband and show interest in his day or agreeing to spend an afternoon or evening with one's family (O'Leary and Turkewitz' own example)? Since these are potentially enjoyable activities, it is clear that there are factors interfering with this enjoyment. Rather than having partners force themselves to do what one might think they might automatically and normally want to do, it would seem more profitable and more consistent with a good behavioral analysis to discover the interfering fac-

*Margolin (1980) has herself noted this problem.

tors—that is, to find out why these potentially rewarding or reinforcing activities are not rewarding to these individuals.

The wife, it may turn out, does not like hearing about her husband's day because he talks about it in an uninviting or offensive way—compulsively, impersonally, or in a manner that naggingly communicates his anxiety, anger, or depression about his job. More important, the wife may feel inhibited about interrupting him. If she is unable to stop him when she wishes to express her reactions to what he is saying and, in so doing, exert some minimal control over the situation, she is likely to start hoping he will not talk about his day at all.

A similar case could be made about the husband's lack of interest in spending time with his family. He may feel awkward with his kids or anticipate, perhaps correctly, that an outing with his family will inevitably lead to an argument with his wife about how to raise their children.

The wife's reluctance to hear about her husband's day and the husband's hesitancy to go on family outings now becomes apparent. In behavior therapy terms, each is feeling or being "punished" for this behavior. Rather than encouraging these partners to participate in activities that, it now becomes clear, they have good reason to avoid, it makes better sense to direct attention to what happens when they do engage in them.

The error for which I am criticizing behavioral marital therapists, ironically, is their failure to pin down with sufficient precision the aversive conditions and reinforcing contingencies that are motivating partners' behavior. Without knowing it, and presumably without intending it, these therapists may be encouraging partners to engage in behavior that is aversive or punishing to them. This may account for some of the resistance to change that these practitioners encounter in their therapeutic efforts (Weiss, 1978, p. 234) and for the array of therapeutic methods designed to counteract this resistance: lecturing, instruction, rehearsal, exhortation, signed contracts.

COGNITIVE RESTRUCTURING

The previous examples suggest how behavioral marital therapists can overlook important feelings and meanings underlying specific behavior or complaints. Certain contemporary behavior therapists, perhaps noting this problem, have devised a new set of methods, discussed under the general rubric "cognitive restructuring," that seeks to correct this deficiency. My belief is that these methods have not adequately corrected the behavioral bias and often lead to moralistic interventions.* Examples will be considered from Strayhorn (1968), Ellis (1958), and Jacobson and Margolin (1979).

*Cognitive restructuring often has the effect of trying to talk people out of their feelings.

Strayhorn

Strayhorn (1978), employing a cognitive restructuring approach, presents the case of a husband who is upset about his wife's tendency to be late. The traditional procedure would be to arrange a behavioral exchange (i.e., the wife is to be on time in return for something she wants).

Strayhorn does not do this and, instead, explores the meaning of this lateness with the husband. The husband, as it turns out, experiences it as a lack of caring. "If she cared about me," he says, "she wouldn't be late like this." So far so good. Strayhorn has modified the traditional behavior therapy approach in an important way. Attention is drawn to the general feelings (the sense of being unloved) underlying the specific behavior (being late).

There are two directions in which a therapist can then go. One is to pursue the husband's sense of uncertainty about his wife's feeling for him. The other is to plan an immediate solution. Strayhorn chooses the latter and, in so doing, reasserts the behavioral bias (i.e., the emphasis on behavioral definitions of problems and behavioral solutions).

There are two options for change, Strayhorn writes. Either the wife, recognizing that her husband views her punctuality as evidence of love, can arrange to be on time from then on or the husband, realizing that her lateness is merely a habit of her upbringing, can cease experiencing it as an indication of lack of love.

Strayhorn's discussion of how this solution is to be implemented suggests that it might be premature and forced. The planned change is not viewed as automatic and spontaneous, but as contrived and effortful. The wife must "rehearse being on time" and/or the husband must "rehearse" saying to himself, "Her lateness doesn't mean she doesn't love me—she's late because of her own habits and upbringing that have little to do with me. I'll look elsewhere if I want confirmation that she loves me. I still don't like waiting, but it doesn't mean I'm unloved."

Why is rehearsal necessary? If it is true that the husband has been suffering from the misconception that his wife's lateness indicates her lack of caring, wouldn't the discovery that this is not the case immediately resolve the problem and without the necessity of rehearsal, practice, or effort? Why does he need to talk himself into the change?

The answer may be that his sensitivity to his wife's lateness is merely a surface manifestation of a general feeling on his part that his wife really does not care for him. His new understanding of his wife's lateness would not alter his sensitivity to this issue because it would not touch this deeper concern.

The required therapeutic task, then, is not to try to talk this husband out of his sensitivity to his wife's lateness but to use it as a means of exposing the more general issue. The suggestion could be made, in fact, that he may be fortunate to be concerned about his wife's lateness. The greater danger is that he might go through his entire married life without confronting his doubts about his wife's feeling for him. His sensitivity to his wife's lateness may be a useful means, or even a unique opportunity, for contacting this important issue.

Ellis

When behavioral marital therapists write about cognitive restructuring (O'Leary and Turkewitz, 1968; Margolin and Weiss, 1978; Strayhorn, 1978; Jacobson and Margolin, 1979), they typically refer to the work of Albert Ellis. Ellis views couple conflict the way he views most other human problems: as a result of the irrational ideas that individuals have about themselves and the world around them. The following example (Ellis, 1958, pp. 27–28) is discussed at length because it gives particularly clear expression to the moralizing that appears to underlie certain forms of "cognitive restructuring."

Ellis describes a husband who was " 'fed up' with his wife's complaints and general unhappiness,. . . believed that his wife should be blamed for her mistakes, particularly the mistake of thinking he was having affairs with other women, when he was not, and also believed that it was unfair for his wife to criticize and sexually frustrate him when he was doing the best he could, under difficult circumstances, to help her." Ellis told him that it was irrational to blame his wife (blaming only makes things worse), that it was unrealistic to expect his wife not to criticize or sexually frustrate him (she was a disturbed individual and this is the kind of thing disturbed individuals do), and if he really wanted to help her he should be kind to and accepting of her.

The wife, as Ellis writes, "was terribly disturbed about the husband's alleged affairs with other women." She was "an extremely neurotic individual who . . . hated herself thoroughly for her incompetency; who severely blamed everyone, especially her husband, who did not love her unstintingly; and who felt that all her unhappiness was caused by her husband's lack of affection." Ellis told her that it was "self-defeating" to believe that she needed to be "inordinately loved and protected," that it was irrational and counterproductive to blame herself and her husband, and that happiness could not come from her husband but only from within.

Ellis brings up an interesting issue. My guess is that few therapists would disagree with his contention that individuals suffer from unrealistic ideas and, in particular, the belief that the partner is to blame for their problems. If we do agree with this, why do we not all do what Ellis described himself doing with these partners and "ruthlessly" and "forthrightly" expose their "nonsensical" and "self-defeating" beliefs "to the merciless light of rationality?" (Ellis, 1958, pp. 27–28).

There are perhaps two major reasons that I do not adopt Ellis' approach. First, it is moralistic, or at least semimoralistic. Ellis (1976) has pointed to the pressured element in neurotic thinking, the voice of self-hate, the feeling of individuals that they, their partners, or their situations are "terrible" or "awful" and must change. He calls this *"must*erbation" and suggests that a "should," "ought," or "must" underlies most irrational thinking. In observing what Ellis is telling clients, however, we find that he comes very close to saying that they should or must change. It would be hard for clients, hearing Ellis' impassioned words, not to feel condemned for clinging to their "irrational" or "nonsensical" beliefs.

Ellis (1962, p. 132) has partly acknowledged his moralistic position. He has suggested, in agreement with Mowrer (1960), that emotional disturbance is caused by the disturbed person's "immoral actions."

Ellis' moralizing is expressed, in part, in the form of preachiness. Statements such as two wrongs do not make a right, blaming does no one any good, and everyone is responsible for his or her own happiness (Ellis, 1958, pp. 27–28), while perhaps true or at least partly true, are the kind of lecturing comments people continually make to each other (and to themselves). Most therapists prefer to avoid such truisms.

The second major reason I do not employ Ellis' approach is that his reasoning does not seem entirely correct. It is true that disturbed behavior is caused by underlying unrealistic beliefs, and Ellis has done us a service by so crisply stating the problem. My own view, however, is that many of the ideas that Ellis substitutes in their place are themselves somewhat faulty, or at least incomplete. Partners in a disturbed relationship need new thoughts, but of a different type than those Ellis wishes to give them.

Ellis, viewing this wife as suffering from the irrational idea that "she had to be inordinately loved and protected," tells her that it is self-defeating to maintain this belief. While it is true that she may have unrealistic expectations about being loved, the more immediate and obvious problem is that she is not able to obtain the most minimal satisfactions that people ordinarily obtain from marriage. She does not even believe that she has her husband's interest. Her fear that he is having affairs with other women appears to be in part a consequence of her feeling that she is too "stupid and worthless" (p. 28) for him to want to have an "affair" with her.

The other major unrealistic idea from which these individuals are suffering is the belief that their partner is responsible for their problems. While it is true that they irrationally accuse each other and that it might be useful for them to realize (if they do not already know it) that this is counterproductive, they also need to appreciate that it is understandable, given the situtation with which each is faced, that they might each feel like blaming the other.

Thus, while I agree with Ellis that the wife has unrealistic expectations about marriage and that both partners irrationally blame the other, these seem to me to be only isolated elements in the problem.

My own inclination would be to suggest to these partners that they may not be appreciating the extent to which they are each being deprived. "Here you are," I might say to this wife, "a woman who felt unloved as a child and with concerns about your lovability. You come to this marriage with the hope of finally being able to feel truly and unconditionally loved. And what happens? Not only is this fantasy hope unfulfilled, you don't even feel you have your husband's interest. You believe he is more attracted to other women."

"And you are in an equally difficult spot," I might then say, turning to the husband. "All you wanted was an ordinary, moderately satisfying relationship. And what happens? You have a wife who, believing you do not love her, criticizes you, blames you for things you feel you have not done (having affairs), and becomes sexually disinterested in you.

"What makes the situation more difficult for each of you is that the one person to whom you might ordinarily turn for help in such a case, each other, is not available as a resource. You don't even get the chance to complain to the other and to feel that the other understands. The other *doesn't* understand and just feels that you don't understand him or her. Given all these frustrations, I can see how one of you might be concerned that the other is having an affair and how the other might be 'fed up.' "

The purpose of this intervention would be to help the partners feel entitled to blame each other so they can stop compulsively trying to free themselves from self-blame.

Jacobson and Margolin

The method of "cognitive restructuring," although designed to enlighten partners, may have the ironic effects of ending productive thinking, turning insight into coercion, and propagating faulty or arbitrary ideas.

Ending Constructive Thinking

Jacobson and Margolin (1979) describe a couples therapy session in which a wife blurts out, "What I really want is to recapture the times we used to have. We were very much in love once. It was romantic. We didn't have a care in the world as long as we had each other."

The therapist, apparently concerned about the unrealistic nature of this wife's wishes, quickly interjects:

I'm not sure I can help you do that. You seldom run into couples who can maintain the romance long past the honeymoon. Don't forget that there was a lot of mystery back then, everything was new, you were discovering each other. Now you know each other, there is not as much to discover. The honeymoon ends in the best of marriages. What you can give each other now is a great deal of satisfaction and fulfillment, and occasional romance. But what you're talking about is going back to an era that is over, an era that is part and parcel of early courtship and the process of getting to know each other. (p. 147)

It is not immediately clear why this therapist felt it was necessary to deliver this lecture. My guess is that the wife could have given it herself, and might have done so if the therapist had asked her if she felt that it might actually be possible to recapture those earlier times. Irrespective of this, however, I would not want to quash this wife's wishes but to find out more about them.

The way she began, with the words, "What I really want," suggests that she might have just been talking about a mundane issue, for example, wishing more help around the house, and then suddenly made contact with a richer and more important set of needs. In asking her more about these early days and how the present is different, it may become apparent that their initial intimacy has almost completely disappeared, that the husband feels this too, and that she and he have not really talked about it until this point. If so, her "unrealistic" expectations might be a valuable opportunity to be used rather than a dangerous belief requiring "cognitive restructuring."

Turning Insight Into Coercion

What Ellis and behavior therapists are trying to do is to convince partners to behave more reasonably. In so doing, they take useful insights (e.g., Strayhorn's recognition that the husband's concern about his wife's lateness is based on a fear that she does not care for him; Ellis' discovery of the voice of self-hate) and turn them into coercions—that is, things that must be changed.* In applying this pressure for change, they instruct, train, lecture, and moralize.

This shift from insight to imperative is clearly seen in the following example. Jacobson and Margolin (1979) discuss a wife who, after three weeks of warm feelings toward her husband, became demoralized when she suddenly felt she no longer loved him. The therapist, in an intervention that was quite consistent with the stimulus–response thinking of behavior therapy, pointed out that love was not an abstract condition, but a response to specific events and, in particular, to her husband's behavior toward her.

---

*Constance Apfelbaum (Apfelbaum and Apfelbaum, 1973) talks about "the reflex-like conversion of insight into moral imperative."

This seemed to me to be an excellent intervention and demonstrated an important grain of truth in behavior therapy. The reason for the wife's loss of feeling of love, it turned out, was the husband's lack of affectionate behavior. "I'm not always good to you," he admitted. "This week I ignored you. I stopped trying. I'm sorry" (p. 145).

Husband and wife had just been given a powerful new tool. In place of the demoralizing view that "being in love" or "not being in love" was something that just happened and about which no one has any control, they had been introduced to the idea that such feelings were directly related to what was occurring in the relationship. The implications of such a new understanding can be quite dramatic and can give partners an entirely different way of experiencing their relationship.

The danger, and it appeared from the husband's reaction that he was already falling prey to it, is that the value of this insight can be subverted by one or both individuals feeling that it is now his or her responsibility, and at whatever personal sacrifice, to behave in a way that will bring forth these loving feelings in the other.

The therapist's task in such an eventuality is to point out that this is happening and to help the individual deal with these self-blaming ideas. Instead of doing this, however, the therapist in the present case did the exact opposite and reaffirmed the husband's self-blame. The therapist said, "You see, John, you have to work to maintain her love. Sometime you'll fail. But lately you've learned that you can do it most of the time" (p. 146).

With this simple comment, although delivered in a friendly, avuncular manner, the therapist nullified much of the value of the original insight (i.e., that the feeling of love is a function of what is happening in the relationship) and turned it into a compulsion. Suppose the husband did not always feel like working to maintain his wife's love? In fact, suppose he never felt like doing it? Why is the therapist telling him what he is supposed to do?

Promoting a Duty-Oriented Philosophy of Intimacy

A third and related characteristic of behavioral marital therapists' utilization of "cognitive restructuring" is the promotion of a particular philosophy or belief about relationships. This belief has already been suggested in previous examples. The therapist's comment, "You see, John, you have to work to maintain her love" and the therapist's quickness in telling the wife her romantic wishes were unrealistic, suggest a view of relationships based on duty and requiring effort, conscientiousness, and a firm grasp on reality.

This is an understandable consequence of the behavior therapy perspective. Disturbed behavior is seen as the result of faulty habits (i.e., defective ways of dealing with reality). Therapy is then devoted to establishing a more adaptive coordination between the individual and the environment.

Such learning or relearning is thought to require discipline, practice, effort, and rehearsal. It is something that one might not naturally want to do.

The emphasis on dutifulness and conscientiousness is clear in Jacobson's (1978, p. 30) example of a husband who, at his wife's request, agrees to ask his mother-in-law at least five questions during the course of an hour's conversation and to make a positive comment both about her physical appearance and the meal she has cooked. This husband is to feign interest in order to make his mother-in-law feel better. In asking your partner about his or her day, Stuart (1975, p. 250; 1976, p. 129) advises, always follow your first question with a second in order to show that you are really interested. This is to be done, apparently, regardless of whether one is interested or wants to ask a second question. Stuart designates this the "two question rule" and presents it as one of a set of "relationship rules" that partners are to follow.

Stuart is drawing attention to an important social truth—the fact that people may ask questions simply to be polite. Their lack of interest is then communicated by their failure to ask follow-up questions. Stuart's solution is to increase partners' skill in feigning interest. The individual is to ask a second question and, in so doing, make it more difficult for the person answering to detect the questioner's lack of interest. The effect may be to drive the problem of their mutual withdrawal further underground and to endorse a style of relating based upon pseudomutuality. Stuart and other behavioral marital therapists appear convinced that politeness and conscientiousness can lead to intimacy. I believe that politeness and conscientiousness may be the cause of the partners' lack of intimacy.

COMMUNICATION SKILLS TRAINING*

Communication skills training is an important element in the behavioral marital therapist's repertoire.** This is understandable. Partners are seen by these practitioners as suffering from faulty relationship habits or deficient relationship skills. The obvious solution is to provide them with the requisite skills.

The Jacobson-Margolin approach to communication training appears to be "training" in a full sense. They offer partners rules to follow, give "positive feedback" if these individuals follow the rules and "negative feedback" if they do not, and take them through practice exercises.

*See Plum, (in press) for a general critique of communication skills training.

**There is a recent tendency among behavioral marital therapists (Jacobson, 1978; Margolin, 1980) to de-emphasize contingency contracting and place major reliance upon communication training and problem-solving training.

Consider the following example of a therapist teaching a husband and wife the communication skill of summarizing what the partner has just said and then checking with this partner about the accuracy of the summary.

T: Don't forget to indicate to her that you understand what she's saying. For example, Helen, tell me what you said you just told John.

W: I told him that . . .

T: No, say it to me, as if I were John, and I will answer as John.

W: I'm worried about what will happen when Don and Linda get back in town. We haven't seen them in seven years, and when we used to get together with them, the two of you ignored me and got very sarcastic.

T: You're worried that when Don and Linda get back in town, things will be like they were before. Is that right?

W: Yes.

T: OK John, go to it. Start again Helen.

W: *(repeats previous remark.)*

H: I can understand why you're upset, but . . .

T: No John, telling her you understand isn't the same as summarizing what she said. How does she know you understand? She has to take you on faith unless you tell her.

H: You're afraid that Don and I will get exclusive and ignore you and be sarcastic, but . . .

T: Check it out with her.

H: Is that what you said?

W: Uh-hum.

T: Good. (Jacobson and Margolin, 1979, pp. 197–198)

What is happening, if one looks at the details of the interchange, is that the husband is being interrupted in his attempt to defend himself. John's first statement, "I can understand why you're upset, but . ..," shows only token compliance with the task of summarizing. The reason, we can imagine, is that he is eager to get to the "but"—that is, to the place where he can begin stating his answer or defense. If the therapist had not been there, John probably would have left out the "I can understand why you're upset" and immediately have started with the defense.

John's next attempt ("you're afraid that Don and I will get exclusive and ignore you and be sarcastic, but . . .") is again halfhearted. While he did summarize what Helen has said, he did not check back with her about the accuracy of it. Here, as before, he seemed impatient to get to the "but."

What the therapist appears to be doing, in essence, is making John wait longer and longer before letting him do what he wants to do—state his defense. This does not seem to me to be a very effective way of dealing with defensiveness and is likely only to increase frustration. A better approach, I suggest, is to comment directly on it, for example, in response to John's original statement ("I can understand why you're upset, but . . .") saying, "It sounds as if you feel Helen is making an unfair complaint, and you want to defend yourself."

Jacobson and Margolin make no mention of the husband's wish to defend himself. The reason, I believe, is that they are attributing his resistance not to defensiveness but to the inertia or resistance that is to be expected when one attempts to extinguish an old habit and replace it with a new one.* Teaching couples communication, these authors write, "resembles instruction in other kinds of technical skills such as learning to operate an automobile" (p. 192). John, it could be argued, in applying this metaphor to his situation, has learned the wrong way of driving a car (i.e., of communicating with his wife). It could take a fair amount of instruction and practice, behavior therapists might suggest, for him to learn the right way.

One problem with behaviorally oriented communication skills training, in other words, is a tendency to overlook important motivational factors (e.g., John's wish to defend himself). Another is a tendency to turn insight into imperative—to go beyond education (i.e., providing information) and begin telling partners how they should communicate. Consider the following intervention.

Partner 1: Well, I think that the best alternative would be for you to . . .

Partner 2: No, I can't go along with . . .

Therapist: Stop. You just interrupted Partner 1. Keep away from interruptions because they frustrate your partner and show that you're not listening well. Listen to your partner, and wait for him or her to finish. (Lester, Beckham, and Baucom, 1980, p. 192)

The therapist provides a valuable service in pointing out how interrupting frustrates people. This can be useful to individuals who do not realize they are interrupting or fail to recognize the effect that this has on their partners. The therapist then goes one step further and tells Partner 2 to not interrupt. This seems to me an unfortunate addition. Suppose this individual feels unjustly criticized and wants to interrupt even while knowing that this may just make the situation worse. In fact, maybe Partner 2 *wants* to make the situation worse in order to express how angry or distressed he or she feels. Why should this person be kept from doing so?

---

*Weiss and Margolin (1977, p. 594) have stated that resistance to or noncompliance with treatment suggestions, assignments, and instructions "may signal nothing more than profound skill deficit."

At issue here is the behavioral marital therapy concern with positive reinforcement. Interrupting has an aversive or punishing effect on one's partner and the therapist is trying to encourage an exchange of positive reinforcers. It is these individuals' own efforts to positively reinforce their partners, however, and to avoid punishing them that may be causing the problem. In their strenuous attempts to be polite and considerate and to avoid starting a fight, people suppress anger and resentment. Partners who suppress "negative" feelings, as it is well known, generally find themselves with little spontaneous "positive" feeling.

The precondition for positive reinforcement, accordingly, may be an increased ability to make complaints.* Behavioral marital therapists picture positive reinforcement in the following pattern: A rewards B, B rewards A, A rewards B, and so on. While this sequence certainly does occur, it is not the only pattern. If partners need to discharge negative feelings preliminary to expressing love or caring, the following pattern might occur: A punishes** B, B punishes A, A rewards B, B rewards A. A well-known example is the warm interchange following a clear-the-air fight.

Certain behavioral marital therapists, recognizing the need of partners to express angry feelings, may allow for limited forms of such communication. O'Leary and Turkewitz (1978) permit expressions of feeling ("I get angry when you leave your clothes around") but not insults ("You're a slob"). They warn about partners who subvert this right to express feelings by saying, "*I feel* you're a slob."

I am not convinced that a statement such as, "I feel you're a slob," is a subversion. The accusing partner may honestly feel at the moment that his or her partner is a slob. What O'Leary and Turkewitz (1978) are saying, I would argue, is that some feelings are okay to express while others are not.

The exclusion of certain feelings is even more clearly demonstrated in another of O'Leary and Turkewitz' "ground rules." "Expressing negative feelings regarding something a spouse cannot change (such as height, family members)," these authors write, "is not likely to be productive and is not encouraged" (pp. 275–276). They are suggesting that complaints must be limited to factors that the accused individual has at least a possibility of changing.

Behavior therapists have an understandable reason for wanting to suppress or tone down accusation and insult. Although the expression of anger

---

*Behavioral marital therapists are worried that partners may "forget" to be nice to each other. I am often more concerned that they may "forget" their complaints.

**"Punish" is being used here in a special sense, to refer to behavior (complaints; expressions of anger) that may appear to an observer to be potentially aversive or punishing to the partner.

can clear the air and set the stage for positive exchanges, it can also lead to irreconcilable, out-of-control arguments.

At issue here is one of the classic problems of couples therapy—how to satisfy the need of partners to express angry feelings while protecting them from the dangers of uncontrolled argument. Behavioral marital therapists deal with this problem by limiting partners' expressions of anger to non-provocative forms. My own preference is to increase the ability of partners to incorporate anger into their relationships—that is, to increase their ability to acknowledge and express such feelings without the situation inevitably and irrecoverably spiraling out of control.

3

Special Characteristics of My Approach

6

The Inevitability of
Fantasy and Alienation

Each of the three major contemporary approaches to couples therapy has made important contributions. The psychoanalytic orientation has produced the basic concepts and methods out of which the field of psychotherapy and the specialty of couples therapy developed. Of particular pertinence to the current orientation are the notions of transference and impulse derivatives and the therapeutic methods of clarification and interpretation. The psychoanalytic approach has been criticized here for its preoccupation with childhood causes and primitive impulses.

The major contribution of the systems theory orientation has been the uninterrupted attention directed to present couple interactions. Systems theory counteracts the tendency of the psychoanalytic approach to drift off into the personal histories and pathologies of the individual partners. It accomplishes this service, however, at what seems to me to be too great a cost, by repudiating individual oriented motivational explanations and requiring acceptance of questionable family and couple oriented explanations, for example, homeostasis. A further problem is the reestablishment, in a new form, of the psychoanalyst's picture of psychotherapy as a struggle between an individual (or partners) seeking to maintain regressive gratification and a therapist seeking therapeutic change.

An important contribution of the behavior therapy approach has been its acknowledgment of the fact that partners in a troubled relationship are in a chronically deprived state and are in insufficient control of the relationship. The major drawback is its inadequate analysis of the psychological meanings of behavior and its subsequent employment of a therapeutic approach based on rule giving, training, moralizing, and forced solutions.

I turn now to a discussion of my own approach. These next five chapters review several general characteristics and assumptions of the orientation. This chapter suggests that fantasy and alienation are inevitable in intimate relationships. Chapter 7 questions the present day emphasis on compromise and indicates the value of not compromising. Chapter 8 describes my position on the individual versus systems issue. Chapter 9 discusses the contemporary predilection for action oriented approaches and presents my argument for an insight orientation. Chapter 10, the key chapter in the series, considers the important issue of disqualification.

This chapter begins with a common couple event—the meeting of partners at the end of a day spent apart—and uses this to suggest that fantasy and alienation are inevitable in an intimate relationship.

COUPLE PATTERNS

A familiar couple event is the meeting of partners at the end of a day. Each has had a difficult day, let us suppose, and is looking forward to this meeting with the fantasy that the partner will compensate for these difficulties.

As soon as the husband walks through the door, however, both sets of hopes are immediately crushed. The wife who seeks rescue from an unpleasant day at home discovers the proposed rescuer is tired, discouraged, and needs to be rescued himself. The husband who wishes to be refreshed by a warm, attentive, nondemanding spouse is faced instead with a series of complaints and requests ("the kids need new clothes," "your daughter needs to be talked to," "the refrigerator doesn't work," "let's go out to dinner") made by a tense and frazzled partner.

Mutual Withdrawal

If both partners respond to the disappointment at the door by withdrawing, the result will be an evening characterized by nonengagement and perhaps suppressed resentment. Both will immerse themselves in independent activities, and, if there is any contact between them, it will be in impersonal or ritualized forms such as silently watching television together.

This is a classic couple pattern. Satir (1972) talks about "placators" and "distractors," partners who are careful to avoid doing or saying anything that may hurt the other's feelings or start an argument. Mace (1972) discusses the marital pattern of "limited interpersonal involvement;" Cuber and Harroff (1965, pp. 46–50) refer to "devitalized" relationships; Weiss (1979) describes the "nothing ever happens couple;" Framo (1965, p. 188) discusses the pattern of silent marital discord; Bach and Wyden (1968) describe such partners as "fight-evaders" and "doves;" and Lederer and Jackson (1968), borrowing a term from Scheflen (1960), designate them "the gruesome twosome."

Haley (1963a) describes the progressive nature of mutual withdrawal.

If a couple is unable to have a fight and so bring up what is on their minds, they are dealing with each other by withdrawal techniques and avoiding any discussion of certain areas of their relationship. With each avoidance, the area that cannot be discussed grows larger until ultimately they may have nothing they can safely talk about . . . When a couple cannot fight, all issues which require defining an area of the relationship are avoided. The couple will then eat together and watch television side by side, but their life has little shared intimacy (p.219).

Mutual Accusation

If both partners respond to the frustration of their fantasy hopes by blaming the other, the result will be an evening of reoccurring or accelerating argument, often about issues only tangentially related to the original disappointment. Compared to the subtle and easily overlooked alienation of the previous partners, these individuals are clearly and dramatically at odds with one another. Each feels unacknowledged, misunderstood, or betrayed by an unreasonable, provocative, insensitive, or selfish spouse.

This pattern corresponds to the cultural stereotype of the troubled relationship. Mace (1976) refers to it as an "artillery duel," Mittelmann (1956) describes it as a "mutual attempt at domination, coupled with a violent defense," and Framo (1965, p. 188) discusses it as the pattern of open marital discord. Fogarty (1976) labels these partners "the openly conflictual twosome," Lederer and Jackson (1965), in their own descriptive style, designate them "the weary wranglers," Satir (1972) discusses them as "blamers," and Bach and Wyden (1968) refer to them as "gunnysackers," and "hawks."

Demanding-Withdrawn

In this pattern one partner responds by approaching, either in a renewed appeal for contact or in anger, and the other by withdrawing (Mittelmann, 1956; Jackson, 1967). The wife, for example, may attempt to rescue some element of her plan for a stimulating evening by making a desperate effort to engage her husband in "meaningful" conversation. The husband's response to this early evening disappointment is to withdraw. The result is a mutually alienating polarization. Fogarty (1976; 1979), who describes this pattern particularly lucidly, calls it the pursuer-distancer interaction. Gehrke and Moxom (1962) refer to it as the "detached-demanding" conflict, Napier (1978) designates it the "rejection-intrusion pattern," and Hiebert and Stahmann (1977) discuss it as the "attaching-detaching marriage." Barnett (1971) appears to be talking about the same type of interaction in his description of the marriage between an obsessional neurotic and an hysteric.

An irony of the demanding-withdrawn pattern, as Fogarty (1976) points out, is that the "pursuer" in one area of the relationship may become the "distancer" in another. Let us imagine that this husband, who did originally have high hopes for the evening, begins to feel that perhaps the night can be rescued with sex. With this in mind, he comes over and caresses his wife. This sudden reaching out after his previous cool detachment comes across to his wife as impersonal and forced. Because of this, and because she is feeling frustrated and resentful, she shrugs him off. His attempts to solve the problem (through sex) conflict with her way of experiencing the problem (loss of interest in sex).

General Comments About These Three Couple Patterns

The first point to make about these three patterns is that they represent distinctive states of couple experience. Each has its own self-reinforcing or even self-generating quality (Jackson, 1967). Cautiousness in one withdrawn partner stimulates cautiousness in the other much as whispering elicits whispering. The attacks of one accusing partner provoke the counterattacks of the other, leading to accelerating spirals of criticism and defense or accusation and counteraccusation. Finally, the demanding partner's demands intensify the withdrawing partner's need to withdraw, and vice versa.

Although there are some couples who seem to adopt one of these patterns as their basic relationship style and exclude the other two, the more common tendency is to shift among them. As Bach and Wyden (1968) noted, periods of accusation are often set up by previous periods of withdrawal ("fight-evading"). It is not unusual for partners to complain about interminable fighting (mutual accusation) one week, lament the loss of feeling for each other (mutual withdrawal) the next, and despair over their "basic differences" (demanding–withdrawn) the third. I have found it useful, accordingly, to think of these couple patterns as states of relationship experience (couple states) that parallel and approximate the shifting mood states (ego states) of individuals.

AFTER THE HONEYMOON

The partners meeting at the door is an example of fantasy expectation in everyday life. The model case of fantasy in relationships, however, is the honeymoon. This could be considered a period of institutionalized fantasy fulfillment (Lederer and Jackson, 1968. pp. 42–43; Framo, 1965, p. 186; Gurman, 1978, p. 453; Ables and Brandsma, 1977, pp. 2–7; Jacobson and Margolin, 1979, pp. 21–22). Each partner is able to overlook the strains and frictions that might interfere with their shared romantic fantasy.

The fate of the relationship then depends on what happens when the honeymoon is over and, in particular, how partners deal with the realization that many of their fantasy based expectations are not to be realized. The sequence of events is very much like what occurred with the partners who met at the door.

First there is a stage of fantasy expectation or fulfillment. This is followed by a period of disappointment and disillusionment and then a reaction or adjustment to this disappointment. The partners who felt so much in love during the courting and honeymoon periods now find themselves mutually withdrawn, mutually accusing, or demanding–withdrawn.

THE INEVITABILITY OF ALIENATION

The common effect of the three troubled couple states is alienation. Mutually withdrawn partners are quietly estranged, mutually accusing partners are openly estranged, and demanding–withdrawn partners are polarized. Here is the tragedy of romantic fantasies. People form relationships in search of intimacy and find isolation.

It would seem a great advantage to avoid this sequence of fantasy, disappointment, and alienation. This turns out not to be easy. Fantasy, the first element, constitutes a major motivating force behind relationships. Most people approach their partners with some sort of fantasy based expectations. Disappointment, the second element, appears equally unavoidable. The imperfection of human life generally prevents these idealized expectations from being realized.

The final element of this tragic sequence offers some possibility for intervention. Alienation occurs when partners act on their feeling of disappointment; they withdraw, accuse, or demand. If instead partners were to share their disappointment, they might be able to short-circuit the alienation.

Although it may be possible to resolve the problem in this manner this is rarely done, at least with any consistency. The pattern of fantasy, disappointment, and alienation occurs with such frequency and subtlety that it often eludes the awareness of even the most insightful couples. The alternative, and this is the approach developed in this book, is to establish ways of coming to terms with this inevitable alienation.

The thesis may seem overstated. It is true that alienation is widespread. In addition to those partners who appear overtly troubled, there are large numbers who keep their dissatisfactions to themselves, perhaps surprising their friends by filing for divorce after several decades of what seemed to be happy marriages. But is it accurate to say that alienation is inevitable? What about those individuals who never expected intimacy in the first place? Is it justifiable to describe them as alienated? And what about those who feel their romantic fantasies are being fulfilled?

An example of partners who may not be expecting intimacy are those who form traditional role oriented marriages. The guiding motivation of these individuals is not the fantasy of romance but the image of living a culturally sanctioned life. Their concern is to fulfill the classic tasks, responsibilities, and role expectations of husband and wife, to do what "happily married" people are supposed to do and in the way they are supposed to do it.

Since these partners are not expecting intimacy, they will not be disappointed by its absence. They may be vulnerable, however, to problems arising from their own particular fantasies. These partners need to feel that their marriage is consistent with the cultural ideal. An important element here, at least in our society, is the maintenance of a cheerful, tactful, uncomplaining attitude (Jackson and Lederer, 1968). The result of such an attitude, as is well known, is pseudomutuality, the model of the alienated relationship.

Another group of partners who do not expect intimacy are those who view themselves as unlovable or as unable to love. These are individuals with reduced expectations. Instead of hoping for intimacy, they may feel lucky or grateful just to have someone who is willing to stay with them (Kubie, 1956). These partners do not feel alienated because they accept alienation as the norm.

Still another group of potentially unalienated partners are those who feel their fantasies of intimacy are being fulfilled. Such a belief generally requires the "bypassing" of considerable contradicting evidence (Apfelbaum, 1977a). Each partner drifts off into his or her own private fantasies about the relationship. The sense of intimacy is thus maintained but at the cost of shutting out part of the relationship and ignoring the partner.

I am not saying that intimacy is impossible in relationships. In fact, nearly everyone appears to have at least short periods of such experience. There is an advantage, however, in assuming that a certain amount of alienation is inevitable. Therapists who have such a perspective will be able to recognize mutual withdrawal, mutual accusation, or demanding–withdrawn polarization as expected, recurrent, and inherent features of relationships and not just as indications of psychopathology.

THE INEVITABILITY OF FANTASY

If, as suggested here, the root of partners' conflicts is their fantasy based expectations, therapy should perhaps be directed to substituting more realistic expectations. The problem with this is that fantasy based expectations appear also to be an integral part of intimate relations. People deal with frustrations in everyday life by recalling past glories and/or anticipating future ones. If individuals do not include their partners in their daydreams it is probably only because they are featuring someone or something else.

The depth analytic view is that fantasy expectations are based on irrational, infantile, or destructive wishes that must be outgrown, renounced, or "resolved" (Sager, 1976; Ables and Brandsma, 1977; Kubie, 1956; Meissner, 1978). The partners who meet at the door hoping to be rescued from difficult days might be seen by these authors as narcissistic or orally dependent persons operating under the omnipotent infantile belief that their partners should drop everything and fulfill their regressive wishes.

The problem with these partners, I believe, is not that they are too deeply committed to their "infantile" positions but rather that they are not committed enough. These individuals were clearly uncomfortable with their fantasy wishes, perhaps because they felt they were not entitled to have them. Rather than telling his wife about his desires, for example, the husband just presented himself at the door with the vague, half conscious hope that she might spontaneously start fulfilling them. The wife did not express her wishes either. She simply listed all the things that had gone wrong that day, perhaps hoping that her husband would somehow figure out that she needed to be swept away. And then, when their fantasy expectations were disappointed, they did not talk about it. In fact, they are likely to have had little awareness of what was happening. All they may have known is that they suddenly felt withdrawn, angry, or lonely.

While Jacobson and Margolin (1979) and Ables and Brandsma (1977), among others, denounce fantasy based expectations, I build the therapy around them. It is partners' own discomfort with these fantasies that is causing much of the problem. The therapeutic goal, in Constance Apfelbaum's words, is to enable these individuals to "inhabit" their relationship — that is, to help them discover what kind of relationship they are having. The fantasies of partners provide critical clues to their experience of the relationship.

7

Love and Compromise

Two beliefs about intimate relationships are particularly widespread: the conviction that they are based on *love* and the belief that they require an ability and wllingness to *compromise.* The first can be considered a romantic view of intimate relationships and the second a pragmatic one.

Contemporary professional opinion rejects the romantic view and bases itself on the pragmatic one. A major difference between couples and therapists, it seems, is that couples typically talk about love and therapists rarely talk about it. If there is one dominant trend among present-day couples therapists, however, it is the value placed on encouraging or teaching couples to negotiate and compromise.

The antipathy of therapists to the notion of love is understandable. "Love" is a concept that can be used in a nebulous and empty way, ending thinking about an issue. In an attempt to explain why they remain in dissatisfying relationships, partners often say, "I guess I just love him (her)." This is supposed to explain everything. Or, "He does this and that cruel thing to me, but deep down I know he loves me" (Framo, 1965, p. 189).

It is probably accurate to say that as much damage has been done in the name of love as in the name of hate. Lederer and Jackson (1968) are perhaps the best known of the authors who discuss the dangers of romantic ideals. The title of their book, *Mirages of Marriage,* suggests this concern, and they begin by describing seven false assumptions to which they attribute major responsibility for contemporary marital unhappiness. Of particular pertinence here are the first three: "that people marry because they love each other, that most married people love each other, and that love is necessary for a satisfactory marriage."

In this chapter I consider how theorists from each of the three major schools of couples therapy arrive at the same general conclusion: that partners in a troubled relationship need to renounce their fantasy based expectations and learn to compromise. My own view, in contrast, is that partners may need to stop compromising and instead pursue their romantic fantasies. I shall consider the generally accepted view first since my own position is in part a response to this general view.

THE PHILOSOPHY OF ENLIGHTENED SELF-INTEREST

Contemporary couples therapists might be thought to have few illusions about human nature. Behavioral marital therapists in particular assume motivational principles no more elaborate nor grand than those that cause rats to press a bar for water or pigeons to peck a disc for food. It is the genius of the behavioral approach, in fact, that so much can be understood from so few principles. Intimate relationships are explained in the same way as other behaviors, as arrangements engaged in by individuals to increase positive reinforcement and decrease aversive consequences. The only substantial difference from the standard rat-in-a-Skinner-box situation is that *two* organisms are involved. The solution to this problem, and it is an ingenious one, is to make each partner the reinforcing agent of the other. The result is the principle of reciprocal reinforcement and the method of contingency contracting.

Don Jackson, a major proponent of systems theory, arrives at the same place but from a different direction. Systems theorists never have had much to say about love and romance, as Ransom (1980) notes. These are needs and feelings associated with individuals, and systems theory is primarily concerned with the need of the system to maintain homeostatic balance. Systems theorists who do appear to consider individuals' needs (Jackson, 1959; Haley, 1963b) talk about power and control rather than love. It is this concern about power and, in particular, the manner in which partners distribute power and control, that leads to the focus on bargaining. In his later work, Jackson (1965a, 1965b) draws attention to the implicit "rules" by which partners determine, among other things, who is to have control in which situations and what each is to give or allow in return for what.

In their book, *Mirages of Marriage,* Lederer and Jackson (1968) turn this notion into a therapeutic technique. The problems of partners—their incompatible wishes, false assumptions about marriage, and efforts to control each other—are to be resolved by establishing the relationship on the firm ground of overtly stated and negotiated *quid pro quo* (something for something) arrangements. Lederer and Jackson thus end up in the same place as the behavioral marital therapists. The concept of *quid pro quo* is related to that of reciprocal reinforcement.

Sager (1976), Martin (1976), Ables and Brandsma (1977), and Kubie (1956), all psychoanalytically oriented practitioners, approach from yet a third direction. Kubie decries the Western tradition of romantic love that "rationalizes and beautifies a neurotic state of obsessional infatuation" (p. 10). The major source of unhappiness between partners, Kubie states, is their unconscious, fantasy based, childhood wishes. One solution, he suggests, is to make these unconscious and unattainable goals of the marriage conscious. It may be possible then "for the married couple to help each other work out a harmonious compromise between their divergent purposes" (p. 40).

While Kubie talks about "a harmonious compromise" between the unconscious and unattainable goals of partners, it was Clifford Sager who popularized the notion of "renegotiating the marital contract." The concept of the marital contract and, in particular, the unconscious marital contract fits quite naturally into psychoanalytic thinking. Psychoanalysts have traditionally viewed marriage, in part, as an effort by partners to gratify unconscious, regressive, fantasy based wishes. The term "unconscious marital contract" is a way of describing this. The goal of therapy for Sager, as it is also for Martin and for Kubie, is to bring this unconscious contract to awareness, to renounce the regressive impulses underlying this contract, and to renegotiate the marital contract on a more realistic basis. This concept is similar to those of contingency contracting and *quid pro quo*.

What these proponents of the three major approaches have done, in a sense, is to formalize conventional wisdom. When partners discuss a problem with a friend, the friend generally tries to advise a compromise. If the husband wants to go bowling and the wife wants him to take the kids to the zoo, the friend may suggest that he go bowling Saturday and to the zoo on Sunday.

This traditional folk view appears to have been accepted not just by the therapists just mentioned but by the field at large. If there is an area of general agreement in this splintered discipline, it is the emphasis on bargaining, contracts, compromise, and the need of partners to renounce their unrealistic expectations.

DISCOURAGING COMPROMISE AND ENCOURAGING ROMANTIC FANTASY

I find myself disagreeing with both aspects of the contemporary antiromantic view—the emphasis on compromise and the attack on fantasy based expectations.

The therapeutic approach of encouraging partners to negotiate and compromise fails to take into account that the partners' own attempts to compromise may be causing much of the problem. It is the adjustments, accommodations, and sacrifices that partners make without telling each other or fully recognizing it themselves—that is, their automatic and unverbalized attempts to compromise and be reasonable—that may lie at the root of the difficulty. What these partners may be needing is to stop compulsively compromising and to develop an ability to complain.

It is possible to show in some cases that the behavior of partner A about which partner B wants a compromise may be the result of an already existing compromise. Jim, who did not like Dorothy's staying late at work, asked her to agree to restrict her lateness to once a week and to phone him and pre-prepare his meals when she suspected she might be late. The problem with this solution is that it grafted a compromise to a compromise. Dorothy had already been compromising. She had felt badly about coming home late and, as a consequence, had done it less often than she would have wanted. Now, with the new "official" compromise, she was to stay late even less often.

A similar point could be made about Dorothy's agreement to phone Jim and arrange his dinners. She and Jim had been operating under classic, though implicit, family rules that they were to keep each other informed about their whereabouts and were to provide certain established services for each other (e.g., she was to prepare his meals). What she really wanted, however, was freedom to come and go without having to check with Jim and without having to worry about his dinners. She had compromised with these overly restrictive family rules by occasionally violating them (e.g., not always calling when she was late and not always preparing his dinners). According to the new "official" compromise, however, she was now to be deprived of even this mild rebellion.

Jim too had made a previous compromise. Dorothy's feeling of being suffocated by Jim, caused in part by their restrictive family rules, had led her to withdraw emotionally. Jim's reaction was to accept this withdrawal and to settle for more modest satisfactions; he made a private compromise regarding his original hopes about the marriage. Although it seemed that he was to be deprived of emotional intimacy, at least he could count on a certain measure of companionship and reliability: a wife who would always be there and who would fix his meals. When it appeared that even this was to be taken from him, it became too much.

The therapist's task, as I see it, is not to arrange or sanction the new "official" compromise but to show how these partners are already compulsively compromising, point out that this is the problem, and draw attention to the underlying issues of oppressive family rules and lack of intimacy.

A similar argument can be made regarding the second major trend of contemporary couples therapy—encouraging partners to suppress or renounce fantasy based expectations. Here too, it is the partners' own efforts to do this—that is, their attempts to suppress unrealistic expectations—that may be causing the problem. The fantasies of partners are efforts to compensate for deprivation and inhibition. A husband who felt unloved as a child, feels unloved by his wife, and is unable to talk in direct and effective ways about these feelings is likely to compensate by imagining some ideal romantic interchange that might somehow convince him he is loved and lovable.

These fantasy hopes, which originally arose to compensate for inhibition and deprivation, may themselves be inhibited. An example is the individuals who imagined being rescued from a trying day by perfectly loving partners (Chapter 6). The problem, I suggest, was not so much that they had unrealistic expectations or that these expectations were frustrated. People are used to frustration and generally take it in stride. The problem was the inhibited manner in which they pursued these fantasies. They just presented themselves at the door somehow hoping the other would guess what they were wanting. And then, when their wishes were frustrated, they did not talk about it. Their response instead was to lose contact both with their original fantasy hopes and with each other. Instead of providing compensation for a depriving day, their fantasy wishes thus led to further deprivation.

The solution to the problem would not be to urge renunciation of these partners' fantasy expectations. The preferred goal would be to enable them to pursue their fantasy wishes more effectively, to stay in contact with these fantasy hopes, and to share and commiserate with each other, not only about the disappointment of these hopes, but also about their respective difficult days. Such mutual sympathy is likely to provide an important element of the rescue they were seeking and, at the very least, would short-circuit the spiraling alienation that had begun to occur.

ROMANTIC LOVE

The major type of fantasy expectation thought to produce couple conflict is romantic love. "Whenever professionals in the marriage field have wanted to point to one factor as being responsible for marital difficulties, romantic love has been cited as the culprit" (Framo, 1965, p. 185). Kubie (1956) distinguishes between love, which he sees as a special capacity of the human being and "the most difficult and important challenge with which the human spirit is confronted" (p. 42), and romantic love, which he views as a tragic flaw of Western culture and "an obsessional state which, like all obsessions, is in part driven by unconscious anger" (p. 32).

My own view is that love and romantic love may be alternative types of responses, neither of which is indisputably advantageous or disadvantageous. It is necessary in developing this thesis to turn briefly to Apfelbaum's (1977a) concept of "bypassers" and "nonbypassers."

Apfelbaum was trying to understand why some people become easily aroused in sexual situations while others do not. "In response to touch," he suggests, "there is one kind of person for whom all worries and grudges are suddenly forgotten; for another kind of person worries and grudges are just as suddenly remembered" (p. 61). Apfelbaum, adapting a term employed by Kaplan (1974), refers to the first kind of person as a "bypasser" and the second as a "nonbypasser."

The notion of bypassing and nonbypassing appears applicable not just to sexual interactions but to couple relationships in general. A bypasser is able to overlook all imperfections in prospective lovers and become quickly swept away in the illusion that the perfect partner has arrived. This is also the individual who views the "bad times" in a relationship as aberrations and the "good times" as indicative of what the relationship is really about. A nonbypasser is acutely aware of imperfections in the partner. He or she discounts the "good times" in the relationship and may be unable to stop thinking about the bad.

With the notion of bypassers and nonbypassers in mind, it is then possible to distinguish two general types of love. In the first type, *romantic love,* the person is able to maintain a sense of intimacy regardless of what happens in the relationship or with only rote participation by the partner. This is the type of love characteristic of bypassers. In the case of the partners meeting at the door, their fantasy hopes of being rescued from a frustrating day were dashed by their initial disagreeable interaction. A good bypasser might be able to disregard the partner's ambivalence and go right on believing the romantic fantasy.

In the second type of love, *reactive love,* the person is sensitively attuned to the partner. The feeling of intimacy comes and goes, increases and decreases depending on what is happening in the relationship. This is the type of love characteristic of the nonbypasser, the individual who cannot overlook grudges and worries. When nonbypassers "fall out of love," that is, lose their positive feeling toward their partners, it is because they are unable to provide adequate expression to negative feelings (see Ransom, 1980, for a discussion of this). For these individuals the maintenance of love requires an ability to make complaints and check out worries. It is trying to stay in love, Apfelbaum has quipped, that causes these people to fall out of love.

We are now in a position to compare the advantages and disadvantages of the two kinds of love—reactive love (characteristic of nonbypassers) and romantic love (characteristic of bypassers). I shall talk about bypassing and nonbypassing in their pure forms. Everyone, of course, shows elements of both.

A relationship between two bypassers might seem at first problem-free. These individuals could conceivably maintain a sense of romantic love indefinitely, tripping off together into their separate fantasies about the relationship. However, bypassing is rarely a completely stable state, as Apfelbaum (1980a) points out, and bypassers can become distressed and hateful if their partners burst the bubble of their romantic fantasies.

A relationship between two nonbypassers is easily susceptible to conflict. These individuals "fall out of love" easily and constantly. They are always noticing imperfections in the other and problems in the interaction. If they are to maintain a feeling of intimacy, these partners need to develop ways of integrating these recurrent feelings of dissatisfaction into the relationship.

These problems are compounded in the relationship between a bypasser (who is experiencing romantic love) and a nonbypasser (who is not). Bypassers feel that everything would be all right if only their nonbypassing partners would "relax a little," "take things as they come," "stop looking at all the problems," withhold their tendency "to always criticize," and "look on the bright side." The bypasser does not require much to maintain the fantasy of love—little gifts perhaps, or other ritualistic expressions of affection—and fails to understand (and may become enraged) at the unwillingness of the nonbypasser to provide them.

Nonbypassers feel equally misunderstood and "oppressed" (Apfelbaum, 1980a). Their partners are having a relationship not with them but with their fantasies of them. When they try to complain, which they need to do to regain a sense of intimacy, their bypassing partners refuse to accept these complaints, since complaints interfere with their own need to feel that everything in the relationship is basically okay. As a result, the nonbypassers feel increasingly less loving and increasingly less interested in providing the tokens of affection so desperately sought by their partners. Apfelbaum's quip thus applies to bypassers as well: it is trying to stay in love by ignoring the partner and having a relationship with the fantasy that, since it alienates this partner and leads to the end of the relationship, causes people to fall out of love.

The advantage of romantic love, in summary, is that it allows individuals who are capable of it (bypassers) to develop a feeling of love almost regardless of what is happening in the relationship. The disadvantages are that the relationship can be impersonal (the individual is having a relationship with the fantasy of the partner) and unstable (the love may turn to hate if the partner does not provide the minimum required to maintain the fantasy). The advantages of reactive love are that it enables individuals to have a highly personal relationship (i.e., these people have no choice but to respond intensely to what is happening in the relationship) and makes them sensitive observers of the undercurrents of the relationship. The disadvantages are that they may be more reactive than they wish and less able to be swept away by an enjoyable romantic fantasy (i.e., they are prisoners of reality).

What then is the solution to these difficulties? The popular contemporary solution, giving up on love and building the relationship on pragmatic exchanges, seems prematurely pessimistic. I prefer an approach that helps these individuals understand their own and their partners' forms of love. Nonbypassers are puzzled and distressed by their loss of positive feeling for their partners and would profit from the discovery that airing complaints may be a necessary prerequisite for regaining such feeling. Bypassers are puzzled and distressed by their nonbypassing partners' "irrational" dissatisfactions and unwillingness to provide the few simple tokens of affection for which they ask. They would profit from the realization that their form of love may have the effect of leaving their partners out and that their need to exclude complaints may interfere with their partners need to express them.

The ego analytic view of love and compromise has at least two general clinical implications. First, the therapeutic task, rather than simply encouraging compromise, is to look for the hidden ways in which partners are already compromising. A wife's concern about her husband's failure to take out the garbage may represent a general feeling on her part of being taken for granted, cut off from her husband, alone in the relationship, and that everything is up to her. If so, the garbage issue is a consequence of an implicit compromise on her part. She is asking only a small fraction of what she might actually wish. As the therapist, I would point this out instead of or in addition to working out a compromise about the garbage. It is often the case, furthermore, that the husband in his own way is also feeling cut off. An issue appearing to require compromise thus broadens to one that does not. These partners are at odds regarding the garbage; they may be agreed on the need to increase intimacy.

The second clinical implication is an increased potentiality for compromise. People who view their partners and themselves in depth analytic terms are at a disadvantage in making compromises. They may be reluctant to make accomodations with partners they see as exploitive, manipulative, narcissistic, or infantile. If they are viewing them in ego analytic terms, however, as deprived, trapped, and isolated, they are more likely to feel sympathetic and to *want* to compromise. A husband who sees his wife's complaint about the garbage not as a wish to dominate but as an indication that she is feeling taken for granted may find himself wanting to take out the garbage. This is most likely to occur, of course, if he feels entitled to his own reactions—that is, if he recognizes his failure to help with the housework not simply as laziness or selfishness but as a result of his own feeling of being taken for granted.

My approach to negotiation and fantasy expectations can thus be seen as a consequence of rejecting depth analysis and adopting ego analysis. Since depth analysts accept the apparent "infantile" behavior of troubled partners at face value, these therapists may have no choice but to counsel compromise and renunciation and to try to convince each partner to behave a little less immaturely. Ego analysis traces "infantile" behavior to ordinary adult needs. One effect can be to remove the need for compromise. The redefined issue may be one in which the partners are no longer at odds.

Another effect is to increase the possibility for compromise. Individuals who have respect and sympathy for their own and for their partners' positions are more likely to find themselves wanting to make adjustments and concessions.

8

An Individual Oriented
Systems Approach

One of the major theoretical issues in couples therapy is whether the problem, and thus the solution, exists in the individual or in the couple. The original view, of course, was that the problem existed in the individual. A disturbed marriage was seen as a symptom of a disturbed individual and the treatment of choice was individual psychotherapy. Systems theory then came on the scene and reversed these two elements. A disturbed individual, the "identified patient," was now to be viewed as a symptom of a disturbed family or couple, and the treatment of choice was conjoint therapy.

Much of what systems theorists say seems correct. Certain couple problems appear to be reinforced or even generated by the internal dynamics of the relationship. As Jackson (1967) points out, one partner's demands cause the other to withdraw and the second partner's withdrawal causes the first to demand. A therapy that does not take this interaction or "system" into account could be seen as deficient.

Practitioners with an individual oriented approach could quickly respond, however, that the determination of which partner becomes demanding and which withdrawn is no accident. Typically both have had their respective tendencies throughout their lives, and it is necessary to take these historic factors into account.

Such therapists could also argue that one partner may be more responsible for the problem than the other (Martin, 1976). Grunebaum and Chasin (1978) suggest that it may be valid and useful to identify one partner as the main patient after all. The withdrawn partner's "basic fear of intimacy" or the demanding partner's "basic hatred of women (or men)" may be thought to undercut and void whatever positive effort the other partner might make.

Most conjoint therapists combine elements of both approaches. Certain systems theorists, it is true, attempt to avoid intrapsychic or individual oriented concepts entirely (Jackson, 1967; Haley, 1967). This is difficult to do, however, and as Keeney (1979) and Friedman (1965) pointed out in Haley's work and Fisch (1979) pointed out in Palazolli's (Palazolli et al., 1978), they are often unsuccessful. Intrapsychically oriented couples therapists are less loath to include systems concepts and appear concerned primarily with providing a balance between the two (Martin, 1976; Sager, 1976; Meissner, 1978).

The use of systems concepts is not entirely new in psychoanalysis. Consider the following remarkable comments:

> It constantly happens that a husband instructs the physician as follows: "My wife suffers from nerves, and for that reason gets on badly with me; please cure her, so that we may lead a happy married life again." But often enough it turns out that such a request is impossible to fulfill—that is to say, the physician cannot bring about the result for which the husband sought the treatment. As soon as the wife is freed from her neurotic inhibitions she sets about getting a separation, for her neurosis was the sole condition under which the marriage could be maintained. (Freud, 1920, p. 150)

> No one who has any experience of the rifts which so often divide a family will, if he is an analyst, be surprised to find that the patient's closest relatives sometimes betray less interest in his recovering than in his remaining as he is. (Freud, 1917, p. 459)

MAINTAINING UNINTERRUPTED FOCUS ON THE COUPLE INTERACTION

The systems approach has a certain advantage. There is considerable value in maintaining an uninterrupted focus on the relationship. The problem with systems theory, however, is that it does this by excluding, or trying to exclude, the individual. Adoption of this approach requires discounting the motivational needs of individuals and subscribing to rather uncertain speculations about the motivational needs of families (e.g., homeostasis). It is difficult to completely exclude individual motivation, and systems theorists continually slip it back in.

The problem with individual motivation and the reason systems theorists seek to exclude it is that it *keeps leading away from the couple interaction.* Therapists who attribute relationship problems to the regressive impulses of partners, for example, or to their unresolved feelings toward their parents may soon find themselves thinking and talking not about the immediate couple interaction but about the separate histories, personalities, and psychopathologies of the individual partners.

The ego analytic approach does not have this problem. Although it is inherently individual oriented, it is also inherently systems oriented. It employs a form of psychodynamic reasoning that, in contradistinction to the traditional depth analytic orientation, *keeps leading back to the couple situation.* Instead of viewing relationship problems simply as expressions of regressive strivings or unresolved feelings toward parents, this approach sees them as (1) understandable reactions to present circumstances, (2) special sensitivities to common couples issues, and (3) distorted expressions of ordinary adult needs. The effect is to focus on the couple's current interaction.

Understandable Reactions to Present Circumstances

It is not difficult to see why couples therapists might conclude that partners in a troubled relationship are gratifying infantile impulses or expressing unresolved feelings toward their parents. These individuals look and act infantile. They argue over trifles, sulk, and rage. What is important to take into account, however, are the conditions under which they are operating. These people are behaving in an "irrational" and "intolerable" manner because they are dealing with an intolerable situation.

One of the more vivid descriptions of such a situation has been provided by Haley (1959). He describes an atmosphere of shared wariness in which no family member ever has his or her perceptions and feelings validated. In fact, no one ever even gets a chance to state them fully. Each statement is immediately interrupted, contradicted, or "disqualified" by everyone else.

> Typically, if one family member says something, another indicates it shouldn't have been said or wasn't said properly. If one criticizes the other, he is told that he misunderstands and should behave differently. If one compliments the other, he is told he doesn't do this often enough, or he has some ulterior purpose. Should a family member try to avoid communicating, the others will indicate this "passivity" is demanding and indicate he should initiate more . . . If one suggests going to a particular place, the other may . . . indicate, "Why must we always go where you suggest?" or the response may be the sigh of a brave martyr who must put up with this sort of thing. (Haley, 1959)

This description is perhaps extreme. Haley himself applies it only to a restricted group of families: those that produce schizophrenic children. What Haley seems to have done in the process, however, is to describe in exaggerated form the pattern of interaction that appears to lie at the root of most family and couple problems. All three of the alienated couple states discussed in Chapter 6 can be described in Haley's terms.

Mutually accusing partners cannot stop arguing (i.e., contradicting rather than listening to each other) because they are feeling too misunderstood, discounted, and disaffirmed by the other. Mutual withdrawal can be viewed as an attempt to avoid such argument. Rather than having their thoughts and feelings disaffirmed or taken too seriously or concretely, these individuals prefer not to express them at all. Finally, demanding–withdrawn (pursuer–distancer) polarization can be seen as a state of reciprocal disconfirmation in which the pursuer disallows the distancer's need or right to withdraw and the distancer disallows the pursuer's need or right to pursue or demand.

The recognition that these individuals are living under intolerable conditions can alter a therapist's view of their behavior. Chronic disaffirmation is one of the more insidious tortures to which people can be subjected. Any response that the individual is able to make to this—rage, withdrawal, or whatever else—seems understandable and in its own way appropriate. The double bind is a classic case of disconfirmation. The appropriate response to a double bind, the originators of this concept suggest, is to double bind back.

Partners' reactions to being disaffirmed, when looked at from this point of view, appear remarkably subdued and constrained. They sulk, nag, frown, and argue over trifles. Furthermore, these individuals generally feel guilty about the toned down expressions they do allow themselves. I sometimes remark that their irritability, sulking, and so on, for which they are criticizing themselves seem extremely mild reactions given the deprivation and frustration they are experiencing.

The "irrational" behavior of partners has been described here as being an understandable and appropriate response to the general conditions of the relationship. It is possible to show in some cases that it may also be understandable and appropriate to the immediate situation. A woman whom I was seeing in therapy became mysteriously enraged when her husband took her to a dancing bar but did not dance with her. She was self-critical in reporting this event, expressing concern about what she felt was an extreme and uncalled for reaction on her part to a very minor provocation. What we discovered, however, was that this incident exemplified her general experience of and complaint about the marriage, her sense that her husband goes through the motions of being a good husband (i.e., takes her dancing), but does not provide any real substance (i.e., does not dance with her).

My experience with such "irrational" partner behavior has led me to approach it with a certain respect. One of my first responses to individuals who are reacting in such a manner, accordingly, is to consider the possibility that they may be seeing or responding to an important underlying issue in the relationship.

Historically Determined Special
Sensitivities to Common Couple Issues

The "irrational" reactions of partners may not only be appropriate to present circumstances or conditions but may also reflect common couple concerns. Partners in a pursuer–distancer interaction (Fogarty, 1976) appear absurd both to themselves and to others. The pursuers cannot stop pursuing even though they know this is driving their partners further away. The distancers cannot stop withdrawing even though they know this increases their partners' need to pursue.

What these partners have done, in essence, is to split responsibility for two classic couple issues. The pursuer has become the specialist in detecting the presence or absence of intimacy and contact. The distancer has become the spokesperson for their joint need to maintain a certain separation and privacy. The problem with dividing up these issues in this manner is the ease with which they can then be attributed to and then discounted as personal defects. The pursuer is likely to be viewed as "oversensitive" and "dependent" and the distancer as "insensitive" and "afraid of intimacy."

A potential solution to this problem, of course, is to point out the universal nature of these concerns and how they are of ultimate interest to both partners.

> In dealing with such clients, it is often useful to congratulate both spouses for having raised all the important issues in the relationship, but then to wonder how each of them got saddled with the responsibility for only half of them. The wife may be the vice-president in charge of separateness, individuality, privacy, and all the other concerns of the "distancer"; whereas he is stuck with togetherness, "coupleship," mutuality, and all the other concerns of the "pursuer." If he can get intrigued with her issues, and she with his, the log jam may be broken and the basis for a differently shaped relationship may emerge. (Taggart, 1979, pp. 99–100)

The determination of which partner gets saddled with which couple issues depends on at least two factors. One is the polarizing effect of accusation. Let us suppose that a husband, perhaps the more verbal of the two, is first to comment on the withdrawal or detachment that has grown up between them that evening. Let us consider further that he does so in the form of an accusation: "Why are you always so silent?" The wife, who may have been on the verge of mentioning the sense of detachment herself, now feels called on to defend herself. She denies that she has been quiet or justifies her right to be so. In doing this, she thus finds herself taking the position of the distancer. These partners, who had been having identical desires for intimacy just a moment before, are now polarized. He is saddled with the responsibility of the pursuer and she with that of the distancer.

Another factor determining which partner is to be spokesperson for which issues is their individual histories. A husband's sensitivity to his wife's distancing may be based on feeling rejected by his father while her reciprocal sensitivity to his pursuing may be built on her early life with an engulfing mother. Whatever the partners' previous experiences with these issues might have been, the fact remains that they are universal concerns with which all couples, at least in our society, must deal. This can be demonstrated by the occurrence of reversals. At moments when the pursuer becomes discouraged with the relationship and withdraws, the distancer may step into the breach and behave very much like the pursuer (Fogarty, 1979). The pursuer, feeling pressured at such times, may then take the role of the distancer.

The effect of relating partners' problems to standard couple issues is similar to attributing them to present circumstances. In both cases, therapeutic attention remains fixed on what is happening in the relationship.

Distorted Expressions of Ordinary Adult Needs

We come now to what is perhaps the most important means by which the present approach directs attention to current partner interactions. The problem with the orientation adopted by traditional depth analysis, as mentioned earlier, is that it leads away from couple interactions. This style of psychodynamic reasoning—attributing the symptomatic behavior of partners to infantile strivings or unresolved problems with their parents—tends to focus attention on these historic factors.

My view, in contrast, is that symptomatic behaviors of partners are distorted expressions of what may be ordinary adult needs and feelings. The therapeutic task is to root out these underlying needs and feelings. Complaints such as "you never tell me you love me," "we don't go out very much," "you never cook special meals anymore," or "this house is a mess" may turn out to be imprecise or distorted ways of raising an important issue of concern to both, for instance, "I've had doubts recently about how much real affection there is between us (or how much you really care about me), and I'm pretty upset about it."

Certain schizophrenic symptomatology can be viewed in these terms—that is, as distorted derivatives of common adult feelings. A husband, who had been relatively free from schizophrenic symptomatology, came to couples therapy with the delusion that his friends were trying to kill him. The source of his terror became clear in the first session when his wife discussed her plan to leave him. His fear that his friends were trying to kill him was a metaphor for or displacement of his feeling that his wife was killing him—that is, that without her his life would be over. Where others might say, "It's hard to imagine what life would be like (or how I could get along) without you," or "losing you is a little like dying," this man was experiencing such metaphorical expressions in concrete terms.

Another husband, who typically reacted to difficulties by becoming delusional, was convinced that the FBI was trying to control his behavior by beaming rays through the wall. He was partially correct. He was being controlled. It was not by the FBI, however, but by his wife or, more correctly, by his fear that if he did not completely comply with each of her whims, she would leave him.

To summarize: the seemingly irrational behavior of partners is seen as having a *hidden rationality.* It is based on or means something important about the relationship. Therapists who adopt this view will thus find themselves returning to the couple interaction to discover the current circumstances, common couple issues, or ordinary adult needs and feelings that lie at the root of the problem.

THE EXAMPLE OF ENVY

The following is an example of how the traditional depth analytic approach leads away from the couple situation and how my approach leads toward it.

A classic couple problem is the envy of one partner for the greater social ability or professional position of the other and the associated fear of being left behind. Colleagues at the California State University, Hayward, Counseling Services have brought my attention to an interesting shift in this regard. In previous years it was generally the husband who, because of more advanced education and professional achievement, was seen as leaving his wife behind. With the recent tendency for women to return to school and develop their own careers, it is now more often the wife who is seen as leaving her husband behind.

A traditional psychoanalytic approach to the issue of envy is to attribute the difficulty to unresolved issues from the past and in particular to sibling rivalry, oedipal jealousy, or penis envy. Ransom (1980), reviewing the psychoanalytic and object relations approaches of Framo (1965), Meissner (1978), and Dicks (1967) writes that "one gets the idea that people do not really relate to one another, but to ghosts, and that they are not in love with one another, but with projected aspects of their unfulfilled love for their parents."

In a related approach already discussed, symptomatic envy is traced to a generalized "developmental defect" (Ables and Brandsma, 1977). The common problem of "the wife of the graduate student who feels left out and jealous when her husband's time and energy are invested in work outside the home," for example, may be seen by such authors as being "rooted in the failure to resolve early symbiotic ties and the subsequent failure to complete successfully the separation–individuation stage" (Ables and Brandsma, 1977, p. 24).

An alternative approach, the one adopted here, is to relate "pathological envy" to present conditions, to consider the possibility that it might be in part an understandable response to these conditions, a special sensitivity to a common couple issue, or a distorted derivative of a common adult feeling. I have frequently found in my work with couples that all three factors can enter into the picture.

There is often an important grain of truth in these individuals' sense of being left out. Many people who become involved in work or graduate studies do exclude their partners. The effect can be more insidious if, as often happens, these individuals feel guilty about neglecting their partners and make forced efforts to spend more time with them. This generally comes across as patronizing and increases the partners' sense of being unimportant and a burden to their mates.

"Envious" individuals may also be correct in their sense of being left behind. Their partners, who are expanding their professional or social horizons, may privately believe they are outgrowing their mates but feel too bad about it to admit that they think this. It is often the case, in addition, that people's tendencies to increase involvement with work or friends may be a direct consequence of and reaction to problems in the relationship. The envious partner would thus be justified in taking this neglect or withdrawal personally.

Envy is a common couple issue. Most people place considerable importance on their relationship with their partners and are understandably concerned when the exclusiveness or intimacy of this relationship is challenged. In addition, partners, because of their centrality in people's lives, generally become one of the major frames of reference by which they judge their own accomplishments and capabilities. It is thus a common tendency to identify with partners: to be proud of their successes, to back them up, to work for their benefit, and to take pleasure in their pleasure. At the same time, people also compare themselves to, compete with, and feel threatened by their partners' successes.

Finally, "pathologic" envy may be a distorted derivative of ordinary adult envy. Feelings of envy are generally benign and unremarkable when experienced and expressed as they arise. I can imagine a partner saying, "I am really pleased at your success; I'm also very envious!" and by so stating obtain some sense of resolution to these feelings. If these thoughts are suppressed or repressed, however, they tend to reappear in offensive or exaggerated forms, as whiny complaints or sudden enraged demands. It is the attempt to be nonenvious, in other words, that may lead to pathologic envy.

THE REGENERATION OF PAST PROBLEMS IN THE PRESENT

The ego analytic approach provides the possibility of examining the symptomatic behavior of partners in terms of current circumstances. But is this desirable? Suppose envy has been a life-long problem for a particular individual, arising in early childhood and occurring with every friend or partner this person ever had. Wouldn't focusing on the present situation be too superficial and restricted?

And what about the childhood conflict and developmental defect models described earlier? Is it not well established by now that psychological problems are rooted in the past, that couple relationships are, in large part, attempts to repeat, correct, or compensate for relationships with parents, and that partners in a troubled relationship are functioning at a reduced organizational or developmental level?

My answer is to agree with all of this and to suggest that focusing on the present relationship may be a particularly good way of exploring these factors. Personal problems, whatever their original source, keep being regenerated in the present, as Wachtel (1977, pp. 51–55) has suggested, and it is the study of these regenerated forms that generally provides the best access to these problems. This is the kind of reasoning that has led psychoanalysts to base their therapeutic approach on the development of the transference neurosis. As Freud has said in speaking about the advantage of dealing with the childhood neurosis in its reactivated form (i.e., in the transference), "when all is said and done, it is impossible to destroy anyone *in absentia* or *in effigie*" (Freud, 1912, p. 108).

Neurotic symptoms are sometimes viewed as holdovers from the past, as a continuation into the present of anxieties and conflicts that were appropriate only to earlier years. The therapeutic approach, then, is to relate these present symptoms to those early causes and to demonstrate to the individual that the danger or conflict no longer exists.* The issue becomes more complex when we include the factors of developmental arrest (in which these early anxieties or conflicts interfere with important developmental tasks and achievements) and secondary gain (in which the symptom, whatever its original cause, comes to have a motivating value in itself). But let us exclude these complicating factors for now.

My own view, in contrast to the holdover-from-childhood theory, is that the original causal conditions are continually being repeated or recreated. An important source of a woman's envy, for example, may have been her sudden displacement as the most prized member of the family as a result of the sudden arrival of a new baby brother or, more accurately, her inability to provide adequate expression to her feelings about this and to have these feelings accepted by others. Her parents may have interrupted and prevented such expression by telling her to stop being so selfish and greedy and to learn to love her new baby brother. She was thus in an untenable

*Some psychoanalytically oriented therapists pay little attention to these childhood experiences in themselves and deal with them exclusively in their reactivated form in the transference.

position. She had insistent needs and feelings that the people most important to her (her parents) felt were completely unacceptable —a view that she, incorporating her parents' attitude, soon came to share.

The same conditions may continually reoccur today. Now, as before, this woman may be unable to provide adequate expression to ordinary envious feelings.* Her "pathological envy" is recreated in each new relationship because each new person treats her feelings in the same way her parents did. An underlying factor is her sense of unentitlement to her envious feelings and her effort to ward them off. As generally happens with suppressed feelings, they reemerge in inhibited and distorted forms. These are then mistaken by the new friend or lover as an indication of a deep-seated, pathological, and primitive envy. Her original experience with her parents has been recreated.

The problems with "pathologically envious" individuals, then, is their inability to integrate ordinary envious feelings into their relationships. What these people need is a different way of thinking about their envious feelings. They need to be able to view them not as antisocial, pathological, and an indication of personal weakness but as understandable everyday feelings that signify something important about the relationship and cause problems only when they are warded off.

The traditional view is that resolving childhood conflicts by sorting out wishes and feelings about one's parents will have beneficial effects on one's present relationship (Bowen, 1972; Framo, 1976). If, as suggested here, the problem is continually being regenerated or rerooted in the present, then the reverse may also be true; resolving present conflicts (sorting out wishes and feelings about one's partner) will have beneficial effects on one's relationship with one's parents. The problem is not so much toward whom these individuals are envious, but how they feel about their envy. Once they resolve this issue with one person, they can conceivably resolve it with anyone.

There remains the issue of developmental defects. As mentioned before, Ables and Brandsma (1977) attributed the graduate student's wife's feelings of jealousy and abandonment to her failure to resolve early symbiotic ties and to complete successfully the separation–individuation stage. Referring to such a problem as a "developmental deficit" as these authors do, seems to me inexact and unfortunate. The effect is to denigrate the individual's reactions, to isolate these responses from the context that gives them their meaning, and to elicit the image of fixed and profound pathology.

What Ables and Brandsma refer to as a failure in separation–individuation, I would describe instead as a sense of unentitlement to certain feel-

---

*I would suggest that not even infants have infantile problems. The task for infants, as it is for adults, is to provide sufficient expression to standard human feelings and to obtain adequate control of interpersonal situations.

ings resulting in an inability to acknowledge, accept, or express these feelings. In fact, this is what "developmental defects," or at least a large proportion of developmental defects, may turn out to be. People remain symbiotically attached to others, for example, when they are unable to accept feelings of envy, ambivalence, or resentment toward them.

WHY ISN'T THE RELATIONSHIP CURING THE PROBLEM?

The current relationship is described here as a useful context in which to examine partners' problems. But what about problems that have to do with the partners as individuals—work difficulties, for example, or lifelong depression? In some instances, of course, the apparent personal problem is a couple problem in disguise. Even if this is not the case, relationship factors almost always enter the picture.

A woman complaining of recent depression attributed it to increased pressure at work, a difficult class schedule at school, and problems with her children. When she was asked whether talking about these problems with her husband helped, she said she rarely discussed such matters with him. He would just give superficial advice, she explained, or would become abrupt, accusatory, and unsympathetic.

What her depression about school, work, and children may have done, in part, was to point out an underlying problem in her marriage, an inability to use her husband as a resource and, perhaps, a general inability to talk with him. It is possible, then, that she was particularly vulnerable to difficulties in other areas of her life (school, work, children) because of the lack of contact she felt with her husband. This appears to have been the case. When, as a result of a couples therapy session, her husband did begin to understand and appreciate how she felt, she became much less depressed. Her relationship with her husband thus appeared as much a cause of her depression as did her school pressures or any of these other factors.

Implied here is a general theory of intimate relationships. A major value of relationships is that they provide a setting in which partners can review distressing and unresolved issues of the day and can celebrate successes and achievements. Partners have different ways of doing this. Some run through the events of the day in a semiformalized manner and immediately upon meeting. Others are silent at first and then spin or spill out these events in the course of the evening, during dinner, just before bed, the next morning, or the next month. Such mutual confiding appears to be a common need of marital partners.

The couple relationship is thus presented here as providing a general reviving and resolving function. It may also serve a longer range curative potential. The fantasy expectations with which many people approach relationships, the hope that they might correct or compensate for dis-satisfactions experienced with their parents, is not entirely fanciful. In fact, there may be as much tendency to underrate the curative potential of an intimate relationship as there is to overrate it. A withdrawn husband claimed that the punishment he received during childhood when he expressed his feelings to his parents taught him to keep his mouth shut. The stories he told about this made it clear that staying quiet may have been a good idea. He has maintained the habit ever since, he went on to say, even though he was unhappy about this because it placed a barrier between him and his wife.

Since it seemed clear that this man had married with the hope that things would be different with his wife, I suggested that we look at examples of what happens at those times when he does express his feelings to her. Per-haps we could figure out why his relationship with his wife "was not curing the problem." What we discovered, as one might guess, is that the punish-ment he used to receive from his parents was being repeated in his inter-action with his wife though in much milder and more obscure forms. The wife, recognizing her husband's sensitivity, had been suppressing every-thing that might hurt his feelings. As generally happens with such suppres-sive efforts, they backfired. At just those moments when he was most sensi-tive to her reaction—that is, when he would tentatively begin expressing feelings—her suppressed criticism would break through. Part of the reason was the scared and inhibited manner in which he approached her at such times. His comments had a tentative and unappealing tone and she re-sponded with subtle "digs."

The curative potential of couple relationships can also be stated in more formal terms. Symptoms are classically conceptualized as split off or warded-off impulses and feelings. The goal of individual therapy is to in-tegrate these impulses and feelings into the personality. The goal of the kind of couples therapy described here is to integrate such impulses and feelings into the relationship. These goals are parallel and in some sense synonymous.

CONJOINTLY ORIENTED INDIVIDUAL THERAPY

Systems theory made conjoint therapy respectable. Practitioners who met with couples and families prior to systems theory did so without a formal or supporting tradition and often with the concern that they might be pro-viding a second class form of therapy. Systems theorists, by locating the problem in the family or couple unit, provided the necessary rationale and tradition. They established family and couples therapy not merely as acceptable therapeutic modalities but as treatments of choice.

My own view is that conjoint therapy is not always such a good idea. A major disadvantage, as one might suspect, is the inhibiting effect the presence of the partner may exert on certain individuals. There are some people whose fear of negative consequences or concern about hurting their partner causes them to withhold information that must be made available if anything else about the relationship is to be understandable.

One woman, although extremely competent and articulate in her professional life, talked in a diffuse and distraught manner that neither her husband, I, nor she herself could fully understand. After several sessions, she wisely suggested that she meet with me separately. It took only three minutes of our first individual session for her to say, though indirectly, the one thing that would have made everything else she had been saying clear: that she had lost all feeling for her husband and was wondering whether she wanted to continue the marriage.

Some systems theorists argue that individual therapy is counterproductive because the partner who is not being seen will view the therapy as a threat to couple homeostasis and will sabotage the whole enterprise. Much depends, of course, on what the therapist is doing. If the therapist takes the side of the attending partner, it is understandable that the nonattending partner might strike back. A major purpose of this book is to suggest how the therapist might be able to take the side of one partner without necessarily criticizing the other. I like to think that it would be possible for nonattending partners to listen to tapes of the therapy sessions and not feel threatened.*

Couples therapy can be thought of from one point of view as showing individuals a new way of having a relationship. It could be argued, consequently, that both partners should be there. While this is often helpful, it is not absolutely necessary. It is possible for the attending partner to teach the nonattending partner what he or she has learned.

THE TRANSFERENCE NEUROSIS OF EVERYDAY LIFE

At the heart of classical psychoanalysis is the notion of the transference neurosis. The client's symptoms become transformed into feelings and fantasies about the therapist. These feelings and fantasies are then analyzed

---

*One woman, who really wanted couples therapy, was seeing me individually because her husband refused to come with her. In an effort to show him that useful things could happen and that she and I were not ganging up on him she played him a tape of one of our sessions. Not only did he realize that he was being fairly treated, he saw that his side was being represented better than he had been able to do himself. He came to the next session with her.

and eventually "resolved." The problem with bringing one's partner into an analytic session, it could then be argued, is that this alters, disrupts, and impedes the development and analysis of the transference neurosis.

My response to this objection is to recommend a broadening of the notion of transference neurosis. Several of the concepts discussed in this chapter are related to those of the transference neurosis: the idea that people's problems are continually being regenerated or rerooted in the present and the notion that relationships might be able to "cure" personal problems.

The defining element of a transference neurosis is the idea that all of the individual's thoughts, feelings, wishes, fantasies, concerns, and problems become centered in the relationship with the analyst. But something very much like this happens in couple relationships. There is first the honeymoon stage, a period in which partners are completely wrapped up in each other, or rather, in their fantasies of each other. The honeymoon stage in a couple relationship is very much like the initial period in a classical psychoanalysis, as the following description suggests (Freud, 1917, pp. 439–440).

We notice . . . that the patient, who ought to want nothing else but to find a way out of his distressing conflicts, develops a special interest in the person of the doctor. Everything connected with the doctor seems to be more important to him than his own affairs and to be diverting him from his illness. For a time, accordingly, relations with him become very agreeable; he is particularly obliging, tries wherever possible to show his gratitude, reveals refinements and merits in his nature which we should not, perhaps, have expected to find in him. The doctor, too, thereupon forms a favourable opinion of the patient and appreciates the good fortune which has enabled him to give his assistance to such a particularly valuable personality. If the doctor has an opportunity of talking to the patient's relatives, he learns to his satisfaction that the liking is a mutual one. The patient never tires in his home of praising the doctor and of extolling ever new qualities in him. "He's enthusiastic about you," say his relatives, "he trusts you blindly; everything you say is like a revelation to him." Here and there someone in this chorus has sharper eyes and says: "It's becoming a bore, the way he talks of nothing else but you and has your name on his lips all the time." . . . Under these conditions the analysis makes fine progress . . . The patient understands what is interpreted to him and becomes engrossed in the tasks set him by the treatment; the material of memories and associations floods in upon him in plenty, the certainty and appositeness of his interpretations are a surprise to the doctor, and the latter can only take note with satisfaction that here is a patient who readily accepts all the psychological novelties which are apt to provoke the most bitter contradiction among healthy people in the outside world. Moreover the cordial relations that prevail during the work of analysis are accompanied by an objective improvement, which is recognized on all sides, in the patient's illness.

The next stage in a classical analysis, the full flowering of the infantile neurosis in the transference, is comparable to stage two in a couple relationship, the period of struggle and conflict (Apfelbaum, personal communication). Here is Freud's description of the shift.

> But such fine weather cannot last forever. One day it clouds over. Difficulties arise in the treatment; the patient declares that nothing more occurs to him. He gives the clearest impression of his interest being no longer in the work and of his cheerfully disregarding the instructions given him to say everything that comes into his head and not to give way to any critical obstacle to doing so. He behaves as though he were outside the treatment and as though he had not made this agreement with the doctor. He is evidently occupied with something, but intends to keep it to himself. This is a situation that is dangerous for the treatment. We are unmistakably confronted by a formidable resistance. (p. 440)

> But I should like to say a few words to you to relieve you of your surprise at the emergence of this unexpected phenomenon. We must not forget that the patient's illness, which we have undertaken to analyse, is not something which has been rounded off and become rigid but that it is still growing and developing like a living organism. The beginning of the treatment does not put an end to this development; when, however, the treatment has obtained mastery over the patient, what happens is that the whole of his illness's new production is concentrated upon a single point—his relation to the doctor. Thus the transference may be compared to the cambium layer in a tree between the wood and the bark, from which the new formation of tissue and the increase in the girth of the trunk derive . . . we are no longer concerned with the patient's earlier illness but with a newly created and transformed neurosis which has taken the former's place . . . All the patient's symptoms have abandoned their original meaning and have taken on a new sense which lies in a relation to the transference; or only such symptoms have persisted as are capable of undergoing such a transformation. But the mastering of this new, artificial neurosis coincides with getting rid of the illness which was originally brought to the treatment—with the accomplishment of our therapeutic task. (p. 444)

I believe that partners' reactions toward each other may constitute a true transference neurosis. Each may be focusing all his or her concerns, problems, and wishes, "infantile" and otherwise, "upon a single point—his [or her] relation to the [partner]." While it may be more difficult to make therapeutic use of these partner-to-partner transference neuroses than if they were experienced toward the therapist, it is not impossible. There are also two advantages. First, since the therapist is not the major object of the partners' fantasy wishes, his or her interpretations are likely to be received in a more neutral and less distorted manner (Whitaker, 1975, p. 171). Second, the prolonged initial period in classical analysis devoted to the development of the transference neurosis is no longer necessary. Couples come to therapy with their partner-to-partner transference neuroses already fully developed. The only remaining tasks are their analysis and resolution.

There are perhaps two major differences between the traditional and this modified view of the transference neurosis. One is the suggestion that individuals form transference neuroses not just with analysts but with selected individuals in their natural environments. The other is the notion that transference neuroses may be a normal part of daily life. If, as earlier argued, unrealistic fantasies are inevitable in relationships and not just indications of pathology, then the same might be said for transference neuroses.

Different people have different spheres or "arenas of comfort."* Some who would find it intolerably threatening to see a therapist alone would be willing to come to therapy as part of a couple. If the view just outlined is accepted, it then becomes possible to deal with the transference neurosis in any of three different contexts, each of which has its advantages and disadvantages: the traditional transference setting in which the client, meeting privately with the therapist, considers feelings and fantasies about the therapist; the extratherapeutic transference setting in which the client, meeting privately with the therapist, considers feelings and fantasies about the partner; and the conjoint setting in which the partners, meeting together with the therapist, consider feelings and fantasies about each other.

The purpose of therapy is to be curative, that is, therapeutic. One can argue, however, that intimate relationships themselves have a powerful curative potential. The aim of my approach is to help couples make greater use of this potential.

*This expression was suggested by Joanne Wile.

9

An Insight Approach to
Couples Therapy

In presenting what is essentially an insight approach, it is necessary to acknowledge that such an orientation runs counter to the times. The classic exploratory–interpretive approach, once preeminent, is now widely viewed as an ineffectual academic exercise. The term "insight" has itself become discredited, being generally used these days to refer to ideas that are hackneyed and uninspiring. This repudiation of insight oriented therapy is particularly evident in the field of conjoint therapy. Couples therapists rarely talk about making interpretations to partners.

Each of the three major contemporary approaches to couples therapy has its own distinct attitude toward insight therapy. Behavior therapy is based on the rejection of insight as the central therapeutic change agent and its replacement with behavioral methods. It is true that behavior therapists have made recent attempts to employ interpretive measures and have devised a set of approaches that they call "cognitive behavior therapy." Such methods, at least as applied in behavioral marital therapy, often seem designed to suppress or dispose of thoughts and feelings rather than to develop them.

Systems theorists are just as clear in their rejection of interpretation and insight. If therapists are to have an influence on the couple, these practitioners believe, it cannot be by appealing to the logic, understanding, or judgment of the partners but by the exertion of direct force on the family or couple system (Minuchin, 1974). Bowen (1978) is one systems theorist who does employ insight and understanding. The reason, however, appears to be his incomplete commitment to systems theory (Gurman, 1978; Whitaker, 1975; Steinglass, 1978) and his inclusion of elements of psychoanalytic thinking.

The psychoanalytic approach is one in which we would expect to find unabashed commitment to interpretation and understanding. It was Freud after all who originated insight therapy. Actually, even here the interpretive approach has had a checkered existence. The history of psychoanalysis can be considered from one point of view as a succession of modifications required to deal with the difficulties and failures encountered in applying interpretive methods. Freud describes the task of discovering the conflicts underlying Elisabeth von R's leg pains as "one of the hardest that I had ever undertaken" (Breuer and Freud, 1895, p. 138). The original goal of psychoanalysis, uncovering the forgotten or warded-off experience or impulse, was soon supplemented by the task of analyzing defenses and resistances.

Psychoanalysis appears to have dealt with the problems of insight in two general ways. One was to develop increasingly more refined and sophisticated means of making interpretations—carefully setting the scene, interpreting elements in the right sequence and at the right time, dealing with defenses and resistances, and waiting for the transference neurosis to develop. The other was to supplement or replace interpretive measures with other approaches. Several noninterpretive psychoanalytic techniques have arisen through the years for use in certain situations or with certain patients (e.g., parameters of technique, supportive therapy, and corrective emotional experiences).

ACCUSATORY VERSUS NONACCUSATORY INTERPRETATIONS

The major problem with certain categories of psychoanalytically oriented interpretations and the reason practitioners may hesitate to offer them is that they often lead to client defensiveness. Therese Benedek (1946) describes a successful businessman, whose aggressiveness and exaggerated self-assertiveness concealed underlying "dependent needs." "Any interpretation of his need for dependence," she wrote, "would increase his defensiveness" (p. 175).

> Pointing out to the patient that he was dependent would have meant to him, "You have to learn to master your dependence, not try to satisfy it by turning childishly to a woman for help." This would have constituted a rejection which he could not have tolerated. The omission of interpretation meant, "You may relax and feel dependent," and it was thus the patient took it. (p. 177)

Benedek reports that she never did discuss dependency with him. She presents her case in support of Alexander and French's (1946) hypothesis that interpretation is inadequate or counterproductive for some patients and should be replaced by a "corrective emotional experience." My own view is that it is not interpretation in general that is inadequate but the kind of interpretation that Benedek was considering. Pointing out to this patient that he is dependent is clearly a depth analytic interpretation. Attention is drawn to an infantile need or impulse and, as Benedek correctly anticipates, such an intervention is typically experienced as an accusation.

An ego analytic interpretation would not cause the same problem. Instead of pointing out that this patient was dependent, for example, I, following Fenichel (1941), might suggest that he seems afraid of being dependent. "You appear to have been existing without any dependency satisfaction at all, a remarkable circumstance," I might say to such an individual. "But now that you are becoming aware that you might have some element of such feeling, it's disconcerting to you. I would guess it's hard for you to imagine the possibility of *enjoying* being dependent." It seems unlikely that this individual would feel rejected or criticized by an interpretation of this sort.

Several authors have pointed to the disorganizing effect interpretations can have on certain patients and recommend a shift from an exploratory, uncovering therapy to a supportive or "covering-over" approach. It is possible to argue, however, that the disorganizing effect may be a consequence of employing depth analytic interventions. An example is the student, discussed in Chapter 2, who responded to a poor grade by rubbing himself with feces. Interpreting his feces play as anal eroticism or narcissistic withdrawal is likely only to increase his humiliation and disorganization. It is understandable that therapists who are thinking in these terms might hesitate to make such interventions. An ego analytic interpretation suggesting that this act is an expression of his sense of defeat and humiliation following his lower than expected grade, however, may have an organizing effect. What must appear to this individual himself as horrifying and grotesque behavior is thus placed in the context of understandable human needs and feelings.

Insight and understanding have been given a bad name, I am suggesting, and have been abandoned prematurely because of unfortunate experiences with depth analytic interpretations. The problem is particularly clear in the field of couples therapy. Psychoanalytically oriented practitioners view partners as "symbiotic" (Ables and Brandsma, 1977), having an "insatiable need for acclaim and power" (Sager et al., 1971), or "projecting" their "own infantile, demanding aspects" on their partners (Lloyd and Paulson, 1972, p. 411). These individuals are already feeling discouraged and self-critical about their situation. Being told that they are dependent, competitive, greedy, and so on would increase their alarm and defensiveness. Therapists who think in these terms might indeed hesitate to communicate these ideas.

Systems theorists also tend to picture couples in unflattering, depth analytic terms. The alcoholic husband is seen as manipulating his wife while she is pictured as enjoying his pathological dependency on her. Partners are seen as colluding with or forming coalitions against each other, using "ploys" and "games" to gain control of the relationship, sabotaging the therapeutic improvement of the other in order to maintain homeostasis, or scapegoating or victimizing each other. It is easy to see how therapists who conceptualize couples in this manner might conclude that communicating this picture to them would not be helpful.

The problem with depth analytic interpretations, in essence, is that they tend to be accusatory. Ego analytic interventions are inherently nonaccusatory and, in fact, rely for their therapeutic effect on their ability to make the partners themselves less accusing and more accepting of each other and of themselves. A bitter argument, viewed by certain depth analysts as a "mutual attempt at domination" (Mittlemann, 1956) may be seen by ego analysts as a reaction to previous dedicated efforts to be tolerant and considerate of each other and to avoid arguing. Such interpretations are likely to increase individuals' understanding of and sympathy for their own and their partners' positions.

Systems theorists do make occasional interpretations, often of a type that is nonaccusatory. The problem is that they do not believe them. When these therapists make such interventions they do so for manipulative purposes. Virginia Satir (1967) is sometimes credited with pointing out the therapeutic value of redefining the couple's problems in positive terms, suggesting, for example, that partners' fights are a sign of involvement with each other. The technique is often discussed as "reframing." Haley develops this procedure further, presenting it as a gambit or strategy for producing change. Nagging is relabeled an attempt to reach out or achieve closeness (Haley, 1963a, p. 226) or as the "concern of an altruistic person for the well-being of the spouse" (Weiss, 1979).

Such tactical stretching of the truth seems to me to be of questionable value and, in any event, is unnecessary. It is my experience and conviction that an accurate analysis of a couple's troubled interactions paying attention to the effects of the partners' efforts to suppress what they believe to be unacceptable feelings and wishes will in most cases automatically recast their behavior in more positive terms.

To summarize, the attitude of practitioners toward insight therapy depends on the manner in which they conceptualize the couple's problems. If partners are viewed as compulsive pursuers of infantile and destructive gratification (the psychoanalytic approach), as mindless victims of superordinate forces (the systems approach), or as inexpert reciprocal reinforcing agents (the behavioral approach), the therapist's task is to correct the respective conditions. The psychoanalyst will help partners renounce or outgrow their infantile impulses, the systems theorist will attempt to change the pathological couple system, and the behavioral marital therapist will teach the couple better relationship habits.

In none of these cases, however, are insight and understanding thought to play the critical role. The psychoanalytic approach comes closest. These practitioners assume the existence within individuals of at least the rudiments of an observing ego, an ability to see beyond immediate infantile needs. It is this healthy or autonomous ego to which interpretive effort may be directed. Many psychoanalytically oriented couples therapists doubt the power of the healthy ego, however, and place major reliance on noninterpretive therapeutic approaches such as corrective emotional experience, modeling, or renegotiating the marital contract.

Therapists adopting an ego analytic approach view partners in terms that lead to useful interpretations. This is not to say that ego analysis immediately solves all the problems of an interpretive approach. The inhibition of partners in expressing their doubts and reservations about what the therapist says and the desperation with which they cling to what they see as their last hope may cause them to simply disregard or dismiss the therapist's interpretations. Therapy then depends on how the practitioner responds to this.

10

Resistance and Disqualification

In the first part of this chapter, I describe how interventions made by proponents of the three major schools may have the effect of disqualifying partners' feelings and reactions. The second part deals with the rationale these therapists may have for employing such methods—the belief that forceful procedures of this sort are necessary if therapists are to deal with resistance. I then suggest how it might be possible to deal with resistance without being coercive or disqualifying.

DISQUALIFYING PARTNERS' FEELINGS

The core problem of relationships is the tendency of individuals to "disqualify" (Haley, 1959; Sluzki et al., 1967) their own and their partners' wishes and feelings. They suppress certain of their feelings (withdraw), blurt out others (demand, accuse), and discount those of their partners. Mutual withdrawal, mutual accusation, and demanding–withdrawn polarization are three classic forms of reciprocal disqualification. A primary task of therapy, accordingly, is to provide partners with usable knowledge about how they unknowingly disqualify their own and their partners' reactions.

Disqualifying feelings is not just a danger of partner-to-partner relationships. It is also a hazard of therapist-to-partner interactions. The following are examples of how methods and concepts employed in each of the three major contemporary approaches may have the effect of invalidating partners' responses.

Mention has already been made about this tendency in certain psychoanalytically oriented approaches. Attributing partners' reactions to regressive impulses, unresolved childhood conflicts, or developmental defects may have the effect of disqualifying them. Sager's (1976) view of Susan as a woman with "underlying feelings of infantile rage" discounted her seemingly valid complaint that her husband was pleasing her only because the therapist had instructed him to do so. Nadelson's (1978) conviction that Mrs. P's jealousy was a result of an unresolved oedipal conflict overlooked the fact that this jealousy was an understandable reaction to her present situation. Ables and Brandsma's (1977) belief that graduate students' wives' envy is a consequence of a failure in separation–individuation disregarded the possiblility that such wives may have good reason to be envious.

The tendency of behavioral marital therapists to disqualify partners' feelings and perceptions appears to arise from their proccupation with behavior and relative disregard for feelings. Margolin and Weiss (1978, p. 1485) use cognitive restructuring procedures to "reduce the incapacitating emotions" that make dysfunctional behaviors resistant to change. O'Leary and Turkewitz (1978), while allowing certain expressions of negative feeling, discourage those that cannot lead to constructive behavioral change. Disqualification is perhaps most clearly seen when behavioral marital therapists give "negative feedback" (i.e., "punish" partners) and when they lecture and moralize—e.g., "Part of being married is learning that you sometimes have to do things for your partner that you would rather not do, simply to please your partner" or "that belief [that your partner should know instinctively what you want] is pure and utter horseshit . . . you are going to have to give up that hope or you might as well kiss the relationship goodbye" (Jacobson and Margolin, 1979, pp. 146 and 148).

While some therapists inadvertently disqualify partners' feelings and perceptions, certain systems theorists do so on purpose. Jackson and Haley believe that constructive change may require placing partners in "therapeutic double binds" or paradoxical situations. The aim is to counteract these individuals' immediate purposes and intentions and to recast them in a form that achieves the therapist's goal.

Invalidating other people's ideas and feelings is a common practice in life. Nearly everyone does it, and most individuals are used to it. It would seem advantageous for a therapist, however, to do so as little as possible. Disqualification has a numbing effect and leads to compliance or rebellion. Such reactions are generally counterproductive.

DEALING WITH RESISTANCE

These practitioners might argue in defense of their approach that resistance is a serious threat to psychotherapy.* Partners do have irrational ideas, inappropriate wishes, or maladaptive habits, such therapists might say, and these ideas, wishes, and habits must be challenged even if this has the effect

---

*Therapists from the three major contemporary schools talk about resistance in different ways. Systems theorists discuss couples' efforts to maintain their pathological couple systems. Behavior therapists are concerned about partners' reluctance to complete the assigned tasks (Weiss, 1979). Psychoanalytically oriented therapists talk about the ego deficits, developmental impairments, and regressive strivings that prohibit partners from engaging in a collaborative therapeutic relationship (Ables and Brandsma, 1977).

of disqualifying partners' feelings and perceptions. I believe, however, that it may be possible to deal with resistance without having to disconfirm or invalidate partners' feelings and reactions.

Much depends on one's definition of resistance. While depth analysts view it as a reluctance to give up infantile gratifications, I see it as a consequence of inhibition and/or desperation. A wife who is afraid to disagree with a therapist's interpretation or complain about being ganged up on in the therapy will be forced to express her objections in indirect ways, for example, by subtly discounting what the therapist says. It is such indirectness that often gives the impression of resistance. A forthright statement (e.g., "I feel ganged up on") would be clarifying and could be dealt with in a straightforward manner.

The term resistance is also sometimes used to refer to rigidly held convictions. An example is a husband's ingrained idea that arguments should never occur in a good marriage. My own experience is that such beliefs generally conceal an underlying desperation or pessimism. This husband may be afraid that a disagreement between him and his wife might signal the end of the relationship.

A therapist who views resistance as a consequence of inhibition or desperation will be able to intervene on the side of the individual and, in a sense, on the side of the resistance. "Of course you would be hesitant about coming to these sessions," I might say. "If, as I am beginning to realize, you have been feeling ganged up on here, we may be lucky you showed up at all today."

The following are examples of coercive or manipulative attempts to deal with resistance. I suggest how it might be possible to intervene on the side of the partners.

The System as Resistance

Systems theorists view partners as resisting anything that threatens the integrity of the family or couple system. An example is the effort of a husband to sabotage the therapeutic progress, independent strivings, or educational and career plans of his wife. This man is concerned, perhaps with some justification, that his wife might be heading toward divorce and the breakup of the family.

Many systems theorists appear to see little value in talking directly about the problem. They assume that the husband will deny opposition to his wife's efforts toward personal fulfillment and independence and will then deceitfully undercut them. The therapist must find some way of counteracting or working against the husband's efforts and intentions.

My own experience is that such husbands are not wholeheartedly against their wives' growing independence. They have mixed feelings about it and if approached in the right way are willing to talk about it. They are deeply threatened, it is true, and it is difficult for them to fully support their wives' new career plans. However, they generally do not want to be the kind of husbands who stand in the way of their wives' happiness. Furthermore, they often approve of many of the changes. Their wives are now more spirited, less depressed, and more interesting. As one husband put it, "I like the changes. I just want to be included in them."

Once some element of the husband's mixed feelings is expressed, it becomes possible to sympathize with his dilemma. I might say the following: "You want to be able to support you wife's career efforts, as you said, and you are doing so in several ways. But it must be hard to put your heart into it when the ultimate result, or at least your fear, is that she may leave you." This intervention, which acknowledges the husband's motives and feelings, is quite different from the traditional Jackson-Haley approach that attempts to circumvent these motives.

According to the systems concept of the "identified patient," the emotional disability or symptomatic behavior of one member is seen as being required for family stability. The family will thus resist and sabotage any attempts to improve the psychological well-being of this individual (Haley, 1963b; Jackson, 1957). It has been my experience, however, that partners are as likely to be relieved and grateful as they are to be threatened and resistant when a problem they had attributed to the "identified patient" is redefined as a general couple problem. This is only true, of course, if the couple problem is stated in a nonaccusatory manner.

Both partners of a couple I saw agreed that their only major problem was the wife's "neurotic symptoms"—her periodic worries about death and her inability to get along with her husband's mother, whom both agreed was a difficult woman. As soon as the wife began talking about either issue, the husband would interrupt and try to talk her out of these concerns, suggesting that she should take life as it comes. Although she may have felt vaguely misunderstood, she agreed he was probably correct.

The couple's idea about therapy was that we should look at the wife's early family experience to uncover the source of her "neurotic symptoms." When I suggested that these symptoms might also have to do with their present relationship, the partners did not become resistant as the systems model might have predicted but were intrigued and encouraged. This is not hard to understand. Their definition of the wife as the "identified patient" left them helpless to do anything about the problem. The suggestion that the difficulty might have to do with their ongoing relationship gave them hope that they might be able to deal directly with the situation.

The wife's fears of death turned out in part to be her way of experiencing the alienation that had arisen between herself and her husband. Once this was established it became relatively easy to suggest that her fears could be used as a sensitive instrument, a relationship barometer, for detecting issues or events about which it was important for them both to know. The husband, for his part, needed to talk her out of her fears because he felt that any unresolved problem between them might end their marriage. Once he had a chance to state this concern, a concern she also shared, it became an issue they could talk about rather than one on which his only alternative was to act.

The wife's other "symptom," her difficulty in dealing with his mother, turned out also to be a function of the marital relationship. The wife would have been able to manage his mother and help her husband in his own attempt to deal with this difficult woman if only she felt her husband were on her side and understood her feelings about it. The husband, convinced that no one could possibly want to help him in the unrewarding task of dealing with his mother and feeling guilty about exposing his wife to this problem, had been devoting all his efforts to instructing his wife not to take her seriously. The effect of this, however, was to convince his wife that he did not understand her feelings and that there was something wrong with her for not being able to follow his recommendations. The problem was not the difficulty of dealing with his mother but rather their inability to be resources to each other in this common task. Once the problem was stated in these terms it became much easier to resolve.

Certain systems theorists view the couple system, couple rules, homeo-static functioning, and the establishment of an "identified patient" as resistant to therapeutic change and as requiring coercive or manipulative countermeasures. My own belief is that it is generally possible to talk use-fully with partners about their couple system, couple rules, and so on, with-out necessarily having to take a stand against them.

Gratification as Resistance

Certain analytically oriented couples therapists are concerned that partners might obtain too much gratification from therapy to be willing to change. Gratification is thus seen as constituting a resistance. It is important not "to assuage their [the partners'] anxiety too much or to gratify them un-duly," Ables and Brandsma (1977, p. 12) write. "The therapeutic climate must be benign but not overly gratifying" (p.66). This is clearly a depth analytic view. An ego analyst, seeing partners as deprived and frustrated, would not be worried about providing too much gratification.

One form of gratification that partners might obtain from therapy is fantasy gratification. Many individuals begin therapy by turning away from their partners and talking directly to the therapist. Ables and Brandsma are concerned that a therapist's acceptance of this might play into the partners' "infantile wishes for an omnipotent parent who will straighten things out by telling them what to do" (p. 48).* Such individuals hope to elicit the therapist's help in forcing the other to change. These authors describe an argument between partners (and particularly the husband) who want to present their cases to the therapist and a therapist who keeps insisting on the importance of their talking to each other (pp. 43–46). The argument is clearly counterproductive.

My own view is that this therapist is overly concerned about playing into partners' fantasy expectations. Such individuals have generally been struggling unsuccessfully with their problems too long to really believe that anyone can help them or that their problems are even solvable. Coming to therapy is often a desperate act undertaken without much real hope and only because there does not seem to be an alternative. Ables herself comments on the desperation of these individuals (p. 57).

Rather than opposing this husband's desperate effort to present his case and prove his wife in the wrong I would simply talk about it. "Perhaps you feel that if you are clear enough in stating your case against your wife I will be convinced and then, in some way or in some manner, help you get your wife to change?" The husband is likely to agree, perhaps after some hesitation, that this is what he had in mind, at least in part, but that thinking about it now, it seems doubtful to him that it would really work that way.** This could then lead to a discussion of how both partners are feeling pretty frustrated with the other and hopeless about the situation.

Instead of viewing these partners' desire to talk to the therapist (rather than to each other) as an attempt to gratify fantasy wishes and as a resistance to the therapy, I see it as an understandable response to their situation. The wife told the therapist that she and her husband had talked to each other about their problems many times before and it seemed futile to do it again. The therapist acknowledged her discouragement, but pointed out that it would be different this time because he or she (the therapist) would be there to help (p. 46). My preference, rather than countering the wife's argument so quickly, would be to focus on the feeling of discouragement, develop it further, and legitimize it. "I can understand the problem," I might say. "Each of you feels the difficulty lies primarily with the other. The obvious task, then, is to try to convince the other of this. This is impossible, how-

---

*Sluzki (1978, pp. 372–373), though employing a systems approach, expresses a similar concern.

**Even if the husband retains some hope that he can get the therapist to take his side, this probably is not a serious threat to the therapy. Fantasy expectations are generally only a problem when they are unexpressed or unrecognized.

ever, because the other thinks that the problem is mostly *your* fault. I can see why you might have given up talking to each other and would prefer to state your cases to me."

Ables and Brandsma view the husband's refusal to accept the therapist's instructions as an indication of his "persistent need to maintain control and his difficulty using therapeutic interventions" (p. 46). This husband's behavior may also be seen, however, as a reaction to an unnecessary and arbitrary requirement. Why should he be prevented from stating his case to the therapist? Bowen (1978), in fact, takes the opposite position. He asks that partners talk directly to him. He would agree with this couple that partner-to-partner talking is likely to be unproductive.

My response to Ables and Brandsma's effort to deal with this couple's resistance is thus twofold. First, I would not necessarily see it as resistance. Second, rather than opposing (i.e., disqualifying) their wish to state their cases directly to the therapist I would try to understand and justify this wish.

Resistance to Assignments

The task of behavioral marital therapy is to get partners to interact in new ways. Once this is done and "the natural reinforcing contingencies take hold," these practitioners believe (Weiss, 1979), the individuals will want to maintain this new, positively reinforcing behavior. Problems occur, however, when partners refuse to experiment with new behavior, resisting the prescribed tasks and assignments. This is a serious difficulty for behavior therapists, striking at the very heart of their orientation and requiring effective and forceful countermeasures. Weiss (1979) suggests the value in certain cases of adopting the strategic methods of the systems theorists. "The issue of resistance in BMT [behavioral marital therapy] is truly complex," he writes, "and probably now involves more artifice than many of us would like to admit." It is necessary in some cases for "the therapist to become a master manipulator, an impression manager, and an expert in metaphor" (pp. 4–6).

Haley (1977), whose systems approach has a strong behavioral element, is rather firm with partners who do not complete assignments. "Generally," he writes, "a therapist should not easily forgive people who have not done what he has asked" (p. 64).

One way to deal with task failure is to tell the family members that the task was very important and that for their sakes it is too bad they did not do it. The therapist can tell them that now they cannot know how beneficial it would have been to them. If they say they did not think the task would do any good, the therapist can say they can never know that now, because they did not do it.

Throughout the interview, when they bring up problems, the therapist can point out that naturally they have those problems because they did not do the task. His goal is to get them to say they would like to have the opportunity to try again and do the task. If they do say this, the therapist can tell them that opportunity is gone and can never come again—they cannot do the task now. In this way, he sets up the situation so that the next time he asks them to do a task they will do it. (p. 64)

The message communicated by Haley and certain behavior therapists is that the partners are being uncooperative and unreasonable in resisting assignments. The effect is to dismiss or disqualify partners' hesitancy or disinclination and to attribute it to inadequate commitment to solving their problems.

Resistance is partly a function of the therapeutic system. It often occurs when therapists need clients to behave in certain ways. If the behavior therapy approach did not require partners to fulfill assignments successfully, the refusal of these individuals to do so would not constitute such an impediment or "resistance" to the therapy.

My own predisposition, were I to employ such assignments, would be to make therapeutic use of partners' reluctance or failure to do them. Mention is made in Chapter 5 of the assignment in which a wife was to show interest in and ask questions about her husband's day and he was to spend an afternoon with the family (O'Leary and Turkewitz, 1978). Suppose the husband came to the next session reporting that he had not kept his side of the agreement. Certain behavior therapists might react by reaffirming the importance of the assignment and encouraging him to try harder the next week. My approach would be to justify and clarify his noncompliance. It may turn out that his initial efforts in spending an afternoon with the family had led to a fight with his wife about how to raise their children. Husband and wife might then realize that this is what typically happens when they spend time together with their children. His failure to do the assignment could thus be used to correct or improve the therapist's behavioral analysis of the situation by providing further information about the reinforcement contingencies motivating the husband's behavior.*

There appear to be at least two general ways of dealing with resistance. A traditional method is to oppose it. The alternative recommended here is to validate it, to stand back from the immediate situation (the apparent resistance by one or both partners to the practitioner's therapeutic efforts), and to show how it makes sense.

---

*It is the value that sometimes comes from examining the failure of partners to complete assignments that led Martin H. Williams, a psychologist working with Apfelbaum, to remark, "Not doing the assignment is one way of doing the assignment."

4

Major Forms of
Intervention

From *Couples Therapy: A Nontraditional Approach* by Daniel B. Wile. (John Wiley & Sons, 1981), pp. 110-147.

11

Clarifying Each Partner's Position

Having considered the special characteristics of my approach, I turn now to the specific interventions a therapist adopting this orientation would make. It is possible to distinguish three general types of intervention: clarifying each partner's point of view (to be described in this chapter), taking the side of each partner (Chapter 12), and developing a shared frame of reference (Chapter 13).

An important initial task in couples therapy is to develop each partner's position on the issues that divide them. Although all couples therapists devote some effort to this, there are differences among practitioners in the emphasis given to this job. Some view it as a preliminary measure, a prerequisite to the major therapeutic activity of making paradoxical interventions, for example, or arranging a compromise. I believe, however, that establishing each partner's point of view may have a powerful therapeutic effect in itself, in that the main problem of partners is their inability to embrace their own positions fully (C. Apfelbaum). This is the key principle of ego analytic couples therapy (Apfelbaum, 1980c).

The purpose of this chapter is to describe how developing each partner's point of view may: (1) solve the therapist's major dilemma: how to exert sufficient therapeutic force without being coercive or disqualifying, and (2) provide a direct though temporary solution to the partners' major problem: their feeling of unentitlement to their own positions.

THE NEED FOR A FORCEFUL THERAPY

In Chapter 10 I suggest that there is an advantage in intervening on the side of the partners. The argument could be made, however, that this fails to recognize the forcefulness of the pathological couple system and the need of therapists to exert a sufficient counterforce. My answer, paradoxically, is that establishing and developing each partner's position may constitute a very powerful counterforce.

There is no doubt that an active, initiating therapeutic approach is necessary. When psychotherapists first turned their attention to treating couples and families, they found themselves beseiged, outnumbered, and in danger of losing their therapeutic neutrality. Family members would gang up on the therapist, engage in interminable squabbling, disqualify everything that they and everyone else were saying, deny the family had any problems, and either ignore the therapist completely or integrate the therapist into their "pathological" family pattern (Satir, 1967; Minuchin et al., 1967).

Therapists who tried family or couples therapy usually responded in one of two ways. Some concluded that conjoint therapy was unworkable and, when faced with the possibility of family or couples therapy on future occasions, suggested instead that one or more family members go into individual psychotherapy. Others reacted by becoming increasingly active, countering the family's or couple's insistent denial with even more insistent accusations, or by functioning as a kind of family traffic cop.

The problem with these more active measures was that they conflicted with the accepted therapeutic model of the day that valued nonjudgmental listening and noncoercive interventions. It was here that family systems theory served a valuable historic function. The systems approach provided a new model that legitimized the kind of forceful and dramatic measures that were necessary if couples and family therapy were to be at all feasible. The metaphor of a powerful family system relentlessly pursuing homeostatic balance not only reflected the conjoint therapist's experience in doing family and couples therapy, but provided justification for engaging in sufficiently strong countermeasures. It was not family members whom these therapists felt they were challenging, but family systems.

These practitioners, although perhaps agreeing that they were being manipulative or bullying, would point to the fact that their approach worked. An active, initiating, controlling approach of this sort was absolutely necessary, they seemed to believe, if family or couples therapy were to be possible at all (Jungreis, 1965). Kempler (1968, p. 95), putting it more strongly, said that "Family therapy requires active participation if the therapist is to survive." The same might be said for couples therapy.

I agree that therapists have to be active and forceful if they are to have any effect on families and couples. My suggestion, however, is that the particular methods that systems oriented therapists employ, although perhaps providing a useful first approximation, may no longer be necessary. It is possible to exercise sufficient therapeutic leverage without having to coerce or manipulate, thereby avoiding unfortunate side effects that such methods produce.

My own solution is to be forceful and initiating, but to apply this force to the task of clarifying the partners' own positions. Caution is often required in challenging people's views. Many therapists are careful, for example, in the manner in which they advise partners to stop blaming each other. There is no limit, however, to the pointedness, persistence, and vigor with which practitioners may *develop* the partners' views. A therapist can be unrestrictedly forceful in pursuing the extent and details of each person's conviction that the other is entirely at fault.

It is generally not difficult to take the initiative in clarifying partners' positions. People are inefficient in representing their own points of view. They lose track of them, cling to them in rigidly ineffectual ways, or fail to pursue the implications. A therapist can provide a major service by formulating the partners' positions and keeping them available as a frame of reference. If partners suddenly stop blaming each other and start criticizing themselves, for example, I might ask what happened to their view that the other is at fault.

The issue of therapeutic forcefulness has been discussed as a concern of practitioners. It is an even greater source of worry to clients. A common fear of partners, arising from prolonged and repeated failure in their own attempts to work out problems, is that nothing will help. They come to therapy, and in particular to the initial session, with a great need for "something to happen," for there to be some shift, however mild, that can give them at least the beginnings of hopefulness. The therapist's forcefulness and initiative in helping them develop their respective points of view generally provides this.

A RESPITE FROM RECIPROCAL DISQUALIFICATION

The act of clarifying each partner's position provides a partial solution to the therapist's problem—how to exert sufficient therapeutic force without being coercive—and reassures partners about their major worry: that nothing can help. But it serves an even more critical function—it speaks directly to the problem that brings the partners to therapy.

The core problem of relationships has been alternatively described as alienation, isolation, deprivation, inhibition, inadequate control, the feeling of unentitlement, and mutual disqualification. All these reduce to one basic factor: the inability of partners to accept and express important feelings and to have them acknowledged by the other or, more generally, the inability to jointly "inhabit" their relationship. Mutually withdrawn partners do not discuss their feelings, mutually accusing partners do not accept each other's right to have them, and demanding–withdrawn partners combine both difficulties.

When I first see partners, I immediately begin dealing with this issue by providing as full an opportunity as possible for each to express his or her position. I ask their respective views and feelings about the issue that brought them in, ask follow up questions, and summarize what they say: "Martha, as I understand it then, you feel the problem is Jed's irresponsibility about money and the fact that he never talks to you. Jed, you don't really feel there is a problem, or rather, the problem is that Martha has these complaints." If they correct any part of my formulation or make additions, I alter it accordingly. My goal is to construct as accurate a picture as possible of how each partner views the problem and the relationship.

In addition to expressing their views and feelings, partners need to feel that their positions are understood or appreciated. An important question, once they have expressed their feelings, is whether their partners will accept these feelings or disqualify them. I have learned that I cannot always judge what partners will find affirming or disqualifying. Many who are used to getting no reaction at all from their mates may be happy to get any sort of response, even an argumentative or defensive one.

When I ask partners how they feel about what seems a frustrating and mutually alienating argument, their response in some cases is to say that they are pleased. "I've heard more this past hour than I've heard in ten years," a partner may say. "This is the first time Neil has ever admitted he is angry at me. I'm learning things I never knew before." Or, "We never get a chance to argue like this at home. I guess we feel safer here."

Most partners obtain immediate though perhaps temporary benefits from sessions conducted in this manner. The reason, I believe, is that their relationship has momentarily changed. For a short time at least they feel more in contact (they have had a chance to state their feelings and hear those of their partners), less disqualified (their feelings have been acknowledged by the therapist and to some extent by the partner), and in greater control of the relationship (a consequence of stating their positions and getting a response). It is easy for them to feel that their major problems would be resolved if they were able to have discussions like this every day.

I shall now describe the approach in greater detail, using drifting and slashing couple interactions as examples. This rather common therapeutic intervention—clarifying partners' positions—can be fashioned into a precise and powerful therapeutic instrument.

The Drifting Couple

A common situation in couples therapy is the drifting interaction, a couple state marked by tentativeness, avoidance, and unclarity. The therapeutic task is to intervene, without being coercive or judgmental. My way of doing this is to make direct and pointed comments but to establish the partner as the final arbiter of the truth.

I thus said to one wife, "I get the idea that, to put it a little sharply, you are saying that you have lost all feeling for your husband and are thinking of ending the relationship. You haven't quite said this, but is this what you are suggesting?" "That *is* pretty sharp," the woman replied, "but I guess that is what I feel."

The advantage of such an intervention is that it may bring immediate clarity to an interchange that has been confusing to everyone. Questions could be raised, however, about the propriety of such an intervention. Although this woman was troubled by her feelings, she was seemingly not quite ready to express them. She was concerned that it would be too shattering to her husband. My experience is that partners are generally glad to have me articulate their positions. People who discuss their feelings in obscure ways appear to be caught between a wish to express them and a fear of what might happen if they did. Their solution, conscious or otherwise, is to lay out controversial thoughts in a semidisguised manner and to leave it to others to acknowledge them or not. These individuals may be partially hoping that what they are saying will go unnoticed; they also appear to be wishing it might be picked up.

The husband in this example may report that he had known for some time that his wife lacked feeling for him and that he is glad to finally get it into the open. On the other hand, he might say that he does feel shattered just as his wife feared. Even then he may be happy to be finally let in on the issue and have a chance to respond. He knows he will have to deal with the problem eventually, and the therapy situation is a good place to do so. The only truly unfortunate consequence is if the husband feels shattered but is unable to acknowledge it. He would then be in the same untenable situation as his wife—struggling singlehandedly with a feeling and an issue that can be dealt with only by both.

An overriding assumption of this approach is that almost anything can be talked about (including the wish to not talk), and in a way that gives the individual a greater sense of control in the relationship. Saying that one feels guilty is a good way of beginning to deal with guilt, and saying that one feels shattered is a good way of beginning to deal with being shattered.

The Arguing Couple

Another major situation for which couples therapists need an effective means of intervention is the slashing interaction, the couple state characterized by anger, interruption, and indiscriminate charges. Murray Bowen's (1978) whole couples therapy approach appears to be based on avoiding this couple state. Whereas Sluzki (1978) and Ables and Brandsma (1977) insist that partners discuss their problems with each other rather than with them, Bowen makes sure that they talk to him and not to each other. "I control the interchange," Bowen (1978, p. 248) writes. "Each spouse talks directly to me in the calmest, low-keyed, most objective possible way. In this situation, the other spouse is often able to listen and to 'really hear,' without reacting emotionally, for the first time in their lives together."

I take a middle position on this issue. I am not as concerned as Sluzki and Ables and Brandsma about the danger of taking too much responsibility or as concerned as Bowen about the danger of partners' emotional reactivity. My approach is to listen to their argument at some moments and to intervene and perhaps take control at others.

My goal, as it is with drifting partners, is to help these individuals develop their respective positions. This may seem unwise because the problem at the moment is that they are already stating their respective positions too much or too forcefully. A problem with mutual accusation, however, is that neither partner has the chance to make his or her point. It is in the nature of argument to discount what the other is saying, interrupt the other, and refuse to acknowledge anything. What I do is give both partners a chance to provide a full and complete statement to their positions. One means of doing this is to help each partner make his or her point as crisply and accurately as possible. I described one husband as appearing to feel he was "living in a mine field, never knowing when Rita was going to explode" and his wife as feeling she was "living with someone completely irresponsible, that she was the only adult in the family." Partners may experience a certain satisfaction and temporary resolution at having their feelings understood and represented in such a manner.

A major problem with mutual accusation is the lack of opportunity or failure by partners to deal with the content of their arguments. It is generally not possible to do this when the fight is occurring, as Bowen has pointed out. But it is also difficult to do so when the fight is not occurring. Many partners are hesitant to bring up controversial issues at such times for fear of rekindling the argument. A common pattern is to alternate between periods of indiscriminate accusation and indiscriminate politeness.

A good way of dealing with mutual accusation is to bring up the problematic issues in between fights or, better yet, just after a fight. I frequently wait until some of the intensity of a particular argument has diminished and then ask the details of their complaints. How concerned are they about the issues they brought up? Were these things just said in the heat of battle or were they really meant? And if they were meant, are they minor matters or serious ones, concerns that might even threaten the continued existence of the relationship? How convinced are they that their positions on these issues are correct, and how much do they think there might be some validity to their partners' positions? How would they feel if the problem turned out to be irresolvable and they had 20 years or more ahead in which they would have to struggle with it? Do they ever get a chance to work together on these difficulties—that is, talk about them when they are not angry?

Partners generally appreciate the opportunity to discuss their grievances in this more neutral setting, and their answers to some of these questions can be surprising and enlightening. The goal is to provide fuller and more accurate expression to partners' complaints or points of view than is possible during the fight.

I do not wish to suggest that dealing with accusing partners is easy and that pursuing their experience of the situation is the entire solution to the problem. I have had my own share of failures with bitterly ensnarled couples.* My point at the moment is that even with these very difficult partners it may still be possible to retain therapeutic initiative and to provide temporary relief from their mutual alienation by simply developing *their* positions.

DEVELOPING VERSUS OPPOSING PARTNERS' POSITIONS

A question arises about the limits of such an approach. Are there not occasions when it may be necessary to oppose partners' views? This section discusses situations considered by some practitioners to require therapist opposition. I suggest the possibility, even in these cases, of dealing with the problem by *developing* the partners' positions.

The Accusing Partner

A traditional problem in couples therapy is the flurry of accusations that partners launch against each other. Jacobson and Margolin (1979), O'Leary and Turkewitz (1978), and Ables and Brandsma (1977) among others, deal with such behavior by opposing it. These therapists point out to partners that accusation is "not helpful" (Ables and Brandsma, 1977) and provide guidelines, rules, or suggestions for "more useful" responses.

An alternative approach, and one that does not require opposing partners' behavior, is to point out the feeling underlying their specific accusations. "You have stated a number of complaints about Gene today," I said to Eva, "about how he never brings you flowers, does not compliment you

---

*The approach developed in this book can be considered in part as a reaction to failure with such partners and as an attempt to design a therapy that might be more helpful to them. One of these failures will be described in Chapter 18.

on how you look, never asks you about your day, and seems overly pre-occupied with his work. But I sense from what you are saying that you might have the deeper and more general concern that Gene does not really care about you, that you are not that important to him, and that he would not miss you if you were to suddenly disappear.''

This did in fact turn out to be the worry at the root of Eva's accusations and we were now able to deal with it directly. It also became clear why Eva had limited herself to specific complaints. Her first response to my state-ment was to say tearfully, ''That's almost too frightening to think about.'' It was thus possible to have a very powerful effect by developing, rather than challenging, her position.

A Hidden Agenda

Another partner whom it is sometimes thought necessary to challenge is the individual who comes to therapy with the goal of proving the relationship untenable on his or her hidden agenda. These are people who feel they are not entitled to divorce or separate unless they have thoroughly pursued every other avenue. Couples therapy is seen as one such avenue. Compared to most partners who are upset if the initial session ends without something hopeful happening, these individuals may be upset or disappointed if some-thing hopeful does happen.

My own experience (and here I differ from therapists who expect part-ners to conceal such a motive—that is, maintain it as a hidden agenda) is that these individuals are often able to talk about it. This may require some work on the therapist's part. The partner, let us say a wife, may not herself have fully realized that her main purpose is to prove the relationship un-workable. She may then be surprised when she finds herself reacting to a rather hopeful and promising therapeutic interchange with disappointment. The only indication of her feeling may be a slight hesitancy or frown. A comment about this hesitancy by the therapist is often all that is necessary to elicit her admission that she is upset about the positive turn of events. It may be possible, then, to have a conversation about the fact that she has come to therapy to justify ending the relationship.

The "Identified Patient"

Al and Lynn came to therapy with the complaint of Al's drinking. ''I am here,'' Lynn said, ''to do whatever I can to help.''

Most couples therapists, recognizing that Al has been placed in the role of the "identified patient," would consider it their task to redefine the issue as a couple problem. This can be done by informing partners directly that drinking usually signifies a relationship problem or by gradually working toward this revised formulation.

While I too would be concerned about the need to recast the problem in couple terms, I would be even more concerned about the danger of talking partners into something that they did not really believe. In fact, if Lynn began to think that she might be involved in the problem after all, I would ask whether she had truly changed her mind or whether she had been talked or pressured into this change and still believed at an important level that it was basically Al's problem.

My approach was simply to ascertain what Al and Lynn did believe. Lynn appeared initially convinced that it was entirely Al's problem. He came from a family of alcoholics, she said. Al admitted he had a drinking problem but related it in part to Lynn's nagging.

There is the danger here of "premature" termination by Lynn. She may conclude that there is no real way in which she can help her husband in therapy and stop coming in with him. However, this is not always such a bad thing. It is unclear whether therapy that begins by forcing an individual to admit what he or she does not believe or is not prepared to acknowledge can be effective.

As it turned out, Lynn did continue and soon began developing her side of the problem. She talked about feeling excluded in the family. She was seen as a prude and as someone who had to be worked around if you wanted to have any fun. While she and the children would gang up in condemning Al's drunken behavior, he and the children would gang up in rebelling against her restrictions.

We thus arrived at a more sophisticated view of the situation. Al and Lynn's problem was not simply Al's alcholism but an interaction and polarization between her conscientiousness and uprightness and his irresponsible/playful disregard. Here, as in many cases, background issues were a factor. He came from a family of alcoholics, and her parents were extremely puritanical.

Partners with Incompatible Goals

Certain therapists require that both partners have at least a minimal commitment to continuing the relationship. Since I accept whatever position partners take, I do not have such a requirement. Ellen initiated couples therapy because she was having difficulty ending her marriage. She said she felt too guilty about hurting Bob to do it on her own and hoped to be able to convince him that it would be best for both of them. Bob agreed to come to therapy with her, but his sole interest was to find some way of convincing her to continue the relationship.

This situation is perfectly compatible with my approach. The goal is to start from each partner's current perspective and to work from there. The fact that their aims are diametrically opposed need not change this. Although each partner may be distracted by the other's efforts in the opposite direction, there is often a special usefulness in their developing their positions and plans in the presence of the other.

I considered with Ellen, and with comment from Bob, how she planned to get Bob's agreement to end the relationship, why it was so necessary to get his agreement, how much hopefulness she had that she would be able to get it, what she would do if she were not able to get it, and how certain she was that she really did want to end the relationship. I considered with Bob, and with comment from Ellen, how he planned to convince Ellen to continue the relationship, how much hopefulness he had that he would be able to do it, how he would feel if the relationship were to end, why he wanted to continue the relationship when Ellen seemed so dead set against it, and how he would feel if she were to agree to stay with him but only because she felt too guilty to leave.

An important result was a recognition by Bob of the extent of Ellen's unhappiness. Their usual way of discussing their problems—by accusing and defending—had prevented him from seeing this. The calm and serious manner in which she now talked about her sadness made an impression on him. He began to wonder how he could have felt satisfied all these years with a marriage that had been so unsatisfying to her.

Partners with Impossible Goals

What if a partner's goals or plans for achieving these goals are, in the therapist's judgment, clearly unrealistic or unworkable? Don't therapists have a responsibility to point this out, and, even if not, how can they be truly neutral about them?

An example is partners who come to therapy saying in effect that they want to learn to be nicer to each other. They wish to control their tendencies to be irritable, whiny, or inconsiderate so that they can be a better husband and a better wife. Such a presenting complaint places the therapist in a dilemma. Most practitioners like to be responsive to partners' objectives and goals, but this particular goal seems unrealistic and counterproductive.

The dilemma in some cases can be easily resolved. It may be a simple matter to suggest that it is the partners' efforts to be nice to each other that may be causing the difficulty. What they might need is greater freedom or permission to be irritable, whiny, and inconsiderate. Certain partners get a great deal from this simple intervention.

However, such an approach may fail to appreciate the depth of commitment these individuals may have to the cultural ideal, the image of the good husband and the good wife as being uninterruptedly cheerful, considerate, giving, gracious, and uncomplaining. Partners and therapist may then find themselves in conflict. While the partners are trying to solve their problems by being nicer to each other, the therapist sees such effort as the major problem.

My response to partners who are committed to such a relationship philosophy is to help them deal with the problems they encounter in trying to apply it. If they criticize themselves, for example, for not having more spontaneity in their relationship, I might point out that this is one of the drawbacks in their approach to marriage, and it is too bad that they have to blame themselves for it. If they chastise themselves for occasional irritability with each other, I might comment on the difficulty of the task or rule they have set themselves—to remain uninterruptedly cheerful and polite—and the inevitability of periodic violations of it.

Partners Who Set Conditions

An example of therapy that did not go well is one in which a husband agreed to his wife's request for couples therapy but only under the condition that nothing too controversial be discussed. When, in the third session, she hinted at possible separation, he restated his condition that it was okay to talk about minor things in therapy, but he wanted to leave major issues like that for just the two of them to discuss. In the next session she became extremely frustrated, left in the middle of the hour, and never returned. He mentioned rather sadly as he got up to leave that he was surprised at her behavior because things had been looking up. They had had a good week together, or so he had thought. He had not known until just then that she had been suppressing complaints the whole time.

It could be argued that it was a mistake to have begun couples therapy under the conditions he set. The failure was not my acceptance of his conditions, however, but my not more actively developing their views and feelings about these conditions. If I had done this, we might have been able to articulate what was happening—how he half complies with her wishes (agreeing to come to therapy but under the condition that nothing important be discussed) and how she then half complies with his conditions and then suddenly rebels—and to recognize this sequence as a typical pattern. His usual response to her complaints was to agree to make changes but on his terms: she was to stop complaining and give him a chance to change. She would half agree to this, withhold her complaints for a time, and then suddenly become frustrated and enraged. Instead of my talking with them about this pattern, I simply sat by passively and let it happen.*

Questioning Partners' Statements

The recommendation to pursue partners' own points of view does not mean that the therapist must automatically accept the first thing individuals say.

Pete and June came to their first therapy session attributing their problems to their parents. June's mother was continually interfering in their lives, visiting them unexpectedly, bringing gifts they did not need, and offering advice they did not want. Every time they looked up, it seemed, there she was. Then there was Pete's family. As a child, he had been deserted by his mother and she and the rest of his family have remained unavailable or unreliable to this day.

The partners' initial statement presents a problem to the therapist. These individuals have come to couples therapy but are not describing a couple issue. The concerns they are discussing are not with each other but with their parents. In fact, they seem to be working quite well together in their efforts to deal with these parents.

I said to them, "Your parents do seem to be difficult to get along with and there is a lot we can go into about this. I had the impression, however, since you asked for couples therapy, that there were issues in the relationship between you. Is this true or *did* you want us to focus on these problems with your parents?" What keeps this intervention neutral and noncoercive is the fact that I am prepared to accept either response the partners might make. If they were to say that there was a problem between them and go on to detail it, that would be fine. If they were to say that they did not have a couple problem, but that they did have a problem with their parents and that they had come to therapy as a couple because they wanted to discuss it together, that would be fine too.

"Our parents are a problem to us *as a couple*," Pete and June answered, "because we get depressed by them. And we also get depressed by what happens between us." This last comment caught my attention and I asked more about it. They then went on to describe a demanding–withdrawn pattern. June typically wanted to have more time to herself, especially when she came home tired from work. Pete, in contrast, always wanted them to

---

*This experience, which occurred early in my career as a couples therapist, remains in my memory as a dramatic reminder of the importance of adopting an active therapeutic approach.

spend more time together. He often followed her around the house trying to talk.

I was correct, it turned out, in suspecting that there might be a problem between them in addition to or instead of their presenting complaint. However, they were also correct. Their problems with each other were the same ones that they had been having with their parents. Pete, who had been and continued to be abandoned by his mother, was sensitive to June's tendency to withdraw. June, who had been and continued to be engulfed by her mother, was put off by Pete's pressure for more contact.

Part of the value of clarifying each partner's position, however irrelevant or defensive it may at first appear, is that it does generally point toward the central couple issues.

12

Taking Each Partner's Side

PAIRED BINDS INTERPRETATIONS

The first task of couples therapy, as just described, is to provide partners with an opportunity to state their positions. In some sessions this might be all the therapist needs to do. Partners who have been unable to discuss problems, express feelings, and make complaints may take full advantage of the chance to do so in therapy.

The situation is different with partners who respond to efforts to clarify their respective positions by engaging in the same sort of stalemated interactions that have been frustrating them at home. Certain individuals may simply restate traditional criticisms, accusing each other or themselves of being "irresponsible," "neurotic," or "self-centered." It is necessary in such cases to proceed more forcefully.

My way of doing this is to go beyond simply clarifying partners' respective positions and to actively defend or justify them. The effect is to intervene on the side of each partner against his or her self-criticism and, in a sense, against the criticism of the other. A major problem with siding with one partner is that this might have the effect or give the impression of siding against the other. The solution to this difficulty is to take the side of both partners simultaneously. The purpose of this chapter is to suggest how this can be done.

INTERPRETING INTERACTING SENSITIVITIES

Betsy and Tom are planning to be married and are looking forward to their wedding with the usual mixture of excitement and apprehension. Tom deals with his apprehension by withdrawing. He finds himself with less desire to see Betsy. He phones less frequently and has less to say when he does. He visits her less often, finds reason to leave early, and spends most of the time with her watching TV. Betsy deals with her fears in the opposite way. She seeks to reassure herself about his love for her, her love for him, their general compatibility, and the wisdom of their decision to marry by having continuous contact, long intimate talks, and lots of flowers, affection, and sex.

There is a tragic irony here. Each of their solutions to the problem intensifies the problem of the other. The more Tom withdraws, the more Betsy needs reassuring contact. The more she seeks contact, the more he needs to withdraw. A useful way of discussing this situation is to suggest the existence in Betsy and Tom of reciprocal and interacting sensitivities. Betsy is sensitive to withdrawal and reacts with demands; Tom is sensitive to demands and reacts with withdrawal. The problem is a serious one. These partners are likely to become increasingly distressed and ultimately may be forced to separate.

People develop ways of managing stress in their relationships. When one becomes particularly upset about an issue or event, the other generally becomes comforting and supportive. The problem arises, however, when both are particularly upset at the same time. This can be a recurrent phenomenon when, as in the case of Betsy and Tom, the sore spot, raw nerve, or special vulnerability of one inflames, stimulates, or intensifies that of the other.

Such reciprocal sensitivities are extremely common and may exist in various forms in all couples. A familiar example is the disagreement between partners about whether to continue an argument. One individual, who worries that the dispute will get increasingly out of control, may seek desperately to cut it off. The other, who resents the first's attempts to end the discussion or who fears that stopping without resolution is preliminary to divorce, may seek just as desperately to continue (Ackerman, 1979).

The issue to which each partner is sensitive often has an historic significance. George, who felt that all the important decisions in his childhood had been made for him and without his knowledge, became upset and a little irrational whenever his wife, Deborah, arranged even a minor matter without first consulting him. Deborah, who had been ineffectively dealing with an irrational father throughout her life, became rattled whenever George acted upset and a little irrational. She dealt with him in the same way she dealt with her father, by keeping more of her thoughts to herself. This, of course, increased the probability of her arranging matters without first informing him. Deborah's special sensitivity to excitable and irrational men thus interacted with George's sensitivity to having things done behind his back.

A particularly dramatic example of historic factors is that of an engaged couple, Dick and Susan, whose respective sensitivities had roots not only in childhood but also in their first marriages. Dick felt rejected by his parents and was clearly rejected by his first wife; she left him for another man. What particularly unnerved him was the fact that he did not have an inkling of a problem until he found his first wife in bed with his best friend. He came away from this experience with an acute fear of rejection and the sense that it could occur at any moment and without warning.

Dick expressed this sensitivity by complaining in a bullying manner whenever he thought Susan had been a little rejecting. Susan, who had a domineering father and an abusive first husband, responded to Dick's bullying by withdrawing, which Dick then took as further indication of rejection. To put the problem simply, Dick was sensitive to rejection and responded by bullying; Susan was sensitive to bullying and responded by rejecting.

If the problem the couple discusses has the general form of interacting sensitivities, it then becomes possible to intervene on the side of each partner at the same time by showing how each in his or her own way is being deprived or provoked. In the domination–rejection pattern, the dominating partner is actually being rejected and the rejecting individual is actually being dominated. And in the demanding–withdrawn pattern (as exemplified by Tom and Betsy, the soon-to-be-married couple), the demanding partner is actually being ignored or left out (Tom is spending less time with Betsy), and the withdrawn individual is actually being pressured (Betsy is complaining about it).

This could be stated to the partners as follows: "Betsy, as you have said, the one thing you want most, and it is perhaps what anyone would want, is a little attentiveness and a feeling that Tom really cares for you. So what happens? This turns out to be the one thing you are not getting. Tom, as you have said, the one thing you need is more time to yourself, an opportunity to slow things down, to withdraw a little. And this is precisely what you are not getting."

The classic hazard of intervening on the side of one partner, the likelihood that this will be taken by the other as a challenge to his or her own point of view, is thus resolved by juxtaposing defenses or justifications of both their positions. A therapist who is conceptualizing the situation in terms of interacting sensitivities will be in a favorable position to do this.

INTERPRETING PAIRED BINDS

It is obvious why reciprocal sensitivities are a problem. As previously suggested, people who are feeling threatened, provoked, or vulnerable in a particular situation or interaction count on their partners to remain relatively objective and to compensate for their condition. If their special sensitivity or vulnerability elicits the special sensitivity of their partners, however, there is no one left to remain objective and the situation may spiral out of control. Systems theorists refer to this as runaway positive feedback.

But there is a further problem. At some point or at some level these partners sense what is happening and seek to stop it. Their attempts may then have the unfortunate effect of compounding the difficulty. The partners who were expressing their apprehensions about their upcoming wedding in incompatible ways may sense that their reactions are having counterproductive effects. Betsy, realizing that her pursuit just increases Tom's withdrawal, may try to not pursue. Tom, realizing that his withdrawal just increases Betsy's pursuit, may try to not withdraw.

The problem with forcing oneself to not pursue, as Betsy tries to do, is that this requires suppressing strong feeling. At some point she is likely to rebel against this self-imposed restraint and blurt out a complaint. Tom is unlikely to obtain much relief from Betsy's efforts to reduce the pressure. He knows what she really wants (i.e., more contact), a fact substantiated by her sporadic blurted out demands.

A related point can be made about Tom's effort to not withdraw. The more he forces himself to see her when he does not quite feel like it and to talk to her when he has nothing to say, the more he may need to rebel against the whole enterprise. In addition, it is difficult for many people to feign enthusiasm. The general result may be a marked divergence between what Tom is subjectively trying to do and his resulting behavior. Although he is struggling to act the part of the devoted lover, the effect of this effort may be simply to reinforce the impression of a detached, withdrawn individual.

These partners are caught in paired binds. Each is faced with two unworkable alternatives. Betsy can pursue or try to not pursue. Tom can withdraw or try to not withdraw. Neither alternative by either partner produces acceptable results. Expressing the particular impulse (i.e., to pursue or withdraw) exacerbates the problem of the other with inevitable repercussions on the first. Suppressing the reaction is difficult or even impossible to do and exposes the person to the unfortunate consequences of suppression: the reemergence of these feelings in distorted or exaggerated forms.

The recommendation often given to troubled partners to "work harder on the relationship" and "to learn to compromise" does not take into account that these individuals are already doing this and that such effort is part of the problem.

A better approach is to interpret their paired binds and show how each partner is in an untenable position. This could be done as follows: "I can see why you are having trouble with this. Each of you has two alternatives, neither of which works out. One thing that you can do, Betsy, and have tried to do, is to deal directly with the issue—to ask Tom to spend more time with you, to complain directly that he never seems to want to talk anymore, and to take events into your own hands by turning off the TV when he turns it on. You are hesitant to do these things, however, because you notice that every time you do, Tom complies briefly and then withdraws further. Besides, as you also said, you feel like a demanding woman. It reminds you of how your mother is with your father, and you don't want to be like that. Your other alternative is to suppress your complaint and to try to be undemanding. The problem is that this requires withholding strong feelings, does not produce the desired change (Tom still remains distant), and, as you have found, is impossible for you and perhaps for anyone to carry out for any length of time.

"Tom, you too are in an impossible situation. You can do what you'd like to do and spend more time by yourself. But, as you said, you must then deal with Betsy's complaints and your self-criticism for letting her down. Also, you can worry, as you mentioned, that there might be something wrong with you, that you are 'basically afraid of intimacy' and will never be able to marry anyone. Your alternative, as you suggested, is to go along with Betsy's wishes and your own image of how you *should* be behaving and force yourself to bring her gifts, see her more often, and think of interesting things to say. But this is hard to do and sometimes makes the situation worse. Betsy feels that you are doing these things just to please her and resents your not *wanting* to do them."

This may seem to the reader to be a rather long and involved formulation. If done well and if accurate, it is not long and involved to the partners. It takes what they have been saying and reorganizes it in a manner that defines, perhaps more compactly and accurately than they have been able to do, the frustrating situation they are in. A common problem in discussions between partners is the failure to convince the other of the merits of one's position in combination with one's own underlying uncertainty about its validity. The value of a paired binds interpretation (or an interpretation of interacting sensitivities) is first the relief that partners may feel in the fact that they have gotten their point across to someone (the therapist). Second, and more important, their position has been stated in a more convincing, more pointed, and less ambivalent fashion than they themselves had been able to do. They thus feel more justified in and sympathetic toward their own position and, at the same time, more appreciative of their partner's point of view.

The concepts of interacting sensitivities and paired binds can be thought of as the natural application of ego analysis to couples. Ego analysis portrays a troubled individual as deprived, frustrated, and lacking sufficient control in his or her life. The concepts of interacting sensitivities and paired binds picture *both* partners as deprived, frustrated, and lacking sufficient control in their relationship.

IS IT POSSIBLE TO AVOID TAKING SIDES?

Among the revolutionary changes in clinical thinking brought about by systems theory was the idea that relationship problems are a consequence of the couple interaction rather than of the psychopathology of one of its members. This proposition has received widespread acceptance and could be considered the "official" view. Concomitant with this, however, is the everyday common sense notion that one partner can be more disturbed and more at fault than the other. Both positions may be adopted by the same clinician. Don Jackson, who has made one of the strongest arguments for the equal participation view (Jackson, 1957, 1967), appears in specific cases to blame one partner. Jacobson (1979), in reviewing a filmed example of Jackson's work, reports him doing precisely this.* Jacobson's review is of special interest because his own opinion is that Jackson is mistaken in blaming one partner for the problem and instead should have blamed the other. It is my opinion that it is possible to justify *both* partners' positions by appealing to the concept of paired binds.

According to Jacobson, Jackson "enters a coalition with the father against the mother, and never seems to come out of it" (p. 73). Jackson's view, Jacobson tells us, is that

> the mother is the real patient or source of pathology in this family and that she is trying to prevent the father from taking a more active role in child rearing. Jackson tends to excuse everything the father does because he works from morning to night, six days a week. Sometimes he seems to be searching for reasons to justify the father's minimal participation in family life, emotional distance from his wife, and angry outbursts against the children. Jackson recognizes the need for greater involvement by the father but sees his alienation as resulting from the wife's tactics. (p. 74)

In contrast, Jacobson writes, commenting on his impression of the interview:

> I saw the mother as an intact but flawed individual trying to cope with a difficult situation in a relatively reasonable manner. She was struggling to cope with a new and large family—including four children and a husband who was rarely home for companionship or help in child rearing. On the other hand, the father appeared to me to be a highly disturbed, alienated, uptight individual who frequently decompensated whenever family problems were discussed in a serious way. (p. 73–74)

In essence, Jackson sees this husband as doing the best he can with a controlling wife, whereas Jacobson views the wife as doing the best she can with a withdrawn and pathological husband. Jacobson seems a little con-

---

*The Hillcrest family: Studies in human communication. Assessment Interview 3 and Assessment Consultation 3. Distributed by Psychological Cinema Register, Pennsylvania State University, University Park, PA 16802.

cerned at the extent of the differences between his own and Jackson's views and suggests that they indicate "how really far we still have to go in psychotherapy research and practice before we shall achieve the truly objective science toward which we are all working" (p. 74).

One way of combining Jackson's and Jacobson's views is to suggest that these partners are in paired binds and that *each* is doing the best he or she can, given the situation. The mother would like assistance from her husband in bringing up the kids as well as more emotional contact with him herself. Whenever she calls on him, however, he just makes matters worse. "He tends to respond to problems with angry outbursts and physical punishment" (p. 73) and "frequently decompensated whenever family problems were discussed in a serious way." The mother is thus left wanting his help, as Jacobson points out, and at the same time rejecting it when he offers it, as Jackson notices.

The father is facing his own unworkable alternatives. He might like to be an active participant in the family but is limited by personal problems (Jacobson's view), his work responsibilities and his wife's "controlling tactics" (Jackson's view), or his awareness that his efforts to help his wife with the kids generally make matters worse. His response is to remain withdrawn most of the time, make sporadic ineffectual efforts to join the family, and devote himself to the one solid contribution he can make to his wife and children—working long and hard and being a good provider.

FINDING THE HIDDEN RATIONALITY

As just suggested, the notion of paired binds provides certain protection against siding with one partner against the other. There are times, however, when I find myself in the same dilemma as Jackson. I too can be caught between my general view (that the problem is in the interaction) and a more immediate impression (that the problem may exist primarily in one partner). The tendency to assign the difficulty to one partner generally occurs when there is a marked disparity between the reasonableness, appeal, or apparent pathology of the individuals. If one appears to be trying to work things out in good faith and the other seems abusive or obstructive, it is difficult not to side emotionally with the first and wonder why he or she is putting up with the second.

While I am prepared to conclude at some point that the problem may lie primarily with one partner, my experience with couples has convinced me of the wisdom of starting with the hypothesis that both are involved in a fundamental way. With this in mind, I look carefully at the seemingly unreasonable or pathological behavior of the more offensive or "disturbed" partner to see if there is a hidden rationality in it. The following are examples.

An Irrational Rage

To demonstrate what she felt was unreasonable behavior on Mike's part, Beth described his rage when she bought a broom for $4 when he had told her not to spend over $3. Mike quickly interrupted to say that it was $4.50 she paid, not just $4. Beth shrugged as if to say, "What's the difference?" Mike then defended himself in a loud, angry, and repetitive manner, saying that he had specifically, clearly, and pointedly told her not to get anything over $3. He suggested that there was something "irresponsible, spiteful," or "just plain dumb" about what she did.

It was difficult not to feel that Mike was completely in the wrong. Beth had gone out of her way to pick up the broom. Although it was somewhat more than the agreed on price, the difference did not seem great. Most importantly, she knew that if Mike did not like it, she could always take it back, which, by the way, she had immediately done. The intensity of his feeling seemed clearly inappropriate. It was not even clear why he was upset.

Since it is easy to be drawn to one partner's side, I adopt the assumption that whatever the situation may at first seem, a paired binds, interacting sensitivity, or some similar two-sided or joint problem lies at the root of it. While it took a deliberate effort to consider the possibility that Mike's feelings might have some validity, it became almost immediately apparent that they did. Mike's rage had developed and persisted because in all his wild accusations he never got a chance to state his main concern. I suggested the following: "What you may have needed to say when Beth came home with the $4.50 broom, was, 'I guess I did not get across to you how important $1 is to me when I am only earning $3 an hour.' " This is exactly what he felt, he said, and my stating it for him seemed to calm him. Beth said she had not known about this—he had not put it in this way before—and it made sense to her that he would feel this way. Mike added that he had felt bad about his low wage and the need to quibble over $1.50.

Mike had found himself with strong feelings that he could not justify. He knew he was upset about the broom, but he did not know exactly why. He then did what many people do when they have strong feelings they do not understand. He cast around for any justification he could find. The weakness of the case he was developing and his inability to really believe it himself may have been responsible for the desperate and unyielding manner in which he held to and multiplied his absurd charges.

A Hidden Truth

Marie and Herb, a couple in their sixties, were at the beach with family and friends. Herb offered to get a pizza and asked Marie to go with him. She grumpily refused. Sarah, their daughter's friend, said she would go and several others also agreed. When they were delayed in their return, Marie became convinced that Herb was having an affair with Sarah.

Marie's belief was patently absurd. Herb and Sarah were with several others, one of whom was Sarah's husband. Nonetheless, Marie's behavior appeared to have a grain of truth. There was a depressed quality to Marie and Herb's marriage, and Marie imagined that Herb might be attracted to someone as cheerful and high spirited as Sarah. She knew she was attracted to good natured men. Marie's delusion was a consequence of her marital relationship as well as intrapsychic factors and was revealing something important about this relationship.

Marie clearly appeared the more disturbed of the two partners. She was chronically depressed and had other fears. My spontaneous feeling, and one I imagine other therapists might share, was to see her as the major problem. Still, the following question could be asked: Is Marie crazy for thinking her husband is having an affair with Sarah or is Herb crazy for continuing 30 years without complaint in a depressed, alienated marriage? If he is not having an affair with Sarah, maybe he should be thinking about it. And maybe Marie should be thinking about one too.

Another example of symptomatic behavior having a hidden truth occurred in the case of Don and Karen. Don seemed considerate, a good provider, the model husband. Karen, however, was subject to crying jags. There she would be, vacuuming the living room rug, tears running down her face. Karen's tears turned out to be a sign of a general dissatisfaction that both had about the relationship. They had been living a culturally sanctioned marriage. Karen had been brought up to believe that "happiness was a clean floor and a new refrigerator." The possibility that her ideal was wrong, or at least not for her, was frightening, and she had difficulty entertaining it. Don too was suffering from the cultural stereotype of what the relationship between husband and wife should be. Karen's weeping, originally seen as the problem, was now viewed as a potentially useful expression, a clue to uncovering an important joint problem.

The possibility that one partner's symptomatic behavior may be revealing something about the relationship is a basic notion of systems theory. In a talk given in 1961, Don Jackson described a family therapy session in which the identified patient, the schizophrenic daughter, screamed out, "Atomic bombs are falling on San Francisco. The whole world is being destroyed!" This, Jackson explained, was an effective way of preventing an argument between her parents. They had begun to bicker but were distracted by their daughter's "psychotic" behavior.* There was also an important truth in what she was saying. If, as the daughter and others in the family feared,

---

*Lantz (1979) has recently described a case in which a 16-year old daughter used compulsive scratching to distract her parents from their arguing.

the argument had led eventually to divorce and the breakup of the family, their world would have been destroyed.

The main point in this example is that a psychotic symptom has been made understandable. It is not a random and meaningless delusion but is about a specifiable danger. Jackson goes further and suggests that it is also an effective means of countering that danger.

The therapeutic task in these cases is to enable these individuals to communicate their message in a more direct and efficient manner and at less personal cost. The daughter's panic attack can be thought of as an imprecise and exaggerated way of saying, "It scares me when the two of you argue and I feel like screaming, going crazy, or doing anything I can to stop you. I'm afraid you'll get a divorce or even kill each other." Jackson is committed to more indirect therapeutic measures, but I would have tried to help this daughter state her feeling in just such a way. Rather than merely distracting her parents from their argument, this might have brought about a direct discussion of the problem by the whole family.

A similar point can be made about the woman who feared her husband was having an affair when he went for a pizza. Her accusations to this effect exasperated him. He might have responded in a more favorable way if she had been able to express her sadness at the state of their marriage more directly, saying that he must feel unlucky to be stuck with such a depressed wife—since she has failed him, he must look longingly at more cheerful women (and especially at Sarah who seems the epitome of youth and optimism)—and that she herself, when she thinks their problems might be his fault, often wonders what life would be like with another man.

DEVELOPING A CASE FOR THE PARTNER WITHOUT A CASE

Whenever possible I try to bring partners in on the task of developing a position or case for the individual who appears not to have one. I would first comment that they seem agreed that one partner is in the wrong. "You both seem to be saying that it was an act of irresponsibility for Joyce to arrive late," or that "Ed is a pushy, spoiled brat who is driving Gloria away with his demands."

If both partners agree that this is what they have been saying, I might then ask whether it might be possible for us to develop a case for the blamed individual. It is generally not difficult to do so. Joyce, who tends to be late and who can be seen as acting "irresponsibly" in many other ways, is likely to be the one who brings spontaneity, casualness, and funlovingness to the relationship. Ed, who is always complaining that Gloria does not spend enough time with him, may be the only one who is aware of the sense of distance and mutual unavailability that can frequently develop between them or that exists as a chronic factor in the relationship.

There is a danger in developing the merits of one partner's position of being seen as taking sides. The way of dealing with this, as Haley (1971) suggested, is for the therapist to make clear what he or she is doing. "Let's see if I can state Andy's case in a way that makes sense to you, Lois (or to both of you)," I might say. Such a statement makes my intention manifest and indicates that I will be taking Andy's side only for the moment. It also makes clear that my purpose, rather than to oppose or defeat Lois, is to appeal to her judgment. If I am unsuccessful in convincing them, I may then say, "I appear to be the only one among the three of us who feels that Andy's case has some merit." Talking with partners about what I am doing and about what is happening between us is my way of avoiding engaging in a subtle argument with them.

CONCLUDING THAT ONE PARTNER
IS LARGELY RESPONSIBLE FOR THE PROBLEM

We finally come to circumstances in which it may be appropriate to attribute major responsibility for a relationship problem to one partner. The symptomatic or irrational behavior of individuals has been shown in several cases to be reflections of or cues to underlying relationship issues or feelings. But what about symptomatic behavior that seems clearly related to conditions or people outside the relationship, a depressed or paranoid reaction following a business failure, for example? If a man decompensates because of his inability to hold a job and, as a result, becomes an impossible person to live with, would it not be reasonable to think of him as the major contributor to their mutual problem? Maybe so. My general impression, however, is that such extenuating factors merely expose and highlight relationship problems that were already there. The partners may have managed to hold things together as long as each basically led his or her own independent life. As soon as one had need to call upon the other for help, the flaw in their relationship became apparent.

Theoretically, any problem can be dealt with in a relationship. Certain problems are harder to deal with than others, however, and some may be so difficult that it is understandable that one or both partners might want to look elsewhere for a relationship.

The problems or symptomatic behavior of partners have been discussed here as being of potential advantage—that is, as providing valuable clues about the relationship. A momentary depression or irritability may signal an underlying conflict or mutual isolation that is important for partners to recognize. There is a point, however, at which the signal becomes a greater problem than the problem itself. People who respond to difficulties or provocations in a relationship by assaulting their partner, making suicide attempts, or becoming psychotic are, it is true, drawing attention to these relationship difficulties. They may be doing so, however, at too great a cost. Their partners may conclude, understandably enough, that no matter what their own contribution to the problem might be and no matter what their partners' behavior might be revealing about the relationship, they do not want to live in a situation where, at any moment, they might be beaten up or required to rush their partner to the hospital.

13

Developing a Shared Perspective

We come now to the third element in my therapeutic approach. The first element, clarifying each partner's point of view, is the ground-breaking task. The therapist develops the partners' own thoughts and feelings as far as it is possible to take them. This task is basically one of clarification.

The second element is employed when the first has run its course. The therapist describes the partners' interacting sensitivities and paired binds, showing how each individual is in a depriving, frustrating, no-win situation. The general effect is to make them less condemnatory of themselves and less hateful of each other.

The third element is a natural outgrowth of the other two. Partners who are discussing their respective positions and interacting sensitivities are talking collaboratively about their problems. What the therapist has done, in essence, is to have helped them establish a two-person observation post from which they can view their relationship.

HAVING A RELATIONSHIP ABOUT THE RELATIONSHIP

There are certain comedians—Johnny Carson is the best recent example—whose humor appears to be largely based not so much on good jokes as on recovery from bad ones. The masterful way in which Carson deals with a difficult situation—telling a joke to a room full of people and having it fall flat—is more entertaining than if the joke had been a good one. It is possible to suggest, in fact, that Carson would lose much of his effectiveness if all his jokes were good.

Carson is having two relationships with the audience. The first is on the content level. He tells a joke and waits for laughter. The second is on the process level. He interacts with the audience about his joke—noting how and why they might have liked it, jokingly threatening them if they do not laugh, making humorous excuses for particularly poor jokes, and so on. It is this second level that, at least for Johnny Carson, is the critical one.

Applying the example of Johnny Carson to couple relationships, I suggest that the process level, having a relationship about the relationship and making partners observers of their own interactions, may be a major part of the solution to partner difficulties. "We've sure got ourselves painted into a corner," one husband said with a sad smile after I had restated what they had been talking about in terms of their paired binds. "Maybe we should say we've got ourselves painted into opposite corners and we're glaring at each other across the room," the wife replied with her own sad smile. The tone of this interchange—a kind of mutual sympathy for their situation—was in marked contrast to the alternately sulky and vituperative one that had characterized the session to that point. These partners had shifted, at least temporarily, into an entirely new form of interaction. They were standing back from the immediate situation and were observing it together.

Another example is of the husband who ordinarily alternated between helplessly sitting by unable to talk and leveling indiscriminate accusations against his wife. He startled both her and me at one point by interrupting a particularly bitter argument between them with: "We're feeling too ripped off to listen to each other now." The fight immediately stopped, and there was a brief period of collaboration. He had taken an idea I previously suggested and, stating it in a more concise and in some sense more eloquent manner than I had done, applied it at an appropriate moment.

The ideal couple relationship can be thought of as consisting of two general states. In the first state, partners are able to abandon themselves to the passions and promptings of the moment. When they feel troubled by a particular interaction, however, they are then able to shift to a plane in which they can talk to each other *about* the relationship.

Paul and Ann typically interacted on the content level. Their fights had a general pattern. Ann would get upset for reasons neither she nor Paul truly understood. She would storm through the house yelling and slamming doors. Paul, frightened by her out-of-control behavior, stuck to his side of the house, waiting for her to calm down. This would be succeeded by two or three days of hostile silence in which Paul would be angry at Ann for her outburst and Ann would be angry at Paul for she was not quite sure what. Ann would eventually apologize and things would be quiet until her next outburst.

It slowly became apparent what Ann's anger was about. She felt that responsibility for their lives—their relationship, the management of their home, and the care of their five children—was completely in her hands and that Paul gave only token assistance. She thus felt alone in the relationship. Since she had never fully recognized this feeling, however, she and Paul had never had the opportunity to talk about it.

Their fights, it then became apparent, could be explained in terms of interacting sensitivities. Ann was sensitive to feeling abandoned and unsupported by Paul and responded with rage. Paul was sensitive to being yelled at by Ann and responded by abandoning her. This discussion of their pattern was particularly intriguing to Paul. He had become discouraged about what he felt was Ann's completely irrational behavior and was reassured by the discovery that it had a meaning.

Ann and Paul's next fight showed the effects of this discussion. Ann came home prepared to spend the whole evening studying for an important school exam only to discover that two of her daughters had been infected with lice. Precious time was required treating these daughters, sterilizing the bedclothes, and so on. When Paul came home from work, she asked for his help. Paul said he would but needed five minutes to relax. Ann became furious and went on one of her rampages, storming through the house, banging doors, and throwing things on the floor. Paul behaved in his usual way. He kept his distance and waited for her to calm down. What usually followed, at this point, were several days of angry silence.

This time, Paul approached Ann later in the evening when things had settled down, and tried to work it out. What led him to do this, he said, was a vague memory about how discussing such events had helped in therapy. The effect on Ann was immediate and positive. She no longer felt abandoned. In their attempts to puzzle out what had happened, they discovered that each of them had come from a difficult day. Ann became angry, they realized, because she thought that Paul was going to relax not just for five minutes but for the whole evening and that she would be left to deal with the lice alone.

The discussion could have gone one step further, and we added this step in the therapy session. It would have been helpful for them to recognize how this interaction had touched each of their main concerns about the relationship. Ann is always in danger of feeling alone and that everything is up to her. Paul, correspondingly, is always in terror of Ann's explosions and becomes psychologically incapacitated when she has them. A goal of the therapy is to make them joint experts in observing this problem.

Developing an effective shared perspective is a difficult task. Some individuals have such little confidence in being able to put their arguments in perspective that they do not try. Their response, following a fight and a brief cooling-off period, is to act as if nothing had happened, and to hope that their partners will do the same. Others seek some sort of resolution but limit their reconciliatory efforts to "I'm sorry." Although this may reestablish a feeling of mutuality, it also immediately reasserts the very conditions—the conscientiousness, the blame oriented style of thinking, and the sense of duty and obligation—that led up to the argument.

What is required if partners are to develop an effective shared overview is knowledge. If a wife is to listen to her husband's criticisms without getting defensive, she needs to know that these are exaggerated expressions caused by previous suppression and that he is likely, after getting a chance to explode, to feel better about himself, better about her, better about the relationship, and less concerned about these claimed dissatisfactions. If Paul and Ann are to develop an effective shared overview of their fights, they need a way of making sense of them.

Where are people to get this understanding? The therapist may be the major source of such knowledge at first. As time goes on, however, partners may become increasingly adept at generating their own ideas.

A CONTINUING AND DEVELOPING DIALOGUE

The emphasis to this point has been the partners' ability to shift from the content to the process or meta level. An appropriate metaphor in this regard is that of a lookout post or a master control tower. Every time that Ann and Paul fight, for example, it is possible for them to get together afterwards and observe how their special sensitivities became aroused.

Although this is a difficult and important achievement in itself, I have something even more ambitious in mind. Once partners are able to view their relationship from a joint perspective, it may be possible for them to have ongoing and developing discussions about it. Rather than simply recognizing that they once again enacted their typical abandonment–rage pattern, Ann and Paul might begin to notice new elements. They may discover that these fights typically follow periods in which Paul has been preoccupied with job difficulties. Not only does this provide further justification for Ann's reaction–she *is* being abandoned–it also presents an opportunity for both of them to obtain greater control of the relationship. These partners now have the potential, when Paul's work pressures build up, to recognize that Paul is likely to become withdrawn and Ann to feel alone, and they can anticipate this possibility.

What I am recommending, in essence, is that partners develop an increasingly accurate and detailed theory of their relationship. This is not an easy thing to do. This therapeutic approach can be seen from one point of view as an attempt to build such a theory with the hope that partners will continue the effort themselves when therapy ends. As the following extended example will suggest, however, the therapist must generally assume major responsibility for this task, at least at first.

Judy and Jeff, a couple in their late thirties with three children, came to me complaining of "incompatibility." Jeff began the session by criticizing Judy for her dependence and lack of initiative. She was unable to make simple everyday decisions—whether to buy towels for the bathroom or an appointment book for her job—without first consulting him. She agreed it was silly, felt it was being overly dependent, and did not quite understand why she did these things.

Among her comments was one that, although stated casually and overlooked by both partners, seemed to touch on the critical point. She mentioned that she sometimes worried that Jeff would get angry if she made the wrong decision. I drew attention to her comment and suggested that this might explain her "dependent" behavior. Perhaps she checked everything out with Jeff to be sure he would not be angry. This made sense to her. She recalled times when Jeff had gotten angry at some of her decisions and mentioned that she was always just a little afraid of him.

Turning to Jeff, I asked, "How does this sound to you? Does it seem correct that Judy might be afraid of you?" Jeff, perhaps feeling that the blame was being shifted to him, said "Well, she *shouldn't* be!" Pressing the point further I answered, "Well, leaving aside for a moment whether she *should* be afraid, do you think she *is*? Do you think this might explain her otherwise mysterious 'dependent' behavior?"

Jeff's reply was a grudging affirmative. "Maybe so," he said. I commented on the half-hearted nature of his answer. He said that although there was also something about what I was saying that seemed right, there was also something that seemed incomplete. As it turned out, he was correct.

Here is an example of partners reacting in different ways to a clarification. Judy seemed clearly relieved. She now had a way of thinking about her "dependent" behavior other than simply condemning herself for it. In addition, an important undercurrent feeling, her fear of Jeff's angry disapproval, had been brought to the surface. Jeff was only partially pleased. He was glad that Judy's irrational and frustrating behavior had been given some sort of meaning. He would have preferred a different one, however. He was concerned that he might now be blamed for the difficulty. It was important, of course, to get all this clearly stated.

The problem was that my intervention was somewhat one-sided. It was half of a paired binds interpretation. While it explained or justified Judy's reactions (her "dependent" behavior), it did not explain or justify Jeff's (his sporadic criticism of her).

Jeff and Judy left the session viewing their relationship in somewhat new terms and, particularly from Judy's point of view, in a more hopeful manner. As often happens, they felt better about each other immediately after the session. These effects wore off in the course of the week, and they came to the next session feeling discouraged about the relationship and with little memory of the previous hour.

Partners' discussions often have an ahistoric quality. They hash out a problem, perhaps arriving at a useful understanding or conclusion and then lose track of what was concluded. When the issue arises again, they are forced to start from the beginning. Instead of having a progressive and developing discussion about their relationship they keep repeating the first discussion.

An advantage of couples therapy is that there is a third party, the therapist, whose business it is to be what Apfelbaum has called the "relationship historian," the person who remembers what has been said and makes it available for use in later discussions. I reminded Jeff and Judy of what had been concluded the previous time and asked them when and how they might have forgotten. As it turned out, they "forgot" almost as soon as they left my office. Jeff had mixed feelings about what was said anyway and began rejecting the idea almost as soon as he heard it. Judy, whom one might think would be motivated to remember it, had difficulty feeling she had the right to this hopeful idea when she was no longer in my presence.

The next several sessions were devoted to developing another aspect of their relationship. Judy, while in some sense subservient to and frightened of Jeff, had moments when she would become sarcastic and cutting. In fact, it began to appear that much of their home life together consisted of Jeff being careful and, in a sense, walking on eggshells to make sure not to arouse her scornful tirades. This was not their "official" view of their relationship and, in fact, Judy, preoccupied by her feelings of intimidation at the hands of Jeff, was not at all aware of the intimidating effect she was having on him.

She was thus a bit surprised and even somewhat amused when I suggested that Jeff seemed to be feeling that being married to her was like living with a wild beast, never knowing when he was going to be jumped on or torn to shreds. Although this was far from her experience of what she was doing and it was hard for her to really believe that Jeff could be intimidated by her, she agreed that this is what he had been saying and that conceivably he could feel this way. Jeff said that this was pretty close to what he did feel and seemed grateful to me for pinning it down for him and expressing it in a form that made sense to Judy.

"We can now add to the picture we began developing in the first session," I then said. "At that time we said that Judy was afraid of Jeff. It is now apparent that the reverse is also true. In a very real sense, Jeff is also afraid of Judy." The irony of the situation was intriguing to them.

This is an example of the step-by-step manner by which a picture or theory of a couple's relationship can be developed. Each formulation serves as a platform or starting place for further formulations. The new conceptualization may add an element or angle to the earlier conceptualization, as in the present case, or it may have the effect of modifying, providing details or specifications, or even negating the original notion.

The following sessions revealed yet another aspect of their relationship.

In addition to the periods just described in which Jeff and Judy cautiously approached each other, there were times of unrestrained cross-accusation. "You're trying to dominate me," Judy would charge, glaring at him and describing how he tried to talk her out of jobs, friends, and activities. Jeff defended himself and made his own complaints. "You don't even afford me the courtesy and consideration people give to strangers they meet on the street," he said, describing instances in which she was uncaring and cold.

It now became possible to specify what Jeff and Judy were afraid of about each other. Judy was concerned about being dominated and Jeff was worried about being rejected. These were historic issues. Judy had felt dominated by an overprotective mother and Jeff had felt rejected by an undemonstrative father. But these were also current dangers. Judy was actually being dominated by Jeff and Jeff was actually being rejected by Judy.

At issue here were interacting sensitivities. Judy's long experience with her mother left her vulnerable to other people's attempts to influence her. She was sensitive to Jeff's criticisms of her behavior and activities, felt he was being dominating, and reacted with scornful rage. Jeff was sensitive to her rage, felt rejected by it, and reacted by becoming critical and judgmental. The shift from feeling rejected to being accusing is a common one. Instead of saying, "I am feeling rejected," Jeff would state, "You shouldn't get so angry, and also you should spend more time at home and not with those mindless friends of yours."

The interpretation of their interacting sensitivities had a positive effect. Judy enjoyed having someone validate her feeling of being dominated and Jeff appreciated my helping him articulate feeling rejected and stating it in terms that made sense to Judy. It was a rather short-lived understanding, however. As had happened before, they felt much better about each other for the next few days but returned the following week with relatively little recollection of what had been concluded. Their traditional pattern—the automatic, almost instinctive manner in which they reacted to rejection and domination—was not to be altered by a once-stated interpretation.

The following weeks were devoted to the establishment of these interacting sensitivities as the critical factor in their arguments and as the main sore point for each partner. They came to one session, however, feeling warm and loving toward each other. Their usual grudges and fears appeared to have temporarily disappeared. This new mood had begun when Judy expressed special concern over a job difficulty Jeff was having. Jeff was touched by this and responded by becoming particularly responsive to Judy's feelings.

It was now possible to conclude that while a hint of rejection or domination could set off a spiral of anger and alienation between these partners, a hint of acceptance or egalitarianism could at times set off a spiral of collaboration and intimacy.

To review, knowledge of Judy and Jeff's relationship had been developed in a series of sequential steps: the discovery that Judy was afraid of Jeff, the realization that Jeff was also afraid of Judy, the recognition of what they were afraid of and that their fears were to some degree valid (each provoked the special sensitivities of the other), and the discovery that there were also periods in which, in contrast to their interacting sensitivities, they experienced interacting satisfactions.

Judy and Jeff's relationship thus appeared to include at least three different states: a state of caution in which each partner is careful not to get the other angry, a state of pitched battle in which each is feeling exploited by the other, and a period of interacting satisfactions in which each is feeling loving, warm, and glad to be married to the other.

The classic criticism brought against insight oriented therapy is that it is ineffectual. Interpretations may sound nice, they may even be true, but what do they actually do? My answer is that the right kind of interpretation can enable partners to experience their relationship in new ways. When Judy and Jeff used to argue, each had only one thought: "This person is exploiting me and I'm not going to stand for it!" The situation now is different. Instead of having just this one thought available and thus just one option for action, these partners now have several:

They can act on their classic idea and have their usual fight.

They can act on their new knowledge of the other's situation (this person is intimidated by me, is particularly sensitive to the way I am being, is feeling dominated/rejected, and is retaliating) and take the other's behavior less to heart.

They can act on their new knowledge of their own situation (I am feeling intimidated by this person, am particularly vulnerable to the way he/she is being, am feeling dominated/rejected, and am retaliating) and feel less desperate and violated.

Or they can act on their new knowledge of the overall situation (we are both stuck) and commiserate with each other.

It is clear that having all four sets of thoughts will put people in a different position than if they were limited to just the first.

It is not necessary for partners to have these alternative ideas available during a confrontation. Fighting often has a narrowing effect. It is in the nature of argument to be singlemindedly devoted to resisting the other's accusations and to counterattack. The thought and feeling—"This person is exploiting me and I'm not going to stand for it!"—may be perfectly understandable in the heat of the moment.

What is important is that the new ideas discovered in therapy become available afterwards when partners sit down to figure out what happened. It is to this task, integrating the new ideas discovered in therapy into the partners' own spontaneous repertoire of ideas, that major therapeutic attention is devoted.

Partners often respond to a therapist's interpretation by saying that they agree it is true, and it certainly puts their relationship in a new light, "but how is this going to help?" or "what can we do about it?" I generally reply by saying I can appreciate this doubt; they have been struggling with this problem for some time and may wonder if anything can help. "The critical issue," I said to one couple (Molly and Ben), "is how much you really believe this new idea and how much it becomes a part of your own thoughts. If you were to think in such terms the next time you had this fight, the outcome would be entirely different. Since you would be aware that your argument about who is to take out the garbage has to do not just with the nuisance of taking out the garbage (the old idea) but with Molly's feeling that Ben has been unusually withdrawn and uninvolved (the new idea), it would no longer be possible simply to discuss the garbage. And since you, Molly, would be talking about your feeling of being shut out and getting some kind of reaction from Ben, you would no longer be feeling so shut out."

The effect of interpretation can be difficult to ascertain. A relationship may show improvement following a series of interpretations but without clear evidence that it was the interpretations that provided the critical therapeutic factor. I have never been very pleased with this. Partners and therapists are always happy to obtain any improvement in the relationship, but the permanence and ultimate value of this gain seems questionable if not associated with increased knowledge by these partners about their relationship.

I thus make an active effort, following an apparent improvement in a couple's relationship, to establish what in particular may have brought this about. And when change is not occurring, I also make an active effort to understand this. If partners and I arrive at a potentially useful new understanding, and these individuals do not utilize this new knowledge, I ask them about it. This happened with Jeff and Judy. When these partners came to a session and described a recurrent fight pattern, I commented that they did not seem to be thinking about it in the ways we had recently developed. What did they make of this fact?

Judy said that she did not want to think of it in these new terms. She was simply furious with Jeff and was not ready or interested in seeing it in more fairminded ways.

Jeff replied that he did not see how what we had been talking about applied to the present case. It became clear when he said more about this that the ideas we had been developing in the therapy, although making sense to him at the time, were quickly subordinated to the more deep-seated belief that Judy was rejecting and should just stop being so. This fact was in itself an important new discovery. It was now possible to check with Jeff regarding how much he was really convinced by any new understanding and how much he might really believe his previously established views. It was also possible to deal directly with his reservations to new ideas which to that point had remained hidden.

This case demonstrates the difficulty of engaging partners in an ongoing and developing discussion about their relationship. Even when the new ideas make sense at the time, they are easily lost. It took a certain persistence on my part to keep this from happening. What is the possibility then for the more ambitious goal of therapy, the development of an ability of partners to have an ongoing dialogue on their own?

Jeff and Judy showed some ability to do this. They returned to therapy after a short vacation reporting that Judy was feeling much less anger at Jeff and much more fondness for him. Of greater interest was the fact that they had figured out what this was about. In the early part of their marriage, when their children were small and Judy felt particularly dependent on Jeff, she had been passive and subservient. In recent years, now that the kids were older, she had been rebelling against this earlier submission. Such rebellion was difficult; she had to counteract her own underlying view that she did not have a right to her own wishes and career. She could rebel only in a global way, by reacting immediately and intensely to any beginning signs of domineering, condescension, or criticism on Jeff's part. What was beginning to happen now, they figured out, was a third stage. Having gained greater confidence in the right to her own position, she no longer needed to work as hard to guarantee it. Her anger became less impulsive and global and she found herself feeling more positive about him.

Constructing a picture or theory of the relationship is a familiar procedure in couples therapy dating back at least as far as the early work of Virginia Satir (1967). Whereas Satir devotes specified segments of early therapy sessions to this enterprise, my own preference is to integate the task into the main body of the therapy and to work on it throughout the sessions, adding to it or revising it through the last hour. The establishment of the history and present status of the relationship is not just background data or a starting point for the therapy. It is what partners know about their relationship and, in particular, about their recurrent troubled interactions that provides the therapeutic effect.

THE RELATIONSHIP EGO

A major objective of psychoanalytically oriented individual psychotherapy is the development of an observing ego: an ability to stand back from one's immediate reactions, understand these reactions, and integrate them into one's life. The object of couples therapy is identical except that the focus of therapeutic interest is shifted to the relationship. What partners need to develop, accordingly, is a "relationship ego" or "observing couple ego" (Apfelbaum, personal communication): an ability to stand back from their interactions, understand and discuss them, and integrate them into their relationship.

Partner-to-partner talking has many potential pitfalls. People are continually disqualifying each other's feelings. Some individuals get into their worst fights when they sit down to talk about their relationship. The tendency of discussions to turn into arguments is acutely frustrating, and partners may point to such experiences as evidence that talking is counterproductive.

What makes the goal of talking worthwhile is the powerful curative effect it may have. Expressing feelings is well known to be potentially cathartic—that is, to allow a release of pent-up emotion. More important, however, is its possible clarifying effect, its ability to change the partners' understanding of a situation. A husband was offended by his wife's abrupt demandingness and feared it indicated a deep-seated selfishness. He became less critical and more sympathetic when he discovered that the opposite was true. Her behavior was a consequence of and a reaction to her belief that she did not really deserve to be given things. Talking is valuable, in other words, when it allows partners to replace a depth analytic conception with an ego analytic view.

Another value of talking is its potential for dispelling the isolation that develops between people. Apfelbaum and his colleagues (1980) describe individuals who, finding themselves sexually unaroused during intercourse, try to force themselves to become excited. When these people finally confide to their partners that they are "turned off" and are worried about disappointing these partners, this often causes them to become "turned on." It is the isolated and self-coercive way in which they were trying to deal with the problem that was producing or at least maintaining the problem.

DEVELOPING AN OVERVIEW OF THE THERAPY

Just as I encourage partners to stand back from and talk about their relationship, I encourage them to stand back from and talk about ours. The reason is similar. Partners who can talk to each other about their relationship are in a better position to work out its problems and are less likely to feel isolated. The same is true in the relationship between partners and therapist.

If husband and wife listen politely to my descriptions of their interacting sensitivities but remain quietly convinced that one of them is completely responsible for the problem, I might make our difference of opinion overt: "I guess I'm the only one among the three of us who believes that Joe has a good case too." I am also likely to comment on subtle undercurrents in our interaction: "It looks like we have been having an argument," I might say, or "I have the sense that Max and I may have been trying to force you into something, Diane, and that you have been feeling forced."

Couples therapists often find themselves in the awkward position of not knowing how much to help partners end a relationship and how much to help them try to work it out. My solution is to share the problem with them. I might say, "Sharon has said she has lost all feeling for Doug and doubts she will ever get it back. There are two ways to go on this and I'm not sure which you want us to take. We can conclude the relationship is over—either Sharon will never get her feeling back or is past the point where she wants to try—and attempt to figure out what is keeping her, or both of you, from ending it. Or we can try to understand what is causing the problem with the possibility of putting things back together. It is possible, of course, for us to do both."

Another concern of couples therapists is whether they are being even-handed in their treatment of partners or, and this may be a different issue, whether they are being seen by these partners as evenhanded. Here again, my recommendation is to bring them in on the problem. "The way we've talked so far today, it occurs to me that you, Chris, could be feeling ganged up on. Are you?" Or, "Your comment last week, Joel, about how you were feeling blamed, got me wondering how you feel about this in general. How much do each of you feel that I side with Nancy and how much do you feel that I side with you?"

Such questions may come across as requests for reassurance, the effect of which would be to burden the partners and make it difficult for them to express criticism or anger. I have found that this problem also can be resolved by talking about it. If partners take one of my questions as a request for reassurance, I comment, "It looks like we've got you reassuring me."

Checking with others about how they are being affected by you has a liberating effect. A therapist can be more direct with partners if he/she has a way of helping them complain about and protect themselves from him/her. Practitioners who do not have the option of asking partners if they feel their side is being fairly represented must be careful that their actions clearly demonstrate such evenhandedness. They are thus limited in what they can say and do. Therapists who feel free to ask are less concerned about always appearing completely neutral. They know they can talk about and correct any momentary or apparent onesidedness.

The type of relationship I try to form with partners is similar to the one I am trying to help them develop with each other. My purpose is not to model behavior. I have never placed much reliance on modeling as a therapeutic tool. What therapists actually get across in their attempts to model behavior and whether and in what ways people are actually influenced by such modeling is too uncertain and unreliable. The reason I talk to partners in this manner is that I believe this is the best way to conduct any kind of relationship—marital, family, social, or therapeutic. It is only by checking with others that it is possible to obtain adequate control in the relationship, prevent the development of symptomatic behavior, and avoid a ritualized interaction.

Another important issue for therapist and partners to discuss is the progress or lack of progress of the therapy. Relationship difficulties are caused in large part by partners' inability to talk effectively about their interaction. They withhold grudges and worries and then blurt them out in exaggerated and distorted forms. The same may happen in the partners' relationship with the therapist. They may hold back concerns or complaints and then express them in an unmanageable form, for instance, by suddenly terminating therapy. My solution is to approach the couple from the beginning as if they were a partner with whom I was trying to keep in contact. I thus check on how they feel about what has been happening.

The relationship between partners and therapist is similar to that of cotherapists or colleagues. The discussions about therapeutic progress and therapeutic strategy are one example. The joint construction of a theory of the couple's relationship is another. Some therapists encourage partners to withhold judgment about the value of couples therapy until they have given it a fair trial. My preference is to appeal from the very beginning to these individuals' own immediate sense about the value or potential value of therapy. "Our decision about meeting again," I might say, "depends on whether what we have done today seems helpful to you or at least gives you hope of eventually helping." This centers the therapy where I feel it should be centered—on the partners' own current judgments and feelings.

Conferring with partners about therapeutic decisions and checking how they are experiencing the therapy assume an ability and willingness on their part to engage in a collaborative relationship. This may seem a faulty assumption to those therapists who view partners as dedicated to resisting the therapy, sabotaging therapeutic progress, defeating the therapist, guaranteeing the status quo, pursuing destructive or self-destructive aims, or maintaining infantile gratifications. My own view, as previously stated, is that resistant behavior of this sort is typically a reaction to a therapist's coercion or moralizing or a consequence of the partners' desperation, pessimism, or inhibition. I believe it is generally possible to form collaborative relationships with partners.

5

Application To Classic Partner Types

14

Withdrawn Partners

As discussed in the last several chapters, the therapeutic interventions employed in my approach consist of three general types: (1) clarifying partners' views and feelings, (2) showing how each is in a deprived, frustrated, no-win situation, and (3) indicating the possibility and advantage of developing a shared perspective and a usable joint theory of their relationship. At any given moment in a therapy session the practitioner is attempting to do one or a combination of these.

The purpose of the next three chapters is to describe this approach with specific types of individuals. Withdrawn partners are discussed here, arguing partners in Chapter 15, and demanding–withdrawn partners in Chapter 16.

The first point to make about chronic withdrawal is that it is a dull, lonely, and profoundly deprived state, adopted only because the alternative, communication, is experienced as even more punishing. Withdrawn partners suppress their thoughts and feelings because they are humiliated by them, do not feel entitled to them, or are concerned that stating them will hurt their partners or lead to unmanageable argument. The problem with suppression is that it limits the range of the relationship, requires a careful selection of what can and cannot be expressed, produces an undercurrent sense of impending danger, cuts off partners from each other, deprives them of the satisfaction and control that can come from expressing important relationship feelings, removes much of the spark, interest, and impulse from their interaction, and may leave partners with very little to say.

Prolonged withdrawal requires an unusual ability to tolerate certain extreme forms of deprivation and powerlessness. Many people cannot stand this and are thus not "capable" of extended withdrawal. It is difficult to explain fully why these particular individuals are able to tolerate the frustrations of emotional withdrawal, but the following factors appear to be involved: low expectations, an ability to bypass, and a polarized interaction.

Some individuals, as a consequence of personal experience or social training, have limited expectations about the amount of intimacy that is possible in a relationship or that they feel they can reasonably ask from or experience with another, given their restricted opinion of their self-worth or personal capacity. Since they are not expecting much, they are not likely to be disappointed. In fact, their main feeling may be that of gratefulness for what they have.

A second factor is an ability to bypass (Apfelbaum, 1977a). As mentioned before, some people are able to overlook or discount worries, problems, and grudges and maintain a positive view of the relationship. Certain individuals are able to picture themselves as intimately involved with their partners while actually being withdrawn or isolated. Cynthia ignored the unmistakable indications of a growing distance between herself and her husband, Glen, and took a few ritualized tokens of affection on his part—little gifts and thoughtful acts—as proof of their deep love and intimacy. "We were made for each other," Cynthia said ironically, when we had uncovered this pattern. "I've always been a sucker for little tokens and Glen was brought up to provide them. It took us three years to discover that we had lost all feeling for each other."

A third factor is the common tendency for one partner to take full responsibility for the issue of intimacy. A wife's quickness in accusing her husband of being withdrawn put him in a defensive position. It was only when she went back to school, became preoccupied with her studies and, as a result, stopped criticizing him that he became aware that he too was concerned about the lack of intimacy in their marriage.

SUPPRESSING COMPLAINTS

Therapy with mutually withdrawn partners has a character all its own. Compared to the active, slashing, chaotic quality of interviews with mutually accusing partners, sessions with mutually withdrawn individuals are often characterized by listlessness, caution, and vacuity. The practitioner's problem with accusing partners is that too much is happening. The therapeutic task is to slow the action and establish some sort of order. The practitioner's problem with withdrawn individuals may be that not enough is happening. The therapist's task here is twofold: to make their caution itself an object for study and to serve as an energizing force.

The following is an example of the persistence and forcefulness with which it may be necessary to approach certain of these partners. Janet and Brad came to a session reporting a problem from the week—an evening of distant silence—but were unable to say very much about it. This is in contrast to individuals who have a continuous flood of ideas, can hardly wait for their partners to stop talking so they can give their version, and make it difficult for the therapist to get a word in.

In talking about their inability to say much about the unpleasant evening, Janet and Brad said that this was characteristic. They often felt that something was wrong between them but could rarely pin it down. I suggested we try to piece together what happened and asked how the evening began. Janet said she did not remember. Brad, however, suggested the problem started when Janet came home from work depressed.

Since Brad's tone implied that the whole problem might have been a result of Janet's depression, I asked whether he was suggesting this. When he said he kind of was, Janet scowled. I commented on her facial expression and she said she did not think the problem was entirely her fault.

Certain mutually withdrawn individuals interact by limiting their complaints to hints, allusions, and nonverbal expressions and ignoring the hints, allusions, and nonverbal expressions of their partners. The therapist's task is to pursue these loose ends and half expressions to see where they lead.

Since Brad had brought up the issue of Janet's depression, I asked if he knew what it was about. Brad said no. He had not asked her, he added, because when he had in the past she usually said she did not know. He suspected, however, that something might have happened at work. Turning to Janet, I asked if she remembered being depressed and, if so, could she recall what it concerned. She did remember being depressed, but, as Brad had predicted, she did not know why.

One way of pursuing this is to reconstruct what happened. I asked her what she had been thinking as she was coming home and as she walked in the door. She said she had been feeling pretty good until she went into the kitchen and saw that Brad had not washed the dishes as he was supposed to have done. She had not confronted Brad with this, however, and instead began washing them herself. When I asked Brad whether he knew she was upset about the dishes, he said that he did—she had clattered them a bit—but he had not connected it to her depression.

The question then became—what happened so that neither of them commented about the dishes? Their first answer was that the possibility of doing this had not occurred to them. Behind this was the feeling that this would not have done any good. Janet said that she would get frustrated at Brad's lame excuses and that he would get upset and pout for the rest of the evening. Brad agreed that this probably would have happened.

It then became possible to describe how Janet's depression, Brad's reaction to it, and the unpleasant evening that ensued were consequences of suppressing complaints. These partners were caught in paired binds. They could express their complaints and have an evening of resentment and hurt feelings, or they could suppress them and have an evening of distant silence.

This particular set of paired binds (i.e., expressing complaints leads to an unmanageable situation but so does not expressing them) appears to be the master conflict undergirding the mutually withdrawn state. It was clearly the core problem of Janet and Brad's relationship. The difficulties they brought up each week almost always came back to this same issue. I was the only one, however, who appeared to be noticing and appreciating this pattern. As mentioned before, partners often live and interact in a basically ahistoric and nonconceptual manner. This may be particularly true in the case of mutually withdrawn partners. These individuals are too preoccupied with the pressures, demands, and dangers of the immediate moment to be able to stand back and take the broader view.

It is the therapist's job, accordingly, to draw attention to this repeated pattern as well as to point out their experience of being endangered. There are different ways of doing this. I might tell partners, after they have stated what has been troubling them in a given week, that I imagine they can guess what I would say about it because it is basically the same thing I have been saying for the past several weeks. Later, I might say that I have come to expect that their problems in any particular week will probably be a variation of the basic conflict we have established. This happens so regularly, I might then add, that I am surprised whenever it turns out not to be. Finally, I might comment that it looks as if they are not as impressed with the ideas we have been developing as I am since I keep talking about them and they hardly mention them at all.

Once partners' attention has been drawn to their lack of interest or in failure to acknowledge these overall patterns, the task becomes to determine the cause or nature of this disinterest or failure. A major factor is the pressure under which these individuals are operating. The preoccupation of of the partners with the dangers of the moment narrows their attention and prevents them from recognizing the general pattern. Another common factor is unexpressed doubts they may have about the value of recognizing and understanding this pattern. It is of critical importance, of course, to bring these doubts to the surface.

The partners appear in some sense to be doing to the therapist what they have been doing to each other. They have reservations and complaints about the therapist's interpretations (they do not see how talking about their pattern can help) but are afraid or hesitant to make these complaints. What they do instead is ignore these interpretations. The therapist is left with the feeling of talking into a vacuum. The practitioner's task is to be a different kind of partner to these individuals than they are being to each other. While these individuals generally ignore being ignored by each other, the therapist directly comments on the fact that his or her comments are being ignored.

CONSTRUCTING THE CONVERSATION THEY MIGHT HAVE HAD

Many partners respond to the realization that their relationship problems are a consequence of suppressing complaints by experimenting with the possibility of expressing them. Some are fairly successful in their efforts. All they may have needed was recognition that this was the problem, realization that expressing complaints is important to the health of a relationship, permission to make complaints, an agreement with their partners to do so, or a safe context within which to function.

Such a context may originally be provided by the therapy situation itself. There is an implicit understanding in coming to couples therapy that this is a place where it is appropriate and even meritorious to express feelings about one's partner. The presence of the therapist may also have a protective effect, reassuring some partners that the interaction cannot reach the intense or violent state that might occur if they were alone. Individuals may thus feel freer to make complaints and may take less offense at those made by their partners.

There are some people who save up their disagreements and complaints from the week for discussion in the therapy session. Others feel freer to make complaints to each other in private knowing that they have their weekly therapy sessions in which they can pick up the pieces if they run into trouble. The ultimate goal, of course, is to make it possible for them to pick up the pieces by themselves.

There are many withdrawn partners, however, who experience a great deal of difficulty in expressing complaints, even when they set themselves to do so. A husband came to a session and proudly described how he had finally confronted his wife about always leaving it to him to walk their dog. It hardly came across as a confrontation to her, however. She did not notice that he had said anything very different, and, as usual, he ended up walking the dog.

The outcome of partners' attempts to express complaints may be merely to clarify why they generally struggle to suppress them. Fred and Cindy decided, as an experiment, to spend half an hour each day expressing their feelings about each other. On the first day of this experiment Cindy became extremely incensed at a complaint Fred made about the way she handled their financial books, and he spent the rest of the evening trying to make up with her. They apparently forgot that they had been conducting an experiment and that they had given each other permission and even encouragement to make such complaints. Instead, both acted as if Fred had made this "unnecessarily hurtful and inconsiderate" statement because of some inherent "meanness." The inability of these partners to deal with complaints in this highly controlled and highly structured situation made it clear how far they were from being able to do so in ordinary everyday life. This was an important realization.

The therapeutic task with such individuals is to find out if there might be ways in which they can express anger and make complaints that do not always lead to an out-of-control argument or unmanageable situation. A popular contemporary approach is to try to educate or train partners to do so. One method is fight training (Bach and Wyden, 1969), in which partners are given rules on how to fight fairly. Another is assertiveness training (Alberti and Emmons, 1976), in which withdrawn ("nonassertive") partners are taught how to state their wishes (be "assertive") without being "aggressive." Still another is communication training, which, among other procedures, teaches partners how to make statements of feeling ("I" statements, e.g., "I am angry") rather than statements of accusation ("you" statements, e.g., "You are wrong or bad") (Gordon, 1970) or, as Guerney and his colleagues (1977) have put it, how to speak in subjective language rather than objective language.

There seems to me to be something unfortunate and limited about the idea of "training" people or giving them rules. This suggests forcing them, though perhaps at their own request, to do something they may not entirely be wanting to do. However, much of the knowledge that such training provides seems invaluable. Particularly useful is the distinction between "I" statements and "you" statements (subjective language and objective language) and the distinction between feelings and statements *about* feelings. My preference is to omit the training but to include the knowledge or information. Rather than giving partners rules to follow and setting up special training exercises, I incorporate the information into the existing content of the therapy.

When partners report a frustrating interaction or enact one right there in the session, I reconstruct with them what happened and supply additional dialogue. This is what I did with Janet and Brad. Turning first to Janet, I asked her what she might have said about Brad's failure to do the dishes if she were *not* worried about his reaction.

After looking nervously at Brad, Janet warmed to the task, saying she would call him "irresponsible, unreliable, and immature." (This is clearly an accusation.) When I asked Brad how he would have responded, he said he would have answered that she had not clearly told him that she wanted him to do the dishes and she had not specified *when* she wanted them done. He said he probably would have gotten to them later that evening. He thus responded to her accusation with a defense. "I'll bet!" she said sarcastically. The argument would have stalled here, each claiming a different version of the facts.

The first point to be made is that this seems a very different couple than the Janet and Brad from a few pages back. In an important sense, they are a different couple. In the terms of this book, they have temporarily shifted from the mutually withdrawn couple state to the mutually accusing, or perhaps accusing–defending, state. This is not uncommon. Few couples maintain the mutually withdrawn stance without occasionally shifting. One way of describing the dynamics underlying mutual withdrawal is that it is an effort to avoid being mutually accusing. At times these partners may slip into the feared state.

What happened in this interchange is that Janet made an accusation and Brad defended himself. A communication trainer might point out that Janet made a "you" statement ("you are irresponsible, unreliable, and immature") and suggest she replaces it with an "I" statement ("I am angry the dishes are not washed"). There does seem something useful in this. Janet, uncomfortable with anger, is unlikely to have thought through the different ways of making complaints. The distinction between accusations and feelings, "I" statements and "you" statements, might be illuminating to her.

The problem, however, is that the phrase "I am angry the dishes are not washed" does not quite capture the flavor of "you are irresponsible, unreliable, and immature." It is possible that Janet is not interested in expressing her feelings—that is, making "I" statements. What she may want to do is to make accusations or state insults—make "you" statements. By suggesting the substitution, the therapist would be attempting to talk her out of her wish to accuse.

A better approach would be to say, "Janet, you appear angry at Brad about the dishes, and, as people do when they are angry, you are accusing him. Brad, you are being accused, and, as people do when they are feeling accused, you are defending yourself. Another way in which you might have expressed your feeling, Janet, and one that might have had a different effect, would have been to say, 'I am angry the dishes are not washed.' Would this have been as satisfying to say, less so, or even more so?" If Janet were to answer, "less satisfying," I would have let the issue go. If she were to say "more satisfying," or "just as satisfying," then the distinction between "I" statements and "you" statements (feelings and accusations) could be usefully discussed.

An even better approach, however, is to help Janet construct her own "I" statement or "feeling" statement. This was done by asking her what she was thinking and feeling when she saw the dishes were not washed and told Brad that he was "irresponsible, unreliable, and immature." Janet's answer was that she knew the dishes would not be washed, that this was typical, that she felt she could not count on him for anything, that she had to do everything herself, and that she often felt alone in the relationship.

I then used what Janet had said to construct a "feeling" statement. "Well, suppose you said that to Brad. Suppose you were to say that you suspected the dishes would not be washed and that this represents your whole experience about the relationship, that you feel you have to do everything, that you feel you are alone in the relationship, and that you are pretty upset about it. Would you have enjoyed saying this?'' Janet replied that she wished she had said this and would have done so if she had thought of it.

I turned to Brad at that point and asked him how he would have felt hearing this. His response was to defend himself. He argued that he did plenty of things around the house and began to list them. I commented that since the statement we put together for Janet could be heard as an accusation, it was understandable that he might want to defend himself and show that she was not correct in saying he did not help around the house. I wondered, however, whether there were any other feelings he might have had in response to Janet's comment. I then took his reply to this question and helped him construct the following ''feeling'' statement: ''I don't feel your criticism is entirely fair, but it is partly, and I feel bad about letting you down. I know I'm not much of a companion and that I don't always do my share around here.''

Turning back to Janet, I asked how she would have felt if Brad were to have said this. She would be surprised, she said. She could not imagine Brad saying this. But if he were to have done so, she would have felt closer to him than she had in some time. She would not feel quite so alone.

I may go back and forth between partners for several successive steps, constructing the dialogue or conversation they might have had if they were able, as perhaps no one ever is, to report all their feelings. The effect is a kind of *in vivo* communication training, or assertiveness or fight training, though without the rules and without the training.

THE THREE TYPES OF INTERVENTION

I shall now describe more specifically how the types of interventions discussed in the previous chapters can be employed with withdrawn partners. Linda and Jack came to therapy describing a feeling of boredom with their marriage and a concern that they were drifting apart. When asked what they thought this might be about, they pointed to a lack of shared activities and hobbies: ''We're just not interested in the same things.''

''Last night was typical,'' Jack went on to say. ''Each of us did our own chores and hardly said a word to each other the whole evening.'' When asked about the details of these events, Jack recalled feeling put out that dinner was not ready on time. He kept this feeling to himself, however, because ''complaining makes Linda feel bad or starts a fight, and, anyway, she has a heavy schedule and maybe I should be making dinner for her.'' Linda was surprised to hear this because she had been thinking that Jack had been having no feelings about her at all. She did not feel like making dinner, she explained, because she had been upset by her boss. She was careful not to tell Jack about this, however, because "he would get upset at my boss and pressure me to quit my job, which I don't want to do."

This brief discussion placed the issue in a new light. The partners' noncommunicativeness with each other was not, as they had stated, the result of their not having anything in common about which to talk. In fact, if the example of the previous evening were typical, it sounded as if they had a great deal to say to each other. The problem was rather that what they did wish to say seemed to them inappropriate, unjustified, or too dangerous. They were suppressing their thoughts and feelings.

This is an example of clarifying partners' positions, the first of the three types of interventions. I responded to Jack's report of the incident of the previous evening by asking what each was thinking and feeling at various points in the interaction. The result was a clearer definition of what the problem actually was.

The situation was now set for the second type of intervention, the recognition that each partner was in a difficult, no-win position and that it was understandable that each would be responding the way he or she was. Jack was correct that complaining about dinner might start a fight and Linda was correct that telling him about her boss might produce the results she feared.

It thus became possible to state the paired binds that lay at the root of their problems. These partners were repeatedly in the position of having to choose between expressing their feelings and precipitating a disagreeable interaction or withholding them and increasing their sense of isolation.* They generally chose the latter (it makes sense that they might), and this then brought about the condition—the mutual withdrawal—for which they were seeking therapy.

Having employed the first two types of therapeutic intervention—clarifying their thoughts and feelings about a particular event and interpreting their paired binds—the situation was now set for the third. The potential solution to the partners' problem lay in the construction of a joint overview. "The problem might be more manageable," I suggested, "if it were possible to develop a way of talking together about the situation. As you were viewing it, Jack, you had two alternatives. You could either tell Linda you were annoyed that dinner was not ready, with the danger of starting an argument, or you could withhold this feeling, with the danger of precipitating an evening of tense withdrawal. But what about the possibility of telling Linda about your dilemma? Suppose you were to say that you were annoyed that dinner was not ready but that you were afraid that if you were

---

*As mentioned before, this is the defining conflict of the mutually withdrawn condition.

to tell her this she would get angry. I can then imagine you adding what you said here, that you wouldn't even blame her if she got angry. With her difficult schedule, you would continue, maybe you should be glad to have any dinner at all. In fact, maybe you should be making dinner for her.''

It seems unlikely that Linda would be offended by such a statement. When I asked her whether she would, she said that quite to the contrary she would have really enjoyed hearing it. This is not difficult to understand. In the statement I constructed for him, Jack was not really criticizing her. He was reporting a feeling—his momentary annoyance—and was talking to her *about* it. In fact, it turns out that Jack was more critical of himself for having his complaint than of Linda for not having dinner ready on time.

There are several related ways of describing the difference between what Jack would have said himself (a complaint that dinner was not ready) and the more extended statement I constructed for him. As just mentioned, the shorter statement is a criticism of Linda and the longer one a description of his predicament. Also, the shorter one is a statement of a feeling and the longer one a discussion about the feeling. Third, the longer statement is an overview statement. What Jack would have been doing if he were to make the statement I constructed for him would have been to stand back from his momentary feeling, view it from a wider perspective, and bring Linda in on the whole process.

The longer, less trouble-producing statement is also the more accurate one. I simply constructed the statement by piecing together what Jack reported he had been thinking and feeling at the time, but had not said. It was not Jack's thoughts and feelings that would have been offensive to Linda, in other words, but his distorted abbreviation of them.

A full statement of a partner's thoughts and feelings does not always solve the problem, however. When I asked Jack how he would have responded if Linda were to tell him what she was thinking—that she would like to be able to complain to him about her boss but was afraid that he would pressure her to find a new job—he admitted that he probably would have done just that, try to convince her to find a new job.

What would be needed at this point would be to take another step back and to discover what Jack would be thinking and feeling to respond in this manner—that is, what would cause him to disregard her wish. One possibility is that he was feeling responsible to do something to help her and did not know what else to do other than advise her to quit. This would mean that he was not convinced that ''just listening'' would really help.

Another possibility is that he was feeling too angry at her boss, too helpless about the situation, too frustrated at her reluctance to do what he would do—that is, quit—or too guilty about his inability to financially support the two of them (in which case she would not have needed the job) to be able to respond in the manner she requested. In addition, he may have felt criticized and rejected by her statement that his natural and usual response—advising her to get a new job—was not desired. He might then react defensively, insisting all the more strongly that this is what she should do.

Elements of all these seemed to be involved, along with a further factor. At the heart of Jack's response were certain moralistic beliefs. He felt that when a problem arose in life, the person should deal with it in a straight-forward and resolute manner—that is, Linda should find a new job. Furthermore, a person should be able to listen to and profit from advice—that is, Linda should pay more attention to what he felt was his good advice.

PARTNER-TO-PARTNER DISQUALIFICATION

We have come to a critical factor in couples therapy and in psychotherapy in general. This is moralistic or judgmental beliefs, the conviction by individuals (and in the present case by Jack) that they or their partners should not be having certain reactions that they are having (or that they should be having certain reactions that they are not having).

Moralistic thinking generally places people at a disadvantage in working out conflicts with others or, for that matter, in dealing with conflicts within themselves. First, it generally brings an end to useful thinking. Individuals who see themselves or their partners as "selfish," "irresponsible," "dependent," or "unreasonable" do not believe there is anything more to understand. They simply feel that they or their partners should stop being that way. According to Jack, Linda should cease complaining about the problem and do something about it.

Second, moralistic thinking has a deadening effect on conversations. A major point of this book is that partners who give full expression to their thoughts and feelings have a good chance of working out their difficulties. We come here to an important exception to this principle. Linda did express her thoughts and wishes. The result, however, was simply to be criticized for having them.

Third, and perhaps most important, moralistic statements tend to invalidate or disqualify an individual's reactions and feelings. Linda is likely to come away from this interchange convinced that Jack does not understand. An even more unfortunate consequence, however, might be an increased tendency on her part to feel that Jack may be correct and that there may be something wrong with her reactions.

Emphasis has been placed on the importance of avoiding therapeutic interventions that impose moralistic judgments upon partners or that disqualify their feelings or reactions. We are now faced with a new issue. If, as has been argued here, moralizing and disqualification have unfortunate effects not only in the relationship between therapist and partners but also, and even more so, in the relationship between partners, is it not incumbent upon therapists to intervene in partner-to-partner disqualification?

One possibility is to intervene in the manner that Ables and Brandsma (1977) suggest and to point out to partners who levy moralistic accusations against their mates that such statements are "not useful," "not helpful," or involve personal standards that should not be imposed upon others. Another possibility is to attribute these moralistic beliefs to unresolved issues in the accuser's childhood or to the projection of his or her own punitive self-recriminations on the spouse. The problem is that such interventions may themselves have a disqualifying effect. The therapist would be preventing partner A from disqualifying the reactions of partner B but at the cost of disqualifying partner A's reactions.

I believe that it is often possible to deal with these issues and considerations without having to disqualify partners' reactions. My approach is to suggest that the partners have different philosophies. I then discuss these philosophies without taking a position for or against either. My emphasis is rather to clarify what each partner does believe and to pursue the implications of these beliefs and the interaction between the partner's respective beliefs.

Jack, I might suggest, appears to believe that there are certain standards of proper behavior that an individual should uphold, such as immediately facing and resolving all problems and listening to and following reasonable advice. Linda, however, seems to believe that respect should be given to one's immediate and intuitive feelings. If a problem looks too difficult, or if an individual does not feel like having to deal with it at the moment, she believes, this person has the right to follow his or her inclinations. This philosophic difference, the view that relationships are based on wishes and feelings versus the belief that they are founded on work, duty, and proper behavior, is a classic one between partners and also occurs among therapists.

Partners may respond in various ways to my statement of the philosophies of relationships to which they are subscribing. Some are pleased by the generalization and feel more convinced by and entitled to their views. Others begin to doubt their position. An interesting example of this is the case of Roger and May. I had just pointed out that Roger appeared to believe that partners should express their feelings while May stood for the importance of being polite and respectful, even if this required holding back certain thoughts. Instead of May agreeing that Roger might be correct, which I would have done if I were in May's position, Roger responded that, deep down, he agreed with May. He had taken the other position, we figured out, because May had accused him of being impolite and he needed a way to defend himself.

Once partners' differing views have been neutrally stated, it then becomes possible to explore the meaning and historic roots of these positions without disqualifying them. "What do you think about having such different orientations?" I might ask. Partners often have a great deal to say in response to such a question. They may discuss their families, their character styles, and the history of their relationship. The result in some cases is an increased tolerance for their partners' points of view and a decreased tendency to take them as personal attacks.

If the statement of the partners' differing philosophies or views does not in itself resolve the issue, the therapist can then suggest that this difference appears to be the critical factor in many of their most distressing conflicts or arguments. I pointed this out to Jack and Linda and described its general form. "You, Linda, as you have said, feel criticized and invalidated by Jack because he does not accept your feelings and instead lectures you. Jack, you agree that you lecture Linda, but you feel convinced that she needs these lectures and that you would be remiss in your duty if you did not give them to her, even though, as both you and Linda agree, these lectures just seem to alienate her and may even be threatening the continuation of the relationship."

What I thus ended up doing was making Ables and Brandsma's (1977) point, that Jack's moralistic lectures and criticisms were not helpful, but without having to invalidate Jack's reactions. Rather than making myself the source of the judgment, I appealed to his own perceptions and judgments. I asked whether he agreed with Linda that his lectures seemed to be driving her away. He admitted that they did. There was no need for me to tell him his behavior was not helpful; he already knew this himself.

Instead of having to recommend that he cease these lectures, an awkward position for a therapist to take, I was then able to consider with him why he was doing something that in his own judgment was counterproductive (i.e., he very much wanted to maintain the relationship). "One possibility," I suggested, "is that you may feel that you will eventually be able to convince her. Another is that you do not believe, when it really came down to it, that she would actually leave you over this. Still another is that you may be so convinced in the correctness of your views that you are willing to stand by them even if this does threaten, or even end, your marriage."

Rather than challenging or opposing Jack's position, an action that is likely to produce a defensive response, I thus approached it in terms of his own views. My hope in suggesting these alternative possibilities was to hit upon the unexamined beliefs that were motivating his behavior and to bring them to the surface so that we could examine them. If we discovered that he had been continuing his lectures in the vague hope that if he was sufficiently persistent he would be able to convince her, we would then be in the position to consider how much hope he actually thinks he has of doing this and whether it is worth the possibility of losing her. The final judgment of these matters, of course, would always be his.

My approach to moralistic, judgmental, or disqualifying beliefs by one partner toward another is thus to make these beliefs an object of study and, in effect, to develop a three-way conversation with the two partners about the implications of these beliefs for the relationship. It was possible to conclude that Jack's position and Linda's reaction to it were leading toward divorce. My purpose was not to criticize Jack for having these beliefs or Linda for having these reactions nor even to suggest that he or she give them up. This would merely replace one moralism with another. My purpose was to provide them with the advantage of knowing what was happening. Jack had mainly one idea about the issue—"The solution to our problem is for Linda to behave more logically and reasonably." We now provided him with a second—"My attempts to convince Linda of this are leading us to divorce."

"FEAR OF INTIMACY"

Withdrawn partners are particularly prone to two types of moralistic beliefs or disqualifying accusations. The first is the stand taken by one or both partners *on the side of the withdrawn individual* and against the non-withdrawn person. The latter is seen as a demanding, pushy, neurotic individual who worries too much, criticizes too much, and always has to analyze everything. The relationship would go better, it is argued, if only this person would loosen up, look on the positive side, and live life rather than having to talk about it all the time.

The second judgmental stand, and the one we shall deal with here, is that taken *against the withdrawn individual.* A common belief about withdrawn, noncommunicative people is that they are afraid or incapable of intimacy, closeness, or commitment. This is a view that their partners commonly have of them. This is an opinion that they often have about themselves. And this is how therapists sometimes view them (e.g., Sager, 1976; Martin, 1976; Ables and Brandsma, 1977). Although these individuals want a relationship, the reasoning goes, they are afraid of intimacy. Their solution is to maintain a distant relationship. They control the degree of closeness by withdrawal and noncommunicativeness.

I have come to believe that the concept "fear of intimacy" is an unfortunate one, and I would not be against discarding it altogether. It is probably impossible to use the term in contemporary culture without implying a certain moralism. People described as being afraid of intimacy are seen as having severe defects in character, as being "closed" individuals—a serious charge given the modern ideal of being open, authentic, uninhibited, and nondefensive—and as unwilling to take risks (i.e., cowardly). It may be impossible to use the term these days without it being experienced as a criticism.

The particular problem with the notion of fear of intimacy is that it disqualifies a partner's position. It suggests that the relationship problem may be entirely his or her fault. "Suppose a man has a basic problem with intimacy or closeness," a colleague argued, "wouldn't this void or undercut whatever positive efforts the wife might make? No matter how she approached him, and she might attempt to do so in many different ways, he would always withdraw. And if she approached him about the problem of his withdrawal, he would be withdrawn and tight-lipped about this too."

The concept is not a problem when used in a strictly descriptive sense—that is, to indicate that a person becomes apprehensive when a relationship develops beyond a certain point. The error occurs in viewing the fear as unjustifiable or unrealistic, a holdover from the past. Intimacy may have been a danger to the individual at one time, it is thought, but it is not now.

A closer look at this person's experience, however, often shows these fears to be currently valid. The individual is afraid of being trapped or engulfed, not merely because of past experiences, but because he or she is continually being, or is always in danger of being, trapped or engulfed now. These are people who, in Apfelbaum's words, "are at a disadvantage in relationships." They are unable to obtain sufficient control in relationships to make them tolerable. They have not established a way and perhaps do not feel entitled to stand up for certain important personal needs, wishes, feelings, and requirements. Their only means of avoiding being used or trapped is "to stay out of range" (Apfelbaum, personal communication).

Roy accused Sally of being "afraid of closeness" and pointed, in particular, to her reluctance to talk about her feelings. Whenever she did tell him about her worries, however, he would criticize her for having them and suggest simplistic solutions. Sally's "noncommunicativeness" and "fear of closeness" could be traced to early rejecting experiences with her father. But they could also be traced to present rejecting experiences with her husband.

The traditional view is that intimacy-fearing individuals refuse to talk about feelings and about their relationships because these are just the kinds of intimate interactions they are attempting to avoid. I have rarely found this to be the case. It is true that people resist talking when they sense the conversation will be punishing, humiliating, or guilt producing. Once they are assured the situation is safe (and such a condition can often be provided in therapy) most people seem willing and even eager to talk.

People withdraw, and are seen as being afraid of intimacy, as has been said, because they are at a disadvantage in relationships. They are unable to assert their needs or establish necessary control or, at least, are less able to do this than their partners are. One factor in this inability may be an idealized notion of what intimacy requires. People who have been brought up to believe that an intimate relationship is one in which you sacrifice your needs and wishes for those of your partner would be understandably apprehensive about establishing such a relationship. These people, and to some degree this may be all of us, are afraid of commitment because of their extreme view of what commitment entails. If people feel they have to be uninterruptedly loving toward their partners or that they should spend all their time with their partners, there will come a point when they no longer want to be with them at all. There is no such thing as too much intimacy or a fear of intimacy unless intimacy is viewed as a state in which an individual feels he or she is no longer allowed to have, express, or gratify certain important feelings and wishes (i.e., anger, dissatisfaction, difference of opinion, or the desire to spend time alone).

AFFIRMING WITHDRAWAL

The purpose of the method described here is to explore the possibility of expressing feelings and complaints. This approach does not *require* that these individuals learn to do this, however. The outcome of these experimental efforts may simply be to reaffirm that particular partners are truly committed to a life based on agreeableness, politeness, self-sacrifice, and controlled emotion. It may be discovered, for example, that these individuals' fears of expressed anger, derived perhaps from exposure to tyrannical parents, may make it presently unrealistic to consider incorporating expressions of resentment into their relationship. I do not remember ever coming to such a conclusion with a couple, but I can imagine the possibility of doing so.

What can be done in such a case is to incorporate fear of anger and mutual withdrawal into the relationship. Much of the difficulty arising from their withdrawal and inability to express complaints comes from the isolated and unintegrated way in which partners experience these problems. They find themselves alone with their thoughts and cut off from their partners.

What is needed in such circumstances is an ability to talk together about the situation. I can imagine a dialogue where one partner says, "Things seem kind of subdued tonight" and the other replies, "Yeah, I noticed that too. I'll bet this is one of those times when we're worried about disagreeing." What these individuals would thus be doing is having a conversation *about the fact* that they are withdrawn.

To the extent that partners are able to discuss their mutual withdrawal, of course, they are no longer mutually withdrawn. They would have incorporated an element of contact and collaboration.

15

Angry Partners

Couples therapists are regularly confronted with two types of difficult situations. The first, just described, is the inhibited couple interaction. Partners in this state carefully avoid conflicts or controversial issues. They respond to direct questions from the therapist with long pauses and vague answers. The experience, from the practitioner's point of view, is like trying to start a fire underwater. The second situation is the explosive couple interaction. Partners in this state take offense at everything the other says or does. Therapist interventions are ignored or turned into ammunition.

The therapist's response to partner fighting depends in part on how this fighting is understood. Partners' anger may be viewed as unprovoked and inappropriate. The reaction may be seen as a displacement of frustration experienced in other areas of life, a release of accumulated aggressive energy (Lorenz, 1966), a projection of the individual's self-hate, an emergence of primitive sadism, an expression of narcissistic rage or oral demandingness, a displacement of anger originally experienced toward parents or siblings, or a manifestation of a basic hatred toward men or women.

The alternative is to consider anger as at least partially pertinent to the present relationship or situation. First, the individual may have been provoked, either overtly or in subtle ways. Second, anger may occur as a consequence of trying to not be angry. This is the familiar case in which suppression or inhibition leads to sudden rage. Third, anger may occur as a reaction to or defense against feelings of hurt or self-criticism. In all three cases, the individual is responding to something going on in the relationship.

The distinction is an important one. Therapists who view anger as an intrapsychic event will draw major attention to the individual's personal character and history. Therapists who see anger as an interpersonal act will direct primary attention to the relationship.

THE RUNAWAY ARGUMENT

Whatever their theoretical differences, however, couples therapists are united in appreciating the practical difficulties in dealing with runaway arguments.

These are disputes that, whatever their original cause, have developed a dynamic of their own. Each partner responds to the attacks of the other by attacking in return. These individuals get very little from the interaction. They feel increasingly provoked, frustrated, and misunderstood. However, they are unable to stop. They feel too stung or outraged by what their partner is saying to do anything other than defend or counterattack.

The therapist is also in a difficult position with regard to runaway arguments. It is clear that partners so engaged are obtaining little benefit from them. In addition, fighting of this nature precludes everything else. The end of the session comes without the sense of anything very useful being accomplished. The therapist thus feels some responsbility to interrupt these fights. The problem is that this may be difficult to do.

One of the more interesting exchanges in the couples therapy literature is a series of papers published in the *Journal of Marriage and Family Counseling* on the importance and means of dealing with couples' anger. It begins with papers by Dayringer (1976) representing George Bach's approach and Mace (1976), who criticizes Bach's view. Ellis (1976) responds two issues later by agreeing with Mace and disagreeing with Bach. L'Abate comes back by disagreeing with all three (L'Abate, 1977; Frey, Holly, and L'Abate, 1979). These papers comprise a useful outline of possible positions on the issue of couples' anger.

Dealing with the Underlying Issue

One approach in dealing with mutually accusing partners is to look past the immediate anger and deal with the underlying hurt, fear, disappointment, or self-reproach. L'Abate (1977) has argued that beneath the "smoke-screen of anger" is the "raw fire of hurt" (p. 14). A husband criticized his wife for "spending all day on the phone." They were arguing about who does the most work around the house and the time the wife "wasted" talking to friends was one of the husband's central points. Behind his accusation, however, was a feeling of hurt and concern. He was worried that she needed to talk so much with friends because she was not getting enough from him.

The hurt, fear, disappointment, or self-reproach motivating the argument would certainly seem important to demonstrate, and L'Abate is correct in pointing this out. My general experience, however, is that these underlying factors usually cannot be discussed when the argument is occurring. And if the argument is always occurring, or is always on the verge of reoccurring, it is possible that they cannot be discussed at all. If it is true, as L'Abate says, that anger is just a smoke-screen, then it is the smoke-screen about which partners seem mainly concerned. It may be impossible to go past the anger to the underlying hurt. The anger may need to be dealt with first.

Teaching Partners to Avoid Expressing Anger

One of the more dramatic pieces in the couples therapy literature is David Mace's 1976 article. He begins by reporting that he has been a marriage counselor for nearly 40 years and has "seen the inside workings of thousands of marriages in trouble" and "hundreds of marriages that were not in trouble" (p. 131). What he has concluded after all this experience and after extensive thinking about this issue is that expressing anger is destructive. "The position at which I have finally arrived," he writes, "is that the venting of anger is inappropriate in a love relationship" (p. 135). In so saying he joins the behavioral marriage therapists who take the same position for theoretical reasons.

Mace gives the example of his relationship with his mother. "My own relationship to my mother, in my childhood years, never became close because she had an explosive temper. She considered this harmless, because her explosions were 'soon over,' after which she 'felt better.' Alas, I could not open my heart to her under those conditions, and remained at a safe distance" (p. 135).

Mace has stated in print what possibly most couples therapists have at one time or another considered. The vicious fights of partners often seem useful to neither. The attacking partner does not seem to be obtaining much satisfaction, particularly since the attack merely provokes a bitter retaliation, and the attacked partner is clearly gaining no advantage from it. When I have witnessed particularly brutal arguments (Mace uses the term "artillery duels"), I often cannot help but feel that everybody would be better off if they were not having them.

What makes Mace's position interesting is that he seems close to recommending suppression. Ellis (1976), in his congratulatory response to Mace's paper, takes this further step. He recommends that partners who are feeling angry distract themselves by counting to 10, going for a drive, cleaning the house, visiting friends, or going to a movie.

Mace's own recommendation is for partners to (1) avoid expressing anger (e.g., cutting comments, bursts of rage) and instead report it ("I'm getting angry with you"), (2) renounce their anger as inappropriate, and (3) ask their partner for help in trying to discover the cause of the anger. The problem with Mace's approach is that it requires that the individuals not be very angry. Suppose they *feel* like making a cutting comment or bursting with rage? Suppose they do not believe, at least at the moment, that their anger is inappropriate? And suppose they are furious at their partners and do not have the least bit of interest in asking them for help?

What Mace is describing is the ideal way in which an argument can ultimately be resolved. After partners have expressed their anger, they may then be in a position to talk about it in a neutral and problem-solving manner. At that point it might be extremely valuable for them to be able to state that they were angry, discuss their doubts about the appropriateness of their anger, and work together to figure out what happened. Mace's concern, it appears, is that the act of expressing ("venting") anger has such an alienating effect on partners that they would never get to the point of resolving the argument. His answer is to skip the expression of anger and go directly to the resolution.

Another way of stating the problem is to suggest that it is precisely the partners for whom a method of interrupting fighting is needed for whom Mace's approach almost certainly will not work. Individuals who are desperately and singlemindedly slashing at each other would have neither the desire nor the perspective to report their anger, cease blaming their partners, or work collaboratively with these partners.

Teaching Partners Genteel Forms of Fighting

A third approach is to allow or even encourage the expression of anger but to structure, channel, or limit it so that it does not lead to runaway argument. The premier example is Bach's "fight-training" (Bach and Wyden, 1969; Bach and Goldberg, 1974). Bach takes partners who fight in uncontrolled, violent, and offensive ways—"unfair fighters," "gunnysackers," and hitters below the belt—and those who do not fight at all ("fight phobic") and teaches both types to fight in a modulated, genteel, controlled manner. For this purpose partners are given rules to follow and are taken through a series of practice exercises. The procedure is similar in many ways to assertion training (Alberti and Emmons, 1976), although shifted a few degrees higher on the aggressiveness scale. The goal is to establish an area of optimal aggressiveness ("fair-fighting" for Bach; "assertion" for Alberti and Emmons) in between overaggressiveness ("unfair fighting;" "aggression") and underaggressiveness ("fight-phobia;" "nonassertion").

Bach's major contribution is to have widened the range of acceptable couple behavior to include certain forms of anger. My major criticism is that he has not widened it very far. When one looks at what Bach recommends as "creative fighting," it turns out to be something less than fighting. "By the time his [Bach's] couples have learned all the rules," Mace (1976) writes, "they are not fighting at all. He says, for example, that it is sometimes best to go into a fight with the intention of losing; and that in the best fights, both win! This seems to me to be stretching the meaning of the word 'fighting' beyond all reason" (p. 134).

Bricklin (1972, p. 181) makes a similar point.

The main reason for my lack of sympathy to the new wave of books teaching mates to fight is that the whole thing seems phony. By the time the various authors get done defining aggression it is no longer aggression. It has been so detoxified by various definitional necessities on how one may properly fight that it is no longer the genuine article. It is like the difference in emotion felt by wrestlers as opposed to boxers—in the latter case the hatred is real, while in the former largely detoxified.

What Bach seems to be recommending is a tongue-in-cheek, twinkle-in-the-eye, not-really-meaning-it kind of fighting. Partners are instructed to prepare for the fight, build up to it carefully, choose the right time (to the extent of making an appointment), and restrict it in stringent ways in order not to offend the other too much. An individual could do all these things, of course, only if he or she is not really very angry. Bach has given partners permission to fight, but it is a limited permission.

Nongenteel Forms of Fighting

The question thus becomes whether it might be possible to integrate "unfair," "below the belt," noncreative, spontaneous forms of fighting in relationships. The problem, as Mace and Bach point out, is the incompatibility between loving and hating. Partners need an opportunity to express anger. However, they also need to maintain a sense of safety, trust, and collaboration. Some forms of anger ("gunnysacking," cutting comments, bursts of rage) may disrupt or destroy this sense of safety, trust, and collaboration.

Mace's and Bach's solution is to limit partners' expression of anger and hate to those forms that do not threaten the relationship. Mace suggests restricting them to the report of being angry, "I'm getting angry with you." Bach goes a little further and includes certain well-controlled and mild forms of fighting.

But there is an alternative. Instead of preventing partners from expressing anger, it is possible to increase their ability to recover from it. Mace and Bach are assuming a need to maintain a certain level of civility and reasonableness at all times. This would not be necessary, however, if partners were to develop an effective way of talking about their arguments afterwards. Such individuals would feel free to abandon themselves to the passions and promptings of the moment. This can include "gunnysacking," cutting comments, and bursts of rage. They would know that after the fight was over they would be able to sit down with their partners and put it in perspective.

"The problem is not that you had these battles," I often say to partners. "In fact, it sounds as if you each got a chance to say things you had been wanting to say for some time. The problem is rather that you did not have a way, after it was all over, to sit down together and make sense of what happened.''

Charny (1972) has criticized the mental health profession for failing to acknowledge that anger and rage are inevitable in an intimate relationship. My approach, following Charny, is to help partners incorporate their anger into the relationship. Rather than encouraging individuals to limit their expressions of anger, the method employed by most couples therapists (Mace, 1976; Bach and Wyden, 1969; Sluzki, 1978; O'Leary and Turkewitz, 1978; Jacobson and Margolin, 1979; and Ables and Brandsma, 1977), my goal is to help partners give full expression to their anger and to assist them in dealing with the consequences.

HELPING PARTNERS FIGHT

I believe that the cause of intractable argument, the reason many partners cannot stop fighting, is that they are not getting a chance to express their feelings or make their point. This can be for any of several reasons. These individuals may not know what their feelings are. They may be afraid to state them with sufficient forcefulness. They may doubt the validity of these feelings. They may be constantly interrupted by their partners. Or they may feel that their points of view are not being acknowledged or appreciated by their partners.

The therapeutic task in part is to help partners get behind their own points of view, develop them more fully, and prosecute them more effectively. The goal, in other words, is to enable partners to express their anger in fuller, more pointed, and more satisfying forms. This differs from a practitioner's intuitive tendency to encourage partners to soften their anger, moderate their exaggerated charges, and be more tactful, compromising, and reasonable.

Therapists can help partners fight in at least three ways: increasing the precision of their complaints, helping them believe their own complaints, and providing an opportunity to fight.

Sharpening Partners' Arguments

Certain arguments are irresolvable because the partners are arguing about the wrong issues. A wife is unlikely to obtain much satisfaction in complaining about her husband's failure to take out the garbage when her real concern is a more general interpersonal issue, her feeling of being unloved or taken for granted. She is also unlikely to obtain much satisfaction in complaining about a general interpersonal issue (the feeling of being un-loved) when her major concern is a concrete issue, not getting enough help around the house. The therapist's task, of course, is to help partners dis-cover the real issues.

Other fights are irresolvable not because partners are arguing about the wrong issue but because they are not stating their grievances with sufficient precision or sharpness. An example is Mike's previously described inability to state his major complaint about Beth spending $1.50 more for a broom than the price on which they had agreed. What he needed to say, we dis-covered, was, "I guess I did not get across to you how important $1 is to me when I am only earning $3 an hour." What I do in a such a situation is improve or strengthen the partner's case—that is, give him or her a better argument.

There are many instances in which both partners are suffering from Mike's problem. Norm and Jan, for instance, while engaged in a furious battle, were not really saying what they needed to say to obtain a sense of resolution or completion. Jan's argument lost punch because her main point —that Norm was domineering—was mixed in a tangle of other accusations. Norm's most telling point, similarly lost among his other statements, was that he was feeling dismissed and rejected by Jan. I used a comment of his—his description of how she hesitated to pick him up when his car broke down —to symbolize and spotlight this feeling.

"If I understand correctly," I said to Jan, "your main complaint is that Norm is a bully—he insists on having things his way, yells at you, argues you out of everything, and is generally domineering. Your main complaint, Norm, appears to be that Jan is uncaring. You mentioned Jan's reluctance to pick you up when your car broke down. As you put it, 'Even a stranger would have helped me out in such a situation.' You feel, in other words, that Jan does not give you the same consideration that she would a stranger off the street.''

The reason the argument has been irresolvable was that neither partner was obtaining sufficient satisfaction from what he or she was saying. Neither was getting a chance to state his or her position pointedly enough and have it acknowledged by the other. My intervention was an attempt to deal with both aspects of the difficulty. I restated what they had been saying in a manner that I believed would be more satisfying to them. The fact that I, an individual other than themselves, was developing their positions seemed likely to provide them with some sense of external acknowledgment.

If my intervention does not accurately represent the core of Jan and Norm's feelings, it is likely to be ignored. These individuals may brush it aside in the same manner as they have been brushing aside each other's statements. But if this intervention does capture the essence of their concerns, it may shift the tone and direction of the session. Feeling that their point has been established, these individuals may settle back and proceed to the next issue.

I am often tempted to go one step further and point out the partners' interacting sensitivities—that is, how Jan is rejecting because she feels bullied and how Norm is bullying because he feels rejected. This does seem important information to get across. My general experience, however, is that it is often unusable to partners when they are still angry. They may not be interested at such moments in viewing their partners' behavior from a neutral or sympathetic perspective and may just feel deprived of their right to complain. It seems best, when partners are angry, to stay with their anger.

Helping Partners Believe Their Arguments

Some individuals, although making a clear and convincing complaint against their partners, obtain little satisfaction because of secret doubts about the justice of their cause. Edna denounced Jim for his physically abusive behavior. Her argument was convincing. She convinced me that he was wrong to hit her. She convinced Jim, although he did maintain a feeble defense. The problem, as we eventually discovered, was that she did not convince herself. She privately believed that his physical abuse was somehow entirely her fault.

Other individuals state their complaints in such an extreme, uncontrolled manner that it is difficult to take them seriously. Doris periodically exploded at Phil, criticizing him for being detached, uncaring, uncommitted, and unavailable. She would dump out complaints from the past few weeks (Bach's "gunnysacking") and dredge up others from 10 years back (Bach's "archeology"). It was easy to view her outbursts as excessive.

Phil's opinion, and the one that Doris somewhat shared, was that her complaints were entirely invalid. He attributed her anger to the pressure of her schedule (she went to school, held a job, and took care of his children by a former marriage) and her menstrual cycle. She resented this reference to her periods but had difficulty launching an effective rebuttal.

The problem was Doris' failure to stand by her own position. Her outbursts appeared to be based on an important grain of truth. There *was* a distance and separation between the two of them. Phil was in some ways "detached, uncaring, uncommitted, and unavailable." Since Doris did not trust her sense about this, however, she was unable to present it to Phil in the calm, consistent, and forceful way that would have been necessary to get his attention.

The therapeutic goal was to help Doris deal with her own and Phil's efforts to talk her out of her feelings. The first task was to justify both partners' positions—to point out how Phil became understandably alarmed at Doris' out-of-control outbursts and how Doris was understandably confused and exasperated at her failure to get her message across to Phil or even to believe it sufficiently herself. The next task was to demonstrate the validity of her message—how she was responding to an important underlying issue in the relationship. This was not difficult. They were clearly leading separate lives together, and neither was really very satisfied with this.

A comment should perhaps be made about Bach's approach to "gunnysacking" and "archeology." He considers these unfair practices that should be discontinued. The problem is that the individual involved is already suffering from inhibition. Suggesting that Doris not express "stored up" or "dug up" complaints might serve only to close off the one means of expressing anger still available to her. The preferred therapeutic task would be to help strain out and make usable the valuable information that may be concealed within the "gunnysacking" and "archeology."

Providing an Opportunity to Argue

A third way of helping partners fight is to provide a structure for the fight. Much of the problem in couple argument is a consequence of its fragmented quality. Margaret accused Joseph of being self-centered. Joseph replied by accusing Margaret of being irresponsible. Margaret then countered by accusing Joseph of being too involved with his parents. If the argument had occurred at home, it was likely to have quickly spiraled out of control. Joseph would state that Margaret was impossible to talk to and storm out of the house.

Since the argument was occurring in the therapy situation, however, it was possible to provide a structure or framework for their interaction. I interrupted to ask Margaret about her feeling that Joseph was self-centered and Joseph about his claim that Margaret was irresponsible. Did they mean these things, I asked, or were they just said in the heat of the battle? And if they did mean them, how did they mean them, and how did the other feel hearing them?

The purpose of my questions was to allow these partners to have a real argument. Margaret had begun with an accusation, Joseph responded with a counteraccusation, Margaret made a counter-counter accusation, and so on. Neither was getting a chance to argue about any of the issues. By slowing the action, allowing one partner to develop a complaint and then turning to the other for a response, it became possible for them to have the kind of full-blown argument they were never able to have on their own. "When one of us gets angry at home," Margaret said, "we go about three sentences, one of us blows, and the other leaves. When we get angry here, there's a break, a pause, you say something, and the discussion goes on. The conversation only exists in some areas because we come here.''

My approach at times is to provide a running commentary or explanatory annotations to partners' arguments. Much of the problem with fights is their nonstated character. A shrug indicating disgust or dismissal is often more provocative than stating, ''I'm just disgusted'' or ''what you're saying is too ridiculous to even answer.'' I might thus give words to the nonverbal expression: ''You look disgusted at what Jack just said or like you don't even think it's worth answering.'' Accusation and defense, charge and countercharge, are particularly offensive to partners when they occur in a slam-bam manner without being labelled as such. I can provide the labels. ''That's a roundly stated criticism, Susan. Tom, how do you feel about it? Are you annoyed by it, do you think there is any truth to it, or what?''

My effort, in some cases, is to have a discussion with partners about their arguments while they are having them. I may acknowledge what is happening. ''Each of you seems pretty frustrated by what the other is saying.'' I may summarize. ''George, if I understand right, your main complaint is that Andrea does not pay attention to you at parties. And Andrea, since you are being criticized, you are defending yourself.'' I may press for further clarification. ''Milt, it is clear that you don't like what Joan is saying. But I wonder whether there is anything in what she is saying that sounds convincing to you, that might be correct even though you wish it weren't correct?'' My purpose is not to get Milt to admit that he partly agrees with Joan. Even if he were to say that he found her point ''completely unconvincing,'' this might still provide a useful context within which the partners could operate. Both he and Joan would then know and have clearly stated between them that he is completely against what she is saying and is trying to demolish it.

The general orientation recommended here is to help fighting partners fight. Such an approach, if workable, has several advantages. First, it rescues therapists from the awkward position of recommending suppression. Second, it produces a broadening of the partners' relationship, enabling them to include previously warded-off feelings and impulses. Finally, it increases the likelihood of learning what the argument is about. Wild accusations are often a rough first approximation, an awkward and inexact statement, of important underlying relationship issues or feelings. Partners who develop a tolerance for such expressions will be in a favorable position to unravel the hidden message.

HELPING PARTNERS RECOVER FROM THE FIGHT

The therapeutic task just described is to help partners obtain more satisfaction from their fights. Another task is to help them recover from them.

A slashing argument is easier to deal with if partners know that they will have a chance to sit down together and put it in perspective after it is all over. The problem is that this is difficult to do, and many couples do not even try. Their response, after a fight is over, is to be glad it is over and to hope that they never have another. Or they may seek a sense of resolution by a ritualized exchange of "I'm sorry."

There are some couples who do not need to sit down after an argument and work it out. These partners—let us call them "natural fighters"—already have an effective way of integrating anger into their relationships. These are individuals who, whether by personal character or family upbringing, are tolerant of almost any kind of angry outburst. They are comfortable both with their own and their partners' hostility, enjoy getting anger "out into the open," and feel better and more intimate afterwards. If their partners make stinging and potentially injurious comments, they automatically discount them as something said in anger. These individuals do not need to recover from their fights because they never take them that seriously. They already have what Bach or Charny would want to teach them—a comfortable attitude toward and sense of humor about fighting.

The rest of us, those who are not "natural fighters," must develop ways of talking about our fights if we are to incorporate anger into our relationships. The problem is that this is difficult to do. Many partners complain that their attempts to discuss their problems never work out. Some couples have their bitterest fights when they sit down to talk about their relationship.

The therapeutic task in such cases is to study examples of partners' attempts to discuss a problem and to discover how and why these attempts go awry. The goal is to develop a mutually understood theory of the points at which their conversations tend to break down. The advantage of such a theory is clear. If partners become familiar with these typical break-down points, they may be able to anticipate them, recognize them when they occur, talk about them, and take them into account.

Certain pieces of knowledge and information are required if partners are to incorporate anger and fighting into their relationships. They need to know, for example, that arguments and fighting are normal and unavoidable. Individuals who view anger as indicating that they have a "bad" marriage will be demoralized by its presence and will be unable to deal with it effectively.*

People need to know that a sudden outburst is often a consequence of previous inhibition or suppression. Individuals who are viewing their partners' angry accusations as nonnegotiable demands for change may have no alternative but to feel threatened and to respond angrily or defensively. If they were to realize, however, that these are exaggerated complaints resulting

---

*The main problem is the belief that what is said in anger is the real truth about their relationship. This is a variant of depth analytic thinking.

from previous suppression and that their partners are soon likely to take a more moderate stance, they may be less threatened by them, may take them less personally, and may simply wait for the explosion to pass.

They need to know that their partners may merely want to complain and feel understood. Individuals who do not realize this may take their complaints too seriously and concretely and may immediately begin offering solutions. This, of course, interrupts the complaining partners' expressions of feelings and causes them to feel that their mates *do not understand.*

They need to recognize the presence of accusation. Individuals who do not know the difference between making accusations and stating feelings ("you" statements and "I" statements) are likely to provoke their partners without realizing they are doing so, without entirely wanting to do so, and without knowing how to stop.

My goal is not to keep partners from fighting but to give them a new way of thinking about the fights they are having. This is the opposite of the classical behavioral approach that puts primary emphasis on behavior. It is not what partners do that is important, I am suggesting, but what they know while they are doing it.

In the case of Ralph, who was complaining loudly about Kay's irresponsible and unloving attitude, my objective was not to make sure that he not say anything too extreme or hurtful or that Kay not say anything too extreme or hurtful in return. I hoped, in fact, that each would have a chance to express what he or she was feeling in as precise and satisfying a way as possible. My objective was rather to increase their knowledge about what they were doing, to change their understanding of their behavior without necessarily changing their behavior.

Ralph may go on a tirade, ending by saying he is sorry he ever married Kay, while at the same time knowing at some level that his statements are overblown, a consequence of having previously held them back. And Kay may allow herself to interrupt him and defend herself even though she too realizes that his tirade is a consequence of held-back feelings and her interruptions may interfere with Ralph's need to vent these feelings.

The fact that these partners have a sophisticated knowledge of the dynamics of anger does not mean that Ralph has to temper his rage or that Kay has to force herself to be tolerant and understanding. In fact, these partners might feel particularly free to express their immediate feelings since they know that they will be able to talk about them afterwards and put them in perspective.

COMBINING THE TWO THERAPEUTIC TASKS

Therapy with arguing individuals has been presented here as involving two discrete tasks—helping partners fight and helping them recover from and talk about their fights. Since these are incompatible tasks—one assumes an adversary partner relationship and the other a collaborative one—questions may arise regarding the manner in which they are to be combined or coordinated. It is in such coordination that the underlying principles of the approach can best be viewed.

A major problem with partner fighting is that these individuals do not always say all that they might want or need to say. The need to defend or attack generally takes precedence and the person may never get a chance to discuss the issue. Bruce felt so criticized by Jane's statement that she felt "taken for granted" that he devoted his full attention to launching a counterattack. He never did get to satisfy his second need—to find out what she meant and to talk with her about it.

"The problem," I suggested to him, "was that Jane's comment about feeling 'taken for granted' elicited two very different feelings within you and you got to express only one of them. You felt accused and angry and wanted to defend yourself. This you did and it was good that you had a chance to do so. But you also wanted to discuss the issue with her."

My recommendation to partners is not to avoid arguments and, instead, have discussions, but to do both. "The ideal, " I said, "would be to express one of your feelings then, as you did (your anger), and the other later. I can imagine your going to Jane that evening and saying some of the things you just said here—that you had not known that she was feeling taken for granted and you are glad that she told you, that you want to find out more about it, that you think there might be some truth in her charge and that you feel badly about it, and that in some ways you feel taken for granted too."

The problem just described is the failure or lack of opportunity to express both needs—to argue and to discuss. Another problem is the tendency to intermix the two. Couples often sit down to discuss an issue and then, without knowing how it happens, end up in an argument. This is frustrating to both individuals and may give talking a bad name. Partners may point to such experiences as evidence that talking is counterproductive.

The shift from discussion to argument is a common event and is only a problem when partners do not see it happening or when they struggle to maintain or regain the discussion when it is clear that one or both needs to have an argument. The therapeutic goals are (1) to enable partners to become experts in detecting at what point one or both begins to become accusing or defensive, and (2) to help them appreciate anger or defensiveness as a valid reaction rather than as something to be avoided or discouraged.

UNMANAGEABLE ANGER

This all sounds very nice, the tolerant reader might say, but the author apparently has not met any brutal, slashing, fight-to-the-death partners whose fangs are too entrenched in each other's necks to pay attention to anything else.

The problem is the same but pitched several degrees higher. These individuals too are having difficulty obtaining sufficient satisfaction from their fights and putting them in perspective. Unfortunately, it may be extremely difficult to help them do so.

The case of Mike, Beth, and the broom has been referred to several times. Mike was an example of a slashing, raging partner. The fast moving, fiercely stated, disorganized nature of Mike's accusations against Beth made it difficult to help him obtain greater satisfaction from his complaints and to enable them to obtain a joint perspective of their problems. My restatement of his feeling about the broom was one of my very few successes in this effort, at least in the beginning of therapy.

The problem in working with Mike and Beth was that there was little room for error. It is possible with most couples to make an approximate interpretation and then, with their help, to make it more accurate. Any imperfection in timing, phrasing, and meaning in my comments to Mike, however, would immediately bring forth defensiveness. The problem with partners like Mike is that they require the therapist to be perfect. It is possible, however, that these brief and isolated periods of better understanding would, over many sessions, become a more frequent and more dominating element in their relationship. This is what happened in this case.

The key to understanding the unmanageably angry partner, I have come to believe, is the recognition of a *hidden desperation*. Underlying Mike's wild charges, we discovered, was a fear that Beth did not love him. Beth gradually and painfully admitted that while she had a lot of feeling for Mike, it was mostly that of concern, like a sister for a brother. This was particularly difficult for Mike to take because he had been unhappy and isolated his whole life, had never formed a real relationship with anyone else before, and was uncertain he ever could again. His rages, we now saw, had been set off in part by subtle indications of Beth's growing withdrawal from him and were expressions of a drowning man who saw his only hope of rescue being pulled from his grasp.

The obvious therapeutic task is to make this underlying sense of hopelessness and pessimism itself a major issue of therapy. This is not always easy to do, however. These individuals may be feeling too desperate to be able to stand back and talk about their desperation, at least at first. There is only one course on which they may have any hope at all—forcing their partners to make the required change—and it is this to which their efforts, interests, and attention may be singlemindedly directed.

INCORPORATING FIGHTING

The effect of the methods suggested in this chapter may be to resolve arguments. The approach does not *require* that the couple's arguments be resolved, however, and does not necessarily seek to do so. The goal, instead, is the establishment of a perspective from which partners can observe their disputes. Even if detailed study of a couple's fights establishes that these individuals clearly disagree on some issues, it is still possible for them to talk collaboratively about this fact. The object of such discussion is to become joint experts in recognizing the existence, significance, manifestations, and vicissitudes of their disagreements. It is in this manner, by holding an ongoing conversation about their arguments, that partners may be able to incorporate them into their relationship.

16

Demanding–Withdrawn Partners

This brings us to the third of the three classic types of troubled couple patterns, demanding–withdrawn (pursuer–distancer) polarization. A prime example, already discussed, is the partners who deal with their fears of marriage in opposite ways. Tom deals with them by withdrawing. He goes to see Betsy less, watches television when he does, and finds reasons to leave early. Betsy deals with her fears by approaching. She seeks to reassure herself about his love for her, her love for him, their general compatibility, and the wisdom of their decision to marry by having continuous contact, long intimate talks, and lots of flowers, affection, and sex.

The interaction, once started, is self-reinforcing. The more Tom withdraws, the more Betsy needs reassuring contact. The more she seeks contact, the more he needs to withdraw. The problem is a serious one. These partners are likely to become increasingly distressed and ultimately may be forced to separate.

The problem has three distinct elements. The first is anger. Each is resentful about what seems to be incomprehensible, irrational, unnecessary, and provocative behavior by the other. The second is self-criticism. At the same time, and at another level, each is alarmed by his or her own reactions. Betsy is worried about being a nagging, demanding woman, and Tom is concerned about being ''afraid of intimacy.'' The third is a sense of incompatibility. Each is troubled by the possibility that the present problem indicates a fundamental difference or conflict between them that would make a long-term relationship impossible.

TRADITIONAL APPROACHES TO POLARIZED PARTNERS

My own approach to demanding–withdrawn couples can best be discussed by contrasting it to traditional orientations. Certain psychoanalytically oriented therapists make genetic interpretations. Partners are seen as acting out childhood problems. Therapy is then devoted in part to drawing attention to these early difficulties (Kadis, 1964; Sager, 1967). Napier (1978), although not generally thought to be psychoanalytically oriented, provides a good example of such an approach.

> In an attempt to break what is essentially a transference panic, the therapist should insist quite firmly that. . . [demanding-withdrawn] partners face their own family histories. This is done most powerfully in the context of a current, emotionally charged incident: "John, when your wife showed up an hour late for your date, your anger was not just at her. You are still remembering all those hours you waited for your mother and felt abandoned by her and Alice is helping you to re-experience all that anger and hurt."
>
> Turning then to the wife: "And when John becomes stern and accuses you of being irresponsible, all of a sudden he isn't John anymore. He becomes your dominating father at whom you are *still* very angry." Many couples resist such moves, preferring to blame the partner, and the therapist needs to be forceful and persuasive in confronting such denial of the historical self. (Napier, 1978, p. 11)

Different therapists choose different points at which to apply therapeutic pressure. Although I agree with Napier that it may be necessary for the therapist "to be forceful and persuasive," I would choose another place. While John's reaction to his wife's lateness is clearly related to early experiences with his mother, it seems to me a mistake to attribute it entirely to these. If John is angry at his wife, I would immediately imagine that he is reacting, at least in part, to important issues in his present relationship with her. Perhaps in some yet unrecognized manner he is being abandoned by Alice as he previously had been by his mother. John's sudden anger suggests that he had been holding back complaints. If suppression of feelings is characteristic of their interaction, as it is for many couples, then it is possible that their relationship contains periods of *mutual abandonment,* times in which each is alone in his or her own held-back thoughts and feelings.

A similar case can be made for the reality of Alice's feeling of being dominated. I usually find myself on the side opposite the one taken by Napier. When partners discredit their reactions, attributing them to unresolved feelings toward their parents, I often suggest that these reactions may have more validity than they may think.

Behavioral marital therapists are likely to deal with polarized partners the way they deal with everyone else, by translating these individuals' abstractly stated complaints into specific circumstances and then into concrete solutions. Thus, "You're a nag!" and "You're afraid of intimacy" are first redefined in operational terms (e.g., "You interrupt me about unimportant matters when I try to read the paper in the mornings" and "You do not spend any time talking to me"). The problem may then be resolved by means of a behavioral exchange where one partner gets an uninterrupted hour to read the paper and the other gets 10 minutes of conversation.

I have no real objection to this approach if it does not produce a forced and insufficient solution. I too might ask partners who are accusing each other of being "a nag" and "afraid of intimacy" whether there are specific situations or events that particularly characterize or symbolize this impression. If they then relate "being interrupted while reading the paper" and "not being talked to" and decide to experiment with changing both behaviors, I would be very interested in the results. If this seems to solve the problem, fine. In any case it is likely to provide further and potentially usable information about the problem and the relationship. The partner who wanted 10 minutes of talking may discover that it is not the existence of talking but what is talked about that is important. The individual reading the paper may learn that it is impossible to relax with the paper knowing that the partner is suppressing a wish to interrupt.

What I would do, of course, is use behavioral change (or the absence of behavioral change) as a means of achieving further understanding. This differs from the traditional behavioral approach that treats behavioral change as an end in itself.

Don Jackson (1967) gives an example of the Palo Alto systems approach to demanding–withdrawn polarization in his discussion of a demanding wife who asks her husband whether he loves her and a withdrawn husband who replies compliantly but unenthusiastically that he does. Jackson refers to this exchange and the hurt and resentment that follow as a "game" and states that husband and wife are helplessly enmeshed in a "self-perpetuating and mutually causative" couple system. Therapy for Jackson then consists of the therapist "behaving in such a way" that this couple pattern "must change" (p. 144). The implication here is that simply talking with them about their situation is not enough.

Watzlawick, Weakland, and Fisch (1974, p. 103), writing from a similar perspective, suggest the tactic of pointing out to such a wife that her demanding behavior, in contrast to what must seem to an outsider as "quiet, kind endurance" on her husband's part, is "making him look good." She, in an effort to stop "building him up in the eyes of others at her expense," stops nagging him which, since the pressure is off, causes him to withdraw less. This is the kind of paradoxical intervention or therapeutic double bind for which this group of therapists is known.

Fogarty (1976) and Guerin (1972), who also employ a systems approach (Murray Bowen's), do feel that there is value in talking directly to partners. Fogarty (1976) recommends that therapists concentrate on the pursuer ("The pursuer is the one who is most anxious and uncomfortable, and therefore most apt to change," p. 326) and, among other things, teach this individual "the operating principle, 'Never pursue a distancer.' The more anyone goes after a distancer, the more he will distance" (p. 326). This operating principle is useful but has certain problems and limitations.

Guerin (1972) provides a vivid demonstration of Fogarty's approach taken from his own life. He noticed that he and his wife were reacting to problems in their extended family in their typical manner.

> In response to this extended family difficulty, my wife predictably pulled back, establishing distance between herself and other family members. Sensing this pulling back, I, according to form, began crowding in on her by repetitive questioning and expert, but unsolicited, supervision on household projects. This method of crowding usually results in increased distance on the part of my wife, and I began taking this distance personally—thereby further intensifying the situation. (p. 447)

> The plan of action I decided upon called for me to cease questioning or commenting on. . . my wife's. . . behavior. Instead I would make such comments in my wife's presence as, "It sure is peaceful to live with someone who doesn't burden me with personal thoughts and feelings," or "I can't stand people who are always talking about their troubles." Immediately after such a comment I would make a quick exit, instead of waiting for or even expecting a response from my wife. (p. 448)

> [The purpose was to] decrease the crowding of my wife. . . while still letting [her]. . . know that I was aware of what was going on. Handling things in this way made it possible for me to view [her]. . . behavior as less of a personal affront. Given enough room, my wife was able to move toward me and open up the issues that were bothering her. (p. 448–449)

The knowledge that "The more anyone goes after a distancer, the more he will distance" (Fogarty, 1976, p. 326) is invaluable for the pursuer to have and Guerin wisely and effectively used this information. My own preference, however, is to supplement it with the opposite notion that "The more anyone withdraws from a pursuer, the more he or she will pursue."

I also question the rule-like tone of the phrase "Never pursue a distancer," although I am not sure whether Fogarty actually meant it to be a rule. I can imagine situations in which individuals cannot stop pursuing or simply feel like doing it. My only recommendation would be the importance of their being aware of what they are doing so that they will not be surprised or confused by the result (their partners' withdrawal) and so they might be able to explain to their partners what happened. This is what Guerin did, in essence, when he jokingly told his wife, "It sure is peaceful to live with someone who doesn't burden me with personal thoughts and feelings." This was his way of explaining to her that he knew he had been crowding her.

This brings up the major modification I would make to the Fogarty-Guerin approach. The most elegant solution to the problem would be for partners to develop a usable *joint* understanding of their pursuer–distancer pattern. Guerin had to go through a somewhat complex set of actions to correct the situation with his wife. With the establishment of a joint understanding, all he would have had to do was point out to his wife that they were engaged in their familiar pattern. Such an understanding would also double the possibility of recognizing the problem. There would then be two people—either Guerin *or* his wife—who could notice what was happening and bring it to the other's attention.

MY APPROACH TO POLARIZED PARTNERS

I would like to suggest the range of interpretations a therapist can employ in his or her attempt to provide partners with a usable joint understanding of their polarized pattern. As mentioned in the beginning of this chapter, polarized individuals are blame oriented (critical of each other and of themselves) and are concerned about their apparent incompatibility. If interpretations are to be helpful, they must deal with these issues.

Reducing Blame

Turning to the issue of blame and, in particular, the tendency of partners to be critical of themselves, it becomes clear why Jackson, Watzlawick, and others might hesitate to interpret these individuals' pursuer–distancer interactions. Many pursuing individuals do not like the idea that they pursue. They often have long painful histories of criticism from others and from themselves for such tendencies. In addition, they may associate this characteristic with a parent whom, at least in this respect, they do not want to be like. Distancing partners generally have similar experiences and sensitivities about their predisposition to withdraw and their alleged fear of intimacy.

The effect of interpreting these individuals' pursuer–distancer interactions, in other words, might merely reconfirm their worst fears about themselves. The result would be to increase their defensiveness and self-criticism. If an interpretation is to be useful, it must have the opposite effect and free them from their blame oriented perspectives.

This is what interacting sensitivities and paired binds interpretations are designed to do. A therapist adopting such an approach might be able to show, in the case of Jackson's couple, that the wife has been struggling between a wish to discuss the lack of intimacy in their marriage and her fear that her husband would feel pressured by this and withdraw further. She deals with this dilemma by suppressing her wish. Since suppressive efforts are never completely successful, the wish breaks through at certain moments in the jarring, highly compressed, out-of-nowhere question, "Do you love me?" Her fear of being demanding, in other words, has led to this intrusively demanding question.

The husband then finds himself in a dilemma: he can either be truthful at the expense of hurting her feelings and precipitating an unresolvable argument, or he can be polite and considerate at the cost of suppressing his feelings. What he feels, we can imagine, is pressured by her question and criticized by the implied accusation that he has been insufficiently affectionate. At least at this moment when he is feeling besieged, guilty, and resentful, he certainly does not love her. This husband, as his wife before him, deals with his dilemma by suppressing his true feelings. These feelings reveal themselves, however, in the toneless and perfunctory manner by which he says he loves her.

Describing the partners' demanding-withdrawn interaction in this manner reduces blaming in several ways. First, these partners had been viewing each other (and perhaps also themselves) as fully committed to the particular offensive behavior, the wife to demandingness and the husband to withdrawal. What now becomes apparent is that each is devoting primary effort to suppressing the very behavior for which he or she is being condemned. The pursuing wife, worried as she is about being too pushy, is spending most of her time trying to not pursue, though sporadically bursting forth with impulsive pursuing efforts. The withdrawn husband, concerned as he is about being too detached, may be continuously—though perhaps unsuccessfully—trying to suppress his tendency to withdraw.

Furthermore, it is the very effort to suppress the unwanted behavior that may be causing the problem. The wife's demanding question "Do you love me?" is a reaction to her attempt to be undemanding and the husband's lackluster response—his compliant answer that he does—is an effort to not withdraw.

This brings us to the next point. A major value in delineating these individuals' concurrent conflicts is that it allows them to recognize that their partners (and they themselves) are caught in difficult dilemmas and are not simply the selfish, unreasonable, malevolent, or unfeeling people they had seemed to be. The wife can pursue or suppress her wish to pursue. The husband can withdraw or suppress his desire to withdraw. Neither alternative works out well for either party. The recognition of their paired binds may increase their sense of sympathy for their mutual situation.

A further way of reducing blame is to show that *both* partners' reactions are justifiable. Since the wife responds to withdrawal with demandingness and the husband responds to demandingness with withdrawal, she is actually being abandoned and he is actually being pressured. Each is provoked by the other in an area in which he or she is particularly vulnerable. The early experience of the wife may have left her especially sensitive to abandonment and that of the husband to demandingness (Napier, 1978).

Still another means of reducing partners' blaming is to point to the essential truth in each of their strivings. The wife's impulsive question, "Do you love me?" may be the closest this couple ever comes to recognizing and discussing the important fact that their life together has not turned out to have the satisfactions and intimacy that both in their own ways had wanted. Everyday married life is filled with moments when one or both partners feel excluded, unappreciated, or disappointed. Couples who do not have a way of recognizing these feelings and talking about them are subject to a gradual buildup of resentment and alienation leading to a loss of feeling for each other and either emotional or actual divorce. The wife's recurrent requests for reassurance can thus be used as a clue that something unsettling or alienating has just happened that needs to be discussed. Considered from this point of view, this woman's wish to ask her husband if he loves her is a valuable asset that the couple may be fortunate to have. Couples in which neither partner is a "specialist" in the moment-to-moment slights, deprivations, and dissatisfactions of the relationship have less chance of recognizing and thus dealing with the alienation that can so easily develop between people.

In a similar manner, the husband's compliant response, his attempts to smooth over difficult issues, and his statement that he does not see the value in talking about their problems, may be the closest this couple ever comes to recognizing that they do not have a way of dealing with conflict. Thus, while the wife is correct that there are critical deprivations occurring in the relationship that need to be talked about, the husband is also correct that they presently have no way of talking about them.

A final way of reducing partners' feelings of blame about their pursuer–distancer interaction is to show it to be an unavoidable and perhaps universal feature of couple relationships. The adoption of the intimacy-seeking role by one partner may lead to the assumption of the privacy-seeking role by the other and vice versa. The wife, who let us say is more skillful than her husband in observing the fluctuating undercurrents between them, notices a strain or detachment. If she were to comment on this, her husband, who at some level is also aware of the strain, might be glad to have it brought out into the open. If they do not have a way of discussing such events, however, she is likely instead to suppress her feeling and then, at a later moment, blurt it out in the form of a complaint or demand—"Why are you always so silent?" or "Why don't you ever tell me you love me?" The husband, feeling accused and threatened, complies perfunctorily and withdraws. Whatever wish he might have had for closer contact is quickly superceded by the more pressing need for self-protection. These partners, who had been having identical desires for intimacy just a moment before, are now polarized.

I am not recommending that therapists make all these points at the same time or at each instance of a demanding–withdrawn interaction. My own practice is to state the one or two that appear particularly pertinent at the moment. There are also occasions when I would make none of these interpretations. Some people are not interested in viewing their partner's position in a more favorable light. They are outraged by this partner and may need to express this outrage. It is when individuals are not completely comfortable with the dispute and might like to be able to view their partner's position in a more sympathetic manner that these interventions are most useful.

Some therapists try to help partners deal with pursuer–distancer interactions by attributing them to male–female differences. They point to the fact that women, being more verbal and social than men, are likely to want more contact, communication, and intimacy in a relationship. While such an intervention may reduce blaming (how can you take personally a problem shared with every other man and woman in our society?), it does so at the cost of exaggerating and codifying what may be only superficial differences. The need of men for intimacy, contact, and communication, if not immediately apparent, is generally only slightly below the surface as is the need of women for separation and privacy. The preferred therapeutic task would be to challenge, not to confirm, this cultural stereotype of a fixed characterological difference between men and women.

Revealing a Hidden Communality

Helping polarized partners reduce blaming is one major therapeutic task. Pointing out the hidden communality underlying their apparent differences is another. As just described for reducing blaming, there are several ways this can be done. Taken together, they too constitute an informal outline of possible interventions.

An analysis of a demanding–withdrawn interaction may reveal that both partners are concerned about the same underlying issue (Sager, 1976, p. 44). The problem of the husband-and-wife-to-be was resolved by pointing out that both were worried about the commitment of marriage but were expressing their fears in opposite ways, she by seeking increased contact and he by seeking more time to himself.

In other cases partners may be expressing similar concerns in different areas of their marriage. The wife in Jackson's case was pressuring her husband for reassurance about his love. It is possible, however, that the husband might be pressing her for something else, let us say sex. Each might be looking for a greater sense of contact, intimacy, and involvement, but in a different aspect of the relationship and, unfortunately, in a manner that offends the other. The wife's attempts to increase intimacy (seeking verbal reassurance) alienate her husband while his attempts (seeking compensatory physical intimacy) alienate her. If these partners were to observe this interaction from a broader perspective, they might be able to recognize that they are both seeking the same thing, an increased sense of intimacy.*

Another discovery that may soften these partners' sense of opposition is the realization that each is taking responsibility for an issue that is of theoretical or potential concern to the other (Framo, 1976, pp. 207–208). In some cases, a kind of division of labor arises in which one partner takes responsibility for certain universal couple concerns and the other takes responsibility for others (Taggart, 1979). The wife in Jackson's example may be speaking for their common wish to establish greater intimacy while the husband is speaking for their common need to maintain the stability and evenness of their relationship and to guarantee a certain measure of separation and privacy. The recognition by partners of an underlying communality may soften the edge of their mutual alienation.

The fact that these issues are of concern to both partners can sometimes be demonstrated by pointing to periods in their relationship when they have taken the reverse positions. I often ask demanding–withdrawn partners if their relationship has always had the present form. They occasionally respond, "Actually, when we were first married, it was just the opposite. *Frank* was the one who was dependent and clingy and *I* was the one seeking more freedom." It becomes possible, by reminding them of this earlier period, to give each a sense of their partner's current experience.

A similar use can be made of reversals occurring in their present lives. There may be times when the pursuing partner temporarily gives up on the relationship and withdraws. The distancing partner may then step into the breach and assume the pursuing role (Fogarty, 1979). I have found these temporary reversals to be an invaluable means of giving individuals a sense of what their partner's typical position is like.

Couples sometimes come to therapy on the crest of a reversal. It is a repeated and interesting phenomenon that the partner who has traditionally been against therapy (generally the distancer) is very often the one who plays the major role in actually initiating it. The distancing husband, realizing that he is about to lose his wife, has become the pursuer. It is now he who wants to talk more, to spend time together, and to work things out.

A final means of demonstrating communality is related to the onesidedness of complaints. A common pattern is for the pursuer to have numerous complaints about the relationship and the distancer to have none. This may further polarize these individuals. As one partner put it, "My husband

---

*Stuart (1969), in an early behavioral approach, reinforced such husbands (gave them tokens) for increased talking and reinforced their wives for increased sexual behavior.

doesn't see any problems between us. That's the problem." The distancer's lack of complaints may be a consequence of low expectations about what a relationship can provide. It is possible in such a case to point out dissatisfactions this individual had been having but had not been set to notice. Establishing that this partner too has grievances and disappointments can provide a useful common ground.

To summarize, a common effect of partners' study of their demanding–withdrawn interactions is a greater appreciation of and sympathy for their own and their partners' positions and the discovery in many cases of an underlying mutuality. More important, however, is the construction of a joint perspective. Individuals who are able to talk collaboratively about their demanding-withdrawn interactions may be able to take them into account, anticipate their occurrence, maintain surveillance of them and, in this manner, incorporate them into their relationship.

The major problem with demanding-withdrawn couples is their alarm at their own reactions. Individuals who view their interactions as signaling unacceptable personal defects in themselves or their partners or as indicating that they have a pathological relationship will be unable to stand back from these interactions and talk collaboratively about them.

Such couples are suffering from the idealized view of intimate relationships promoted in this culture and reinforced by some therapists. Charny (1972) has criticized the mental health profession for failing to recognize that mutually accusing interactions are normal and inevitable. The same point can be made with respect to both demanding-withdrawn interactions and mutually withdrawn interchanges.

A common image of troubled partners—as deviant individuals having deviant relationships—seems inexact or at least incomplete. A more accurate view, I believe, is that these are people who are intensely experiencing universal couple problems that others may be denying or overlooking. There is an important advantage in conceptualizing the situation in such a manner. Interventions made from this perspective are likely to increase partners' feelings of entitlement to their reactions and to interrupt the self-accusation that is intensifying their difficulties.

6

The Ultimate Expression of My Approach

17

Incorporating Problems
Into Relationships

The common sense approach to couple problems, and the one employed by some contemporary therapists, is to try to eliminate or "solve" them. The drawback of such an orientation is that it is partners' intolerance for their problems and their own desperate attempts to eliminate them that may be causing most of the difficulty. The alternative, as shown for withdrawn, angry, and polarized partners, is to stand back from the problem and to incorporate it into the relationship—that is, to acknowledge the problem and the feelings and wishes associated with the problem as an inherent part of the relationship. Rather than, or in addition to, solving problems, the goal is to enable partners to have problems (Apfelbaum, 1980c).*

This chapter discusses the disadvantages of forcing solutions to partners' conflicts and indicates the advantages of building the relationship on these conflicts.

URGING PARTNERS TO BE REASONABLE

When partners argue about who is to blame for a problem, Ables and Brandsma (1977) write, the therapist should direct their attention instead to how they plan to solve it. The general goal among these and many other therapists is to encourage partners to make compromises, give up unrealistic expectations, and, in general, behave more reasonably.

Ables and Brandsma discuss two intrusive wives. One was unnecessarily concerned about her husband's clothing (at least in these authors' opinion) and the other was opening her husband's mail. Ables and Brandsma re-

*Freud (1914, p. 152), making this same point for individual psychotherapy, talks about a patient's developing "a certain tolerance for the state of being ill." "He must . . . direct his attention to the phenomena of his illness. His illness itself must no longer seem to him contemptible, but must become an enemy worthy of his mettle, a piece of his personality, which has solid ground for its existence and out of which things of value for his future life have to be derived."

sponded to the first in their typical manner. They defined this wife's concern with her husband's clothing as unreasonable and pressed her to change her attitude.

> You're going to have to be clear to separate this out, because if he chooses to look bad, et cetera, he's an adult, and that's his choice. . .and that could only reflect on him. So I see you taking over a responsibility you can very well give up. You are not responsible for how he dresses. (p. 129)

This is an example of Ables and Brandsma's attempt to help partners achieve a higher degree of separation and individuation. The problem, however, is that these authors' method of doing this may have the effect of increasing people's self-criticism and trying to talk them out of their feelings. This is what appeared to have happened. The wife became convinced that she should not be so concerned about her husband's clothing but then found herself unable to give up this concern. She became apologetic. "I don't know why it bugs me," she said, "but it does!" (p. 129). She promised to "make a conscious effort" not to let her husband's clothing bother her, but she was uncertain that she would be successful.

These authors dealt with the second wife in an entirely different way. They took what on the face of it appeared to be intrusive, unreasonable, and possibly even illegal behavior (opening her husband's mail) and found a hidden rationality. Opening his mail was her way of expressing a general sense of being left out by her husband. The problem was much easier to deal with once it had been redefined in this broader and more accurate manner.

My recommendation is to apply Ables and Brandsma's second approach to the first case and to every other instance of "unreasonable" partner behavior. Rather than encouraging the clothes-conscious wife to feel less responsible for her husband's clothing, I would want to find out what her feeling of responsibility means. It is possible to speculate from comments she made later in the session that she felt her husband's unkempt appearance was an expression of his lack of pride in himself *and that this lack of pride may be her fault.*

> Well, maybe I feel like I've fallen down on my job to inspire pride in you [the husband]. . . . Maybe I don't have enough confidence and don't build up your confidence in yourself and don't do my part in some ways. I do consider it a reflection on the way I have treated you. (p. 133)

This appears to be the heart of the issue. The wife wants her husband to dress in a more attractive way, it now is clear, because she takes his not doing so as a sign that she has failed in her duty as a wife. Rather than being told that her concern about how he dresses is illogical, she needs the opportunity to express how she feels she has let him down.

One way of describing Ables and Brandsma's approach to the clothes-conscious wife is to suggest that they have taken her behavior out of its dynamic or motivational context and placed it instead in a moral framework. Behavior viewed dynamically is assumed to be understandable and in its own way rational. The therapist's task is to discover the hidden rationality. Behavior viewed from a moral perspective is to be judged as helpful or detrimental, rational or irrational and, if found deficient, to be renounced. Consider the following interventions taken from various parts of Ables and Brandsma's (1977) book.

> Well, you see that's not helpful. It would be better if you would quit talking about problems and talk about specific behaviors and what you can do to work on these. [To wife] If there are problems about your feelings about yourself, that's probably not something you [to husband] can help her with directly, but you can help her by loving her, you can help her by supporting her, you can help her by asking her if there's anything you can do, you know, specifically. (pp. 82–83)

> I guess what would be helpful would be if you could come on honestly enough to say "I don't like them" or "It doesn't sit well with me" without having to add the additional value judgment of whether they're foolish or ridiculous or whatever. (p. 93)

> One of the things you both probably have done, because most couples do to some extent or another, is use labels, and these are very unhelpful—adjectives like "childish," or "immature," and so forth. . . . These are things that you are going to have to start working on, to get them out of your vocabulary, because they are accusations. (p. 175)

> What it requires is caring enough to make the effort . . . . First knowing what it is you need to do—which is part of what we're trying to do—and then caring enough to make the effort. What it means is trying to think about somebody's needs as well as your own. (p. 64)

My major concern with these particular interventions is that many of them are criticisms and all of them impose judgments (they tell partners what they should be doing). Ables and Brandsma have an image or model of what constitutes acceptable or appropriate couple behavior and appear to be trying to impose this model. A husband who complains about his wife is told that it might be better if he were to love her, support her, and ask if there is anything he can do for her. The more "honest" thing to do, certain partners are informed, would be to express their feelings rather than judge each other. What is required, another couple is told, is to care enough to make the effort and to think about somebody else's needs besides their own. If they are unable to change, the suggestion is thus made, it may be because they are too selfish, insufficiently caring, or unwilling to make the effort.

SUPPLYING THE MISSING FEELINGS

The problems of partners are that they too take behavior out of its motivational context and place it in a moral framework (i.e., make judgments about it). The letter-opening wife skipped over her feeling of being excluded by her husband and focused instead on what she felt to be a right to open his mail. The clothes-conscious wife shifted from her concern that she was letting her husband down to an insistence that he dress better which, if he were to do so, might allow her to feel that she may not have let him down so much after all.

This factor—the tendency of partners to skip over important feelings—appears to be a major principle underlying couple conflict. Problems occur between partners when they act on their feelings rather than acknowledge them. This is obvious in the case of mutual withdrawal. Withdrawal can only occur when partners are not talking about the fact that they are withdrawing. A person who says "I feel distant from you" or "I feel like withdrawing" is making a very intimate and nonwithdrawn comment.

The point is almost as clear in the case of mutual accusation. Instead of telling his wife that he is afraid to complain about dinner not being ready because he is worried about starting a fight, a husband talks himself out of it only to suddenly blurt out "Why isn't dinner ever ready?" And instead of responding that this is difficult to hear because she was already feeling bad about not having it prepared, the wife snaps out, "Why don't *you* make dinner for a change!" Finally, instead of mentioning that he feels she has a good point (she does everything around the house in addition to holding down a full-time job) but that he is too angry at the moment to want to admit it, the husband slams the door behind him yelling "You're impossible to talk to!"

The point can also be made in the case of demanding–withdrawn partners. The wife who asks her husband "Do you love me?" (Jackson's case) appears to be feeling a lack of contact and intimacy in the relationship. Instead of telling her husband about this, however, she acts on her feelings and forces out this awkward request for reassurance. The husband, in turn, is not saying what he is feeling. Instead of telling her that he feels pressured by her question and criticized by the implicit accusation that he has been insufficiently affectionate, he replies perfunctorily that he does love her.

Problems develop in a relationship, it seems, when each partner in succession passes over important feelings. The wife in the last example skipped over her sense of a lack of intimacy in the relationship and instead asked her husband to reassure her that he loved her. The husband ignored his feeling that something was amiss and answered perfunctorily that he did. The wife then passed over her sense of disappointment in his response and made an intensified demand or an angry accusation. The husband skipped over his feeling of confusion and looked for a graceful exit.

The therapeutic task is to reinsert the omitted feelings. The practitioner in the present case could interrupt the interaction and ask the wife what she was feeling when she inquired whether her husband loved her. Her answer, let us suppose, is that she felt a lack of intimacy or had recently begun to think that their relationship did not have much romance and excitement. This might seem a very powerful thing to say and may be even more difficult for her husband to handle than what she did say (it is such a fear, in fact, that might have kept her from saying it in the first place). However, it would not have had the same pressuring, demanding, and response limiting quality as did the question, "Do you love me?" In addition, it would tell the husband what his wife was feeling. My guess is that he might be able to make a fairly specific and nonwithdrawn response and, in so doing, temporarily dispel the demanding–withdrawn polarization.

TRYING TO NOT HAVE (OR TO SOLVE) PROBLEMS CAUSES THEM

It is a familiar idea in psychotherapy that the attempts of individuals to solve their problems often causes them. This has been pointed out by Horney (1945) and Watzlawick and his colleagues (1974), among others. In fact, the major principle can be traced as least as far back as Freud and was given particular emphasis by Fenichel. It is defenses that people erect against their impulses—that is, their attempts to eliminate or "solve" these impulses—that produce psychological symptoms.

The present discussion of skipped over or left out feelings provides a useful way of specifying how partners' attempts to solve their problems, or to not have them, may actually cause them. The problem with the wife who asked her husband if he loved her was that she was feeling insufficient contact or intimacy in the relationship. One way she could have dealt with the difficulty, and the way many people do, would have been to try to not notice it. The effect would have been to respond to her husband's withdrawal by withdrawing herself. Mutual withdrawal, a particularly insidious type of problem, is the common consequence of partners' efforts to not have problems (Framo, 1965, p. 188).

Another way she could have attempted to avoid the problem, and the way she did choose, was to try to solve it. She asked her husband if he loved her. Her hope was that, if he were to mouth these words, she might be able to believe him. If so, she could then feel that he was intimately involved with her after all, rather than detached and unavailable as he presently seemed. The result of her attempted solution, of course, was to make matters worse. Her feeling of insufficient contact, a feeling that perhaps could have been discussed, had been converted into a problem.

BEING ABLE TO HAVE PROBLEMS SOLVES THEM

This fact (i.e., that partners' efforts to avoid difficulties may cause difficulties) has an interesting implication for therapy. The task in some cases may be not to try to help partners solve or eliminate their problems but to enable them to acknowledge them, tolerate them, and incorporate them into their relationships. An example was Cecile's feeling of inferiority with respect to Greg—her distress that he could do everything better than she could. He made more money, had more friends, and excelled in sports. Traditional therapeutic approaches might include analyzing her penis envy, pointing out areas in which she was superior, or encouraging her to return to school and work toward a higher status and better paying job. The last two seemed useful areas to explore, and I did ask her if she really felt there was nothing at which she was superior and whether she was suggesting that she might wish to develop a more lucrative and more satisfying career. Much of the problem, however, was her failure to confide in Greg about these feelings. Worries that partners keep from each other have a tendency to become increasingly preoccupying. She experienced considerable relief when she was finally able to tell him about them.

It is not quite correct to say that Cecile had never stated these concerns to Greg before. She had made vague allusions to them, expressed them as sarcastic remarks, and blurted them out in the middle of arguments. However, she had rarely said them in a manner and in a context that would require Greg to take them seriously. The few times she had done so had not produced satisfying results; Greg took them too seriously. He immediately tried to talk her out of the problem, pointing to ways in which she was superior. What was needed, and what was provided in therapy, was an opportunity to acknowledge and the ability to tolerate the existence of the problem.

A paradoxical result of Cecile and Greg's acceptance and discussion of the difficulty was an immediate improvement (Cecile felt less distressed about the ways in which she felt inferior to Greg and began to appreciate ways in which she was competent) and a freeing of her energies and resources (she made plans to go back to school and develop a more satisfying career).

Integrating her problem into the relationship thus led to the beginning of its solution.

Apfelbaum and his colleagues (1980) describe another example. The problem was the failure of an individual to become sexually aroused during intercourse. When this man, who had been struggling in an isolated manner to force himself to become sexually excited, finally confided to his partner that he was "turned off" and was worried about disappointing her, this resulted in his becoming "turned on."

Mike and Beth (the broom example) can be discussed in similar terms. Mike's rage was a consequence of his inability to state his position with sufficient precision. But it was also a reaction to an unspoken issue in the relationship. The issue became clear when Beth finally admitted that she had been holding back complaints about Mike, had lost all positive feeling for him, and was thinking of divorce. Once she had a chance to state her held back grudges and complaints, however, her positive feeling for him began to return.

Isolation, the failure or inability of partners to talk in an ongoing way about their respective concerns, appears to be at the root of most couple problems. Alan was displeased with his fear and awkwardness in social situations. He was too humiliated to discuss it with Georgia, however. He imagined that she must be as disgusted with it as he was himself. These unexpressed worries became increasingly distressing. He came to believe that she was probably sorry she had ever married him and that she was just staying with him through habit.

Georgia did have some dissatisfactions. It was not Alan's social inhibitions in themselves that caused the problem, however, but the failure of these partners to develop a way of talking about them. If, from the beginning of the relationship, Alan were to have taken Georgia into his confidence, telling her that he was concerned about his shyness and was worried that she would be critical of it, then Georgia would have had a chance to say what she was feeling at the time—that while she had moments when she wished he were a more assertive, take-charge kind of man, she mostly liked his quiet, unassuming ways. She would thus have been able to express the reservations and criticisms she did have. Without such opportunity, these reservations began to intensify and solidify. By the time these partners came to therapy, Georgia had herself come to believe that Alan's lack of assertiveness was a serious weakness.

The point can be made sharper by considering the relationship these partners could have had. If Alan and Georgia had developed an effective ongoing way of talking about his nonassertiveness, Georgia's distaste for it would not have intensified. Alan would have come to realize that, though she did have some reservations about it, she was a great deal less upset about it than he was. He might then have been able to use her as a resource or ally in dealing with it. As it turned out, she became a major part of the problem. His greatest, though hidden, concern when he came to therapy was that his lack of "manly assertiveness" would cause him to lose his wife.

The problem, it often appears, is not the identified issue, but the isolation caused by not having a way of talking about it. Paula wanted Jay to spend more time with her. Jay, who claimed a need to work on his graduate school studies, said he was unable to do so. Much of the difficulty, it turned out, arose from their attempt to not notice the problem. Each evening immediately after dinner Jay would disappear into the bedroom to do his schoolwork. Both knew that Paula did not like his doing this, but neither said anything about it. It was not the fact that Jay was leaving Paula to do his homework but the inhibited way in which he was doing it that was causing Paula to feel left out. She was offended by the cautious manner in which he slipped away, as if she were a danger to circumvent. The procedure was also alienating to Jay, and he found it difficult to concentrate on his studies. Paula's original complaint, feeling cut off from her partner, could now be seen as a fully accurate description of the condition experienced by both.

The other major way in which these partners tried to handle the problem—unilateral efforts to solve it—also added to the difficulty. Paula tried to deal with Jay's unavailability and with her concern about being "too dependent" by making plans to do things on her own. Such attempts to prove one's independence, of course, are rarely successful. Although she did go out more on her own, she could not get her resentment and sense of rejection out of her mind. She became particularly incensed when Jay hardly appeared to notice her absence and may even have been relieved by it. Her attempt to become independent and undemanding thus ended in an angry demanding attack.

Jay made his own unilateral attempts to solve the problem with similar results. In an effort to give Paula what she wanted, he planned a picnic. Since it was clear to Paula, however, that he really wanted to be working on his studies, she did not obtain much satisfaction from the outing. This was intensely frustrating to Jay. Since he was already overextending himself to go on the picnic, he had little patience for Paula's displeasure with it. It was now he who became enraged.

The therapeutic goal is to make partners experts in recognizing their patterns and acknowledging them as an inherent part of the present relationship. If Jay and Paula were to know that it was the hesitant, guilty way in which he disappeared into the bedroom that was so offensive to Paula and that both were feeling cut off from the other, they might be able to discuss this. And if they were to become aware of how Paula periodically tried to become "independent" and Jay occasionally planned "duty" outings and how neither effort ever worked out, they might be able to sympathize with each other about this.

Incorporating problems into the relationship can be a difficult task. Partners may be too sensitive about a problem to be able to stand back from it and talk about it. Paula may be too alarmed at the thought of being a "dependent, nagging woman" to do anything other than try to be "independent." Alan may be too self-critical about his inhibitions to admit he has them. Therapy must then be devoted, as Apfelbaum has stated it, to "the development of a capacity to have problems"—that is, to uncovering and contacting the self-hating attitudes or underlying desperation that stand in the way of partners' abilities to acknowledge and tolerate the existence of these problems.

BUILDING A RELATIONSHIP ON A PROBLEM

The general effect of incorporating a problem into the relationship is to make it less of a problem. Cecile's confiding in Greg about her feeling of inferiority led to a sudden decrease in her distressed preoccupation with it. If Alan and Georgia had an effective, ongoing way of talking about his nonassertiveness and their feelings about it, it never would have become a problem.

But what about problems that are not the result, or are not entirely the result, of defective communication and mutual isolation but are issues of acute conflict in their own right? Is it possible to incorporate these into a relationship? Edna wanted children now that she was approaching the upper limits of the usual child-bearing age and was upset that Burt seemed set against it. Burt, who had recently discovered what he really wanted to do professionally, had several years of graduate school and low paying jobs ahead of him. He was thus unable "to make the time, financial, and emotional commitments that would be required to care for a child properly." Although Edna was glad that Burt had finally discovered a profession that really excited him, she was displeased that this stood in the way of having a baby.

The conflict could be considered a displacement of general interpersonal concerns. Edna was uncertain about the extent of Burt's commitment to her, and his reluctance to have a baby could be thought of as symbolizing this. The issue was also significant in its own right. Although Edna had her own doubts about children, she mostly wanted to have them.

The issue of "commitment" was dealt with in the usual way. Both partners had been withholding certain wishes and complaints. The result was a mutual withdrawal that Edna experienced as a "lack of commitment."

The opportunity provided by therapy to express some of the held back feelings had a general enlivening effect upon their relationship.

While Edna no longer took Burt's reluctance quite as personally (i.e., as a sign of his lack of commitment to her), the concrete issue still remained. She wanted a child, or at least mostly did, and he did not. The decision would eventually have to be made one way or the other. What was important then was the extent to which these partners would be able to stay in contact with their reactions to the decision and the degree to which this contact, given the frustration, would be sufficient to keep the relationship viable.

The following possibilities might occur. The danger, if they were to decide against having a child, is that Edna would be subject to sad, lonely musings about babies and that Burt, in reaction, might immerse himself in his studies. This might lead in turn to occasional angry battles in which Edna would condemn Burt for depriving her of children and for being preoccupied with his studies, and Burt would criticize her for being depressed. A similar chain of events might occur if they were to decide to have a baby. It is Burt who might then become sad and resentful, particularly if these increased family responsibilities were to interrupt his graduate training, and it is Edna who, in reaction, might immerse herself in another activity—caring for their baby. The ultimate effect here too might be mutual withdrawal intermixed with sporadic fighting.

Partners who are able to incorporate conflicts into their relationship would be able to keep in touch with each other about them. If Burt and Edna were to decide to not have a child, Burt, seeing that Edna was particularly quiet at a given moment, might ask if she were thinking about babies. It could be relieving for Edna to be able to share her feelings rather than struggle alone with them and, in the process, alienate both herself and Burt. If they were to decide to have a child, it might be Edna who, noticing that Burt seemed unusually remote, might inquire whether he was thinking about what his career would have been like if he did not have to discontinue his studies.

Partners who engage in a continuing dialogue about their conflicts may learn important new facts about them. Burt might realize, once he has expressed resentment about being forced to drop out of school, that the responsibility of a child was not the only reason for doing so. He might have begun to grow tired of graduate school. They may also discover that Burt's sad musings about his interrupted career or Edna's unhappy thoughts about their childlessness are not just random events reflecting a chronic problem but also reactions to present events. Edna would start daydreaming about children whenever she felt slighted by Burt or sensed a disruption in the relationship. This knowledge could allow them to use this daydreaming as a kind of relationship barometer indicating the existence of a subtle difficulty in their present interaction.

Certain troubled feelings may reoccur with such regularity and at such critical moments that it might be useful to consider them as defining elements in the relationship. With one couple I saw, the husband continually felt "abandoned" by his wife while she repeatedly felt that she was "letting him down." Individuals who are aware of their own and their partners' typical relationship feelings may be able to use them as frames of reference. These partners would know, whenever a problem developed between them, that he was probably feeling abandoned and she was likely to feel she was letting him down.

Partners often build their relationship on their positive feelings (their common interests and the good times they have together). I would like to suggest the value of building it also on the negative feelings. It is what partners know about their recurrent dysphoric feelings (e.g., their sense of abandonment or of letting the partner down), and their ability to discuss them rather than just act on them, that may largely determine the quality of the relationship.

It is a well-known psychoanalytic principle that people form relationships to solve certain life-long problems (Kubie, 1956; Nadelson, 1978). Julie, who was raised by intimidating and undependable parents, sought a reliable husband (Clarence) who would not threaten her. Clarence, who lacked spontaneity, sought a wife (Julie) who could supply this missing element. While some therapists argue that seeking personal completion in the personality of one's partner indicates a pathological relationship, my view is that nearly everyone does this, and it appears to be one of the better reasons for forming relationships.

It is true, however, that the attempt to solve problems through one's partner almost always leads to difficulties. The problem with marrying a nonthreatening man, Julie discovered, is that you get a nonthreatening man. Although she liked Clarence's gentle manner, there were times when she would have preferred a more aggressive mate. Clarence, although enjoying and vicariously sharing Julie's emotional responsivity toward the world, now found himself having to deal with her emotional responsivity toward him, a task he sometimes found overwhelming.

Each relationship can be viewed as having its own inherent problems, many of which arise from the very forces that attracted the individuals to each other in the first place. The ideal relationship, then, is one in which the partners appreciate the inevitability of such problems, utilize them as reference points, and, to some degree, build their relationship on them.

18

Incorporating Fantasies into Relationships

This final chapter extends the line of reasoning one step further. The possibility has been suggested for incorporating partners' problems into their relationships. It may also be possible to incorporate the fantasies that underlie these problems.

Fantasy expectations might seem at first glance to be clearly destructive. People who expect the romantic glow of the honeymoon period to persist throughout the marriage, who are convinced that major dissatisfactions and disagreements should not occur in a good relationship, or who believe that people who love each other should know instinctively what the other person wants and needs and should provide it, are thought to be at a serious disadvantage in dealing with the realities of a relationship. Ables and Brandsma (1977), Jacobson and Margolin (1979), and Sager (1976), among others, recommend challenging these expectations.

Consider the following example. A husband and wife have just said that people who love each other should be able to sense what the other needs without having to be told. The therapist responds:

> That belief is pure and utter horseshit. And it is responsible for more divorces down through the ages than you can imagine. You're going to have to give up that hope or you might as well kiss the relationship goodbye. If the only kind of marriage you're willing to accept is a dream world marriage, you might as well divorce each other now and spend your time fantasizing about the relationship based on ESP. (Jacobson and Margolin, 1979, p. 146)

This intervention suggests the vigor and directness with which it is sometimes thought necessary to attack partners' relationship fantasies. My approach, in contrast, is to discover or develop these fantasies, to employ them as a frame of reference, and, in some cases, to incorporate them into the relationship.

UNCOVERING THE HIDDEN FANTASY

The major problem in many cases is not simply the existence of relationship fantasies but their concealment. Behind the irritability, noncommunicativeness, or demandingness of some individuals may be an unexpressed or only partially expressed fantasy wish. A wife may complain about her husband's posture and dull inexpressive ways in an effort, perhaps only partially recognized by her, to make him more like the fantasy ideal she has in mind. By so doing she may hope to quiet her dissatisfactions and suppress her recurring wish to find a more interesting man.

Concealed or unexpressed fantasies of this sort have a befuddling effect upon partners. Neither can get a grasp on the problem. It may be clarifying, therefore, when the hidden fantasy begins to emerge. An example of such an emergence is when a partner whimsically states that he or she would like to recapture the romantic feeling of the early part of their relationship. Ables and Brandsma (1977, p. 211) and Jacobson and Margolin (1979, p. 147) explain to couples that such expectations are unrealistic. My own preference is to welcome such statements by partners and to use them as possible entry points into their background fantasies. "What is the difference between how you were feeling then and how you are feeling now?" I might ask. "What do you think caused the change? Do you see such change as inevitable or do you believe that, with another partner or under different conditions, things might have been different?"

Brenda had the background fantasy that most of her problems might be solved if she were involved with a man who was sensitive to her feelings as she felt her husband, Barney, was not. Her diffuse complaints about him now became clear. She had been trying to turn her husband into such a man and, despairing of this, had become secretly preoccupied with thoughts of going off to find this type of person.

Once partners' background fantasies emerge, I employ them as a frame of reference. When in the following session Brenda appeared much less critical of Barney, I asked what had happened to her dissatisfactions with him and to her thoughts about finding a more responsive husband. Brenda said that she felt it was unfair to expect Barney to change his character and had begun to worry that her expectations of finding a more sensitive man might be unrealistic. The therapeutic task with Brenda, it thus appeared, was not to quash her fantasy expectations (she herself was already trying to do this), but rather to bring them into the open and keep them there.

Brenda suppressed her fantasy wishes for two reasons. She felt guilty about them, and her efforts to discuss them with Barney always led to arguments and hurt feelings. Barney would say that Brenda should accept him for what he was rather than trying to change him all the time. Brenda would argue with this, and the dispute would go on from there.

The therapeutic goal, in such a situation, is to enable these partners to have a matter-of-fact conversation about Brenda's fantasy wishes. This can often be done in the same way as described for problems in general, by supplying the missing or skipped over feelings. I interrupted Brenda's defensive response to Barney's accusations by saying that these accusations must be difficult to take since they reflected some of her own concerns. "It seems that both of you can feel at times," I said, "that Brenda's expectations are unrealistic. Of course there are other times that both of you, or at least Brenda, believe that they are realistic and justified." Barney, apparently feeling less defensive, then admitted that he did worry that he was not as attentive to her as he felt he should be. The interaction had shifted in tone. It became possible, at least for a short time, to have a discussion about Brenda's fantasy wishes.

Such discussion may lead in either of two opposite directions. The first is an increased commitment by Brenda to her fantasy of finding a more responsive man. The opportunity to state and consider what she wants from marriage and what she has with Barney may make it clear that Brenda feels the relationship is essentially over and that she has been remaining with him only through duty or fear. The second and more common outcome is a decreased commitment to this fantasy. Fantasy wishes, given full expression, often become less preoccupying. There is also the possibility, once these wishes have been discussed in a nondefensive manner, of gratifying them in the relationship. Barney's "insensitivity" to Brenda's feelings turned out to be a consequence of their style of interacting. Actually, neither of them was having his or her feelings acknowledged by the other. Once they began to discuss Brenda's fantasy wishes rather than arguing about them or simply not talking about them, they were in this way being more responsive and sensitive to each other's feelings.

FANTASIES AS CLUES TO REALITY

Fantasy wishes and images occur as an ongoing accompaniment to relationships and as potential clues to what is happening in them (Apfelbaum, 1980b). A wife's image of sitting alone on an iceberg may be an accurate representation of her experience with her husband. A partner may react to a disappointment in his or her present relationship by daydreaming about former or prospective lovers. People deal with frustrations, among other ways, by imagining idealized solutions. A man who feels rejected by his wife may daydream about a woman who instinctively gratifies his every wish. A woman who feels pressured by her husband's demands may think about living alone in a woodside cabin. The ideal is for partners to use their fantasies as a means of discovering the relationship they are having—

that is, as an instrument for detecting how each is experiencing the relationship.

A husband's attempt to convince his wife to wear provocative clothing led to a reoccurring and mutually distressing battle. If he were to tell her his fantasy about it, how he has never felt very impressive and really likes being associated with a glamorous wife, he would at least be sharing his feelings with her. There is even the possibility, if approached in this manner, that she might get into the spirit of his fantasy and enjoy acting it out with him.

SHARING UNFULFILLED FANTASIES

If partners are to feel comfortable sharing their unfulfilled fantasies, they will need to develop an understanding about them. Simply stating them may lead to difficulties. If the wife meeting the husband at the door were to say that she had been looking forward to being greeted by a charming, masterful, and rescuing man rather than the depressed, grumpy, and withdrawn individual she found, this husband might feel bad about disappointing her (or be angered by the criticism) and start defending himself. The ensuing argument might then spiral out of control.

What is required is an ability to respond on two levels. This husband, feeling criticized by his wife, might want to defend himself, particularly if his own fantasy expectations are being frustrated. This is understandable. The therapeutic task is not to eliminate the immediate reaction but to provide for an additional period, perhaps later in the evening, when the partners could come together and sympathize with each other about their mutual disappointments.

The value of such a discussion is clear. Each partner has been disappointed by the other. What is left for them, and it is a very considerable compensation, is to commiserate with each other about this. Husband and wife may agree that it is a shame that, on that given evening, or on every evening, neither is able to give the love and caring the other has wanted because, among other reasons, they are both needing to be loved or cared for themselves. They would be comforting each other regarding the human condition—the fact that many of the most important needs and wishes of people remain unfulfilled.

Such sharing of unfulfilled fantasies may have even more dramatic effects. A husband, who had been criticized by his co-workers, had reacted by imagining being accepted or affirmed by his wife to the same degree (or twice as much) that he felt rejected by these others. He had thus come home with a rather extravagant fantasy of how his wife might express this affirmation. It might have taken no more than a kind word from her, however, and a chance to talk with her about the frustrations of the day to interrupt the view of the world he had built up (i.e., as hostile and uninviting) and to substitute a more benign and congenial one. He might no longer need his fantasy expectation to be fulfilled; it would in a sense have been fulfilled.

It is not difficult to understand how this might happen. People often respond to frustration in the sphere of reality by imagining an exquisite gratification in the sphere of imagination. It might take no more than a fragment of real satisfaction (a kind word from his wife), however, to make fantasy satisfaction no longer necessary.

PESSIMISM AND DESPERATION

Most people have a philosophic attitude toward their fantasy wishes. They know, or at least suspect, that their expectations are unrealistic. There are occasional individuals, however, who are convinced that their fantasy based expectations are totally realistic.

Grace was enraged at Edgar's refusal to go to the laundromat with her. She stood on the steps outside their house screaming at him. Behind her wish was a fantasy desire to have an idyllic moment together. Both sets of parents were visiting and this was their only chance to be alone. The irony was that Edgar might have enjoyed sharing her fantasy if he had known about it. The critical question, then, is why did she not simply tell him what she had in mind and, by so doing, induce him to participate? The reason, she said, was that she wanted him to arrive spontaneously at the same fantasy himself. This brought us to the root of the problem. Grace needed Edgar to have independently the same romantic fantasy she was having to counteract an underlying pessimism—her feeling that he had no real affection for her at all.

While pessimism motivates some rigidly held fantasy expectations, desperation underlies others.* In the example of Dick and Susan (Chapter 12) Dick was insistent that Susan write him love letters, call him several times a day, buy him little gifts and in general be as warm, accepting, and attentive to him as he felt he was to her. He devoted the therapy to long, angry lectures insisting on her obligation to relate to him in such a manner. He turned all other discussions back to this major issue and could think of little else.

An irony of Dick's behavior was the unloving manner in which he was trying to get Susan to express her love. He was condemning and in a sense hating her for her failure to express love in the ways he wanted. Susan's reaction was to feel less loved and less interested in providing what he

---

*Pessimism and desperation were previously discussed as factors underlying resistance.

wanted. The mystery was why Dick did not notice this. He was somehow able to discount his continuous carping and to maintain his view of himself as warm and accepting.

Dick's behavior might be characterized as infantile and motivated by a fantasy of narcissistic omnipotence. The real explanation, I eventually came to believe, was his underlying desperation. He needed continuous signs of affection from Susan to be able to maintain even the slightest belief that she cared for him. As discussed, his long-standing doubts about his lovability had been traumatically reinforced when he discovered his former wife in bed with another man.

The approach I took at the time I was seeing this couple turned out to be ill-advised. I pointed out the counterproductive effects of his demands on Susan and challenged his behavior. This seemed a necessary thing to do. His angry complaints dominated the session and prevented anything else from happening. The effect was to convince Dick that I did not understand. He became demoralized and terminated therapy. This was some years ago.* My emphasis today would be on his hidden sense of desperation.

Many couples therapists believe that fantasy wishes are destructive to marriage and must be replaced by realistic expectations. My view is that relationship fantasies are unavoidable, potentially valuable, a source of much of the charm of marriage, and a problem largely when partners are unaware of them or condemn themselves for having them. The goal is not to deprive partners of their wishes and fantasies—a task that is probably impossible—but to provide a perspective from which they can jointly observe them.

CLOSING COMMENT

My couples therapy approach is built on three principles. One is the realization that partners in a troubled relationship are suffering the effects of mutual alienation and bilateral disqualification. This immediately places the therapist on the side of each partner. Instead of being viewed as gratifying infantile impulses and as exploiting each other (and the therapist), these individuals are seen as deprived, trapped, and desperate.

The second principle is the image of the ideal relationship as consisting of two general states. In one state, partners are able to abandon themselves to the passions and promptings of the moment. When they feel troubled by

---

*The approach developed in this book can be considered in a sense as a reaction to this experience and an attempt to design a therapy that might have been more helpful to Dick and Susan.

a particular interaction, however, they are then able to shift to a second state in which they can talk to each other about the relationship.

The third principle is the view of intimate relations as encompassing rather than excluding. The goal of this therapy is not to renounce wishes, end fighting, force compromises, and solve problems but to enable partners to incorporate their fantasies, arguments, and differences into the relationship.

The three principles are interdependent. It is the ability of partners to step back from troubled interactions (principle 2) and to sympathize with their respective positions (principle 1) that may enable them to incorporate their problems into the relationship (principle 3).

The symptomatic or "irrational" reactions of partners are pictured here as having a hidden rationality, as saying something important and valid about the individuals' present relationship and about relationships in general. These couples are experiencing particularly clear forms of the problems that underlie everyone's relationships. While subject to considerable conflict, they at least avoid the subtle and insidious alienation that forms between partners who overlook or deny these problems.

This approach to couples therapy has several implications for individual therapy. First, it raises questions about the traditional psychoanalytic method. In classical analysis the therapist remains neutral while the client acts out his or her infantile wishes and conflicts. These pathological elements are then demonstrated to the client, worked through, and resolved. The problem with this paradigm, from my point of view, is that it typically shows the client to be distorting. The therapist's objective, in fact, is to demonstrate the inappropriateness of the individuals' reactions—that is, to relate them to an earlier era. Since the therapist is thought to be neutral, nearly everything the client feels about the therapist is seen as a displacement or projection. My view is that clients' reactions have a hidden appropriateness and validity. Rather than, or in addition to, demonstrating them as distortions, I show how these responses and feelings may be pointing to an important reality. If a client feels abandoned, rejected, or criticized by the therapist, I consider the possibility that this therapist may be abandoning, rejecting, or critical in ways that he or she may not realize.

A second implication for individual therapy concerns the therapist's attitude toward a client's reports of problems with his or her partner. It is easy in listening to such accounts to conclude that one or the other is at fault. My approach protects against this. If the client, let us say a husband, condemns himself for the problem, it is possible to point out that his apparent "offensive" or "irrational" behavior might be indicating an important truth about the relationship. The situation is similar if he blames his wife. Although I would not interfere with his doing this and might help him consider why he is not responding more directly to her apparent provocation, I would bear in mind that her "irrational" behavior might itself have a hidden validity.

A third implication for individual therapy concerns the therapist's understanding of resistance. A traditional view is that clients are obtaining too much regressive gratification from their pathological patterns to be willing to give them up. I would argue that they are generally getting very little from them. What may appear superficially to be "resistance to the therapy" I view as an understandable consequence of inhibition, pessimism, or desperation or a reaction to the perhaps subtle coercion or moralizing of the therapist.

References

Ables, B. S., & Brandsma, J. M. *Therapy for couples: A clinician's guide for effective treatment.* San Francisco: Jossey-Bass, 1977.

Ackerman, B. L. Relational paradox: Toward a language of interactional sequences. *Journal of Marital and Family Therapy,* 1979, **5** (1), 29-38.

Ackerman, N. W. *Treating the troubled family.* New York: Basic, 1966.

Alberti, R. E., & Emmons, M. L. Assertion training in marital counseling. *Journal of Marriage and Family Counseling,* 1976, **2,** 49-54.

Alexander, F., & French, T. M. (Eds.) *Psychoanalytic therapy.* New York: Ronald, 1946.

Apfelbaum, B. On the etiology of sexual dysfunction. *Journal of Sex and Marital Therapy,* 1977a, **3,** 50-62.

Apfelbaum, B. A contribution to the development of the behavioral-analytic model. *Journal of Sex and Marital Therapy,* 1977b, **3,** 128-138.

Apfelbaum, B. Beyond Dysfunction: A new look at sexuality. Workshop given in Los Angeles. March 1980a. Available on tape. Berkeley Sex Therapy Group.

Apfelbaum, B. Why we should not accept sexual fantasies. In B. Apfelbaum, M. H. Williams, S. E. Greene, & C. Apfelbaum, *Expanding the boundaries of sex therapy: Selected papers of the Berkeley Sex Therapy Group,* rev. ed. 2614 Telegraph Avenue, Berkeley, CA 94704, 1980b, pp. 101-108.

Apfelbaum, B. Ego analysis versus depth analysis. In B. Apfelbaum, M. H. Williams, S. E. Greene, & C. Apfelbaum, *Expanding the boundaries of sex therapy: Selected papers of the Berkeley Sex Therapy Group.* rev. ed. 2614 Telegraph Avenue, Berkeley, CA 94704, 1980c, pp. 9-36, 47-55, 82-83, 101-102, 194.

Apfelbaum, B., & Apfelbaum, C. Encountering encounter groups: A reply to Koch and Haigh. *Journal of Humanistic Psychology,* 1973, **13,** 53-67.

Apfelbaum, B., Williams, M. H., Greene, S. E., & Apfelbaum, C. *Expanding the boundaries of sex therapy: Selected papers of the Berkeley Sex Therapy Group,* rev. ed. 2614 Telegraph Avenue, Berkeley, CA 94704, 1980.

Bach, G. R., & Goldberg, H. *Creative aggression.* New York: Doubleday, 1974.

Bach, G. R., & Wyden, P. *The intimate enemy: How to fight fair in love and marriage.* New York: William Morrow, 1969.

Barnett, J. Narcissism and dependency in the obsessional-hysteric marriage. *Family Process,* 1971, **10,** 75-83.

Bateson, G. A systems approach. *International Journal of Psychiatry,* 1971, **9,** 242-244.

Bateson, G. Comments on Haley's history. In C. Sluzki & D. C. Ransom (Eds.), *Double bind: The foundation of the communicational approach to the family.* New York: Grune & Stratton, 1976, pp. 105-106.

Bateson, G., Jackson, D. D., Haley, J., & Weakland, J. H. Toward a theory of schizophrenia. *Behavioral Science,* 1956, **1**, 251–264.

Beels, C. C., & Ferber, A. Family therapy: A view. *Family Process,* 1969, **8**, 280–318.

Benedek, T. Control of the transference relationship. In F. Alexander & T.M. French (Eds.), *Psychoanalytic therapy.* New York: Ronald, 1946.

Berne, E. *Games people play.* New York: Grove, 1964.

Boszormenyi-Nagy, I. Contextual therapy: Therapeutic leverages in mobilizing trust. In Smith, Kline & French, *The American Family.* Philadelphia, 1979. Unit IV, Report Number 2.

Bowen, M. Toward the differentiation of a self in one's own family. In J. L. Framo (Ed.), *Family interaction: A dialogue between family researchers and family therapists.* New York: Springer, 1972, pp. 111–173. Published under the name anonymous.

Bowen, M. Principles and techniques of multiple family therapy. In M. Bowen, *Family therapy in clinical practice.* New York: Jason Aronson, 1978, pp. 241–257.

Breuer, J., & Freud, S. Studies in hysteria. *Standard edition,* Vol. 2. London: Hogarth, 1955, pp. 1–251. Originally published in 1895.

Bricklin, B. Letter in response to Charny's *Marital love and hate.* In I. Charny, *Marital love and hate.* New York: Macmillan, 1972, pp. 180–182.

Bursten, B. *The manipulator: A psychoanalytic view.* New Haven: Yale University Press, 1973.

Charny, I. *Marital love and hate.* New York: Macmillan, 1972.

Cuber, J.F., & Harroff, P. B. *Sex and the significant Americans: A study of sexual behavior among the affluent.* New York: Penguin, 1965.

Dayringer, R. Fair-fight for change: A therapeutic use of aggressiveness in couple counseling. *Journal of Marriage and Family Counseling,* 1976, **2**, 131–137.

Dicks, H. V. *Marital tension.* New York: Basic, 1967.

Ellis, A. Neurotic interaction between marital partners. *Journal of Counseling Psychology,* 1958. **5**, 24–28.

Ellis, A. *Reason and emotion in psychotherapy.* New York: Lyle Stuart, 1962.

Ellis, A. Techniques of handling anger in marriage. *Journal of Marriage and Family Counseling,* 1976, **2**, 305–315.

Fenichel, O. *Problems of psychoanalytic technique.* New York: Psychoanalytic Quarterly, 1941.

Ferreira, A. J. Family myth and homeostasis. *Archives of General Psychiatry,* 1963, **9**, 457–463.

Fisch, R. Review of Palazzoli et al., 1978. *Family Process,* 1979, **18**, 213–214.

Fogarty, T. F. Marital crisis. In P. J. Guerin (Ed.), *Family therapy: Theory and practice.* New York: Wiley, 1976, pp. 144–153.

Fogarty, T. F. The distancer and the pursuer. *The Family,* 1979, **7**, 11–16.

Framo, J. L. Rationale and technique of intensive family therapy. In I. Boszormenyi-Nagy & J. L. Framo (Eds.), *Intensive family therapy: Theoretical and practical aspects. New York: Harper & Row, 1965, pp. 143–212.*

Framo, J. L. Family origin as a therapeutic resource for adults in marital and family therapy: You can and should go home again. *Family Process,* 1976, **15**, 193–210.

Freeman, D. S. The family as a system: Fact or fantasy? *Comprehensive Psychiatry,* 1976, **17**, 735–748.

Freud, S. Three essays on the theory of sexuality. *Standard edition,* Vol. 7. London: Hogarth, 1953, pp. 125-243. Originally published in 1905.

Freud, S. The dynamics of transference. *Standard edition,* Vol. 12. London: Hogarth, 1958, pp. 97-108. Originally published in 1912.

Freud, S. Remembering, repeating and working-through (Further recommendations on the technique of psycho-analysis II). *Standard edition,* Vol. 12. London: Hogarth, 1958, pp. 145-156. Originally published in 1914.

Freud, S. Introductory lectures on psychoanalysis, Part 3. *Standard edition,* Vol. 16. London: Hogarth, 1963. Originally published in 1917.

Freud, S. The psychogenesis of a case of homosexuality in a woman. *Standard edition,* Vol. 18. London: Hogarth, 1955, pp. 145-172. Originally published in 1920.

Freud, S. Analysis terminable and interminable. *Standard edition,* Vol. 23. London: Hogarth, 1964, pp. 209-257. Originally published in 1937.

Frey, J., Holley, J., & L'Abate, L. Intimacy is sharing hurt feelings: A comparison of three conflict resolution models. *Journal of Marital and Family Therapy,* 1979, **5** (2), 35-41.

Friedman, L. An examination of Jay Haley's Strategies of psychotherapy. *Psychotherapy: Theory, research & practice,* 1965, **2**, 181-188.

Fromm, E. *The anatomy of human destructiveness.* New York: Holt, Rinehart & Winston, 1973.

Gehrke, S., & Moxom, J. Diagnostic classification and treatment techniques in marital counseling. *Family Process,* 1962, **1**, 253-264.

Gordon, T. *Parent effectiveness training.* New York: New American Library, 1970.

Greenberg, G. S. The family interactional perspective: A study and examination of the work of Don D. Jackson. *Family Process,* 1977, **16**, 385-412.

Grunebaum, H., & Chasin, R. Relabeling and reframing reconsidered: The beneficial effects of a pathological label. *Family Process,* 1978, **17**, 449-455.

Guerin, P. Study your own family, Part I. In A. Ferber, M. Mendelsohn, & A. Napier (Eds.), *The book of family therapy.* New York: Science House, 1972, pp. 446-459.

Guerney, B. G., Collins, J. D., Ginsberg, B. G., & Vogelsong, E. *Relationship enhancement: Skill-training programs for therapy, problem prevention and enrichment.* San Francisco: Jossey-Bass, 1977.

Gurman, A. S. Contemporary marital therapies: A critique and comparative analysis of psychoanalytic, behavioral and systems theory approaches. In T. J. Paolino & B. S. McCrady (Eds.), *Marriage and marital therapy: Psychoanalytic, behavioral and systems theory perspectives.* New York: Brunner/Mazel, 1978, pp. 445-566.

Gurman, A. S., & Knudson, R. M. Behavioral marriage therapy. I. A psychodynamic-systems analysis and critique. *Family Process,* 1978, **17**, 121-138.

Haley, J. The family of the schizophrenic: A model system. *Journal of Nervous and Mental Disease,* 1959, **129**, 357-374.

Haley, J. Whither family therapy? *Family Process,* 1962, **1**, 69-100.

Haley, J. Marriage therapy. *Archives of General Psychiatry,* 1963a, **8**, 213-234.

Haley, J. *Strategies of psychotherapy.* New York: Grune & Stratton, 1963b.

Haley, J. Toward a theory of pathological systems. In G. H. Zuk & I. Boszormenyi-Nagy (Eds.), *Family therapy and disturbed families.* Palo Alto: Science & Behavior Books, 1967, pp. 11-27.

Haley, J. Family therapy. *International Journal of Psychiatry.* 1971, **9**, 233-242.

Haley, J. Development of a theory: A historical review of a research project. In C. Sluzki & D. C. Ransom (Eds.), *Double bind: The foundation of the communicational approach to the family.* New York: Grune & Stratton, 1976, pp. 59-104.

Haley, J. *Problem-solving therapy: New strategies for effective family therapy.* San Francisco: Jossey-Bass, 1977.

Haley, J., & Hoffman, L. *Techniques of family therapy.* New York: Basic, 1967.

Hiebert, W. J., & Stahmann, R. F. Commonly recurring couple interaction patterns. In R. F. Stahmann & W. J. Hiebert (Eds.), *Klemer's counseling in marital and sexual problems: A clinician's handbook,* 2nd ed. Baltimore: Williams & Wilkins, 1977, pp. 17-33.

Horney, K. *Our inner conflicts.* New York: Norton, 1945.

Jackson, D. D. The question of family homeostasis. *Psychiatric Quarterly Supplement,* 1957, **31**, (1), 79-90.

Jackson, D. D. Family interaction, family homeostasis and some implications for conjoint family psychotherapy. In J. H. Masserman (Ed.), *Individual and familial dynamics.* New York: Grune & Stratton, 1959.

Jackson, D. D. Family rules: Marital *quid pro quo. Archives of General Psychiatry,* 1965a, **12**, 589-594.

Jackson, D. D. The study of the family. *Family Process,* 1965b, **4**, 1-20.

Jackson, D. D. The individual and the larger contexts. *Family Process,* 1967, **6**, 139-154.

Jackson, D. D. Schizophrenia: The nosological nexis. In P. Watzlawick & J. H. Weakland (Eds.), *The interactional view.* New York: Norton, 1977, pp. 193-207.

Jackson, D. D., & Weakland, J. H. Conjoint family therapy: Some considerations of theory, technique, and results. *Psychiatry,* 1961, **24**, 30-45.

Jacobson, L. I. Communicating about communication: Review of three films about the Hillcrest family. *Contemporary Psychology,* 1979, **24**, 72-74.

Jacobson, N. S. Training couples to solve marital problems: A behavioral approach to relationship discord. Part I. Problem-solving skills. *International Journal of Family Counseling,* 1977, **5**, 22-31.

Jacobson, N. S. A stimulus control model of change in behavioral couples therapy: Implications for contingency contracting. *Journal of Marriage and Family Counseling,* 1978, **4** (3), 29-36.

Jacobson, N. S., & Margolin, G. *Marital therapy: Strategies based on social learning and behavior exchange principles.* New York: Brunner/Mazel, 1979.

Jungreis, J. E. The active role of the family therapist. In A. Friedman et al., *Psychotherapy for the whole family.* New York: Springer, 1965, pp. 187-196.

Kadis, A. L. A new approach to marital therapy. *International Journal of Social Psychiatry,* 1964, **10**, 261-265.

Kaplan, H. S. *The new sex therapy: Active treatment of sexual dysfunctions.* New York: Brunner/Mazel, 1974.

Keeney, B. P. Ecosystemic epistemology: An alternative paradigm for diagnosis. *Family Process,* 1979, **18**, 117-129.

Kempler, W. Experiential psychotherapy with families. *Family Process,* 1968, **7**, 88-99.

Koch, J., & Koch, L. *The marriage savers.* New York: Coward, McCann & Geoghegan, 1976.

Kubie, L. S. Psychoanalysis and marriage: Practical and theoretical issues. In V. W. Eisenstein (Ed.), *Neurotic interaction in marriage.* New York: Basic, 1956, pp. 10-43.

L'Abate, L. Intimacy is sharing hurt feelings: A reply to David Mace. *Journal of Marriage and Family Counseling,* 1977, **3** (2), 13-16.

Lantz, J. E. Extreme itching treated by a family systems approach. *International Journal of Family Therapy, 1979,* **1**, 244-253.

Lederer, W. J., & Jackson, D. D. *The mirages of marriage.* New York: Norton, 1968.

Lester, G. W., Beckham, E., & Baucom, D. H. Implementation of behavioral marital therapy. *Journal of Marital and Family Therapy,* 1980, **6**, 189-199.

Levant, R. F. Family therapy: A client centered approach. *Journal of Marriage and Family Counseling,* 1978, **4** (2), 35-42.

Liberman, R. P. Behavioral approaches to family and couple therapy. *American Journal of Orthopsychiatry,* 1970, **40**, 106-118.

Lloyd, R. A., & Paulson, I. Projective identification in the marital relationship as a resistance in psychotherapy. *Archives of General Psychiatry,* 1972, **27**, 410-413.

Lorenz, K. *On aggression.* New York: Harcourt Brace, 1966.

Mace, D. R. Marriage as relationship-in-depth: Some implications for counseling. In H. L. Silverman (Ed.), *Marital therapy: Psychological, sociological and moral factors.* Springfield, Ill.: Charles C. Thomas, 1972, pp. 159-177.

Mace, D. R. Marital intimacy and the deadly love-anger cycle. *Journal of Marriage and Family Counseling,* 1976, **2**, 131-137.

Mahler, M. S. *On human symbiosis and the vicissitudes of Individuation,* Vol. 1. *Infantile psychosis.* New York: International Universities Press, 1968.

Margolin, G. Contingency contracting in behavioral marriage therapy. *The American Journal of Family Therapy,* 1980, **8**(3), 71-74.

Margolin, G., & Weiss, R. L. Comparative evaluation of therapeutic components associated with behavioral marital treatments. *Journal of Consulting and Clinical Psychology,* 1978, **46**, 1476-1486.

Martin, P. A. *A marital therapy manual.* New York: Brunner/Mazel, 1976.

Meissner, W. W. The conceptualization of marriage from a psychoanalytic perspective. In T. . Paolino & B. S. McCrady (Eds.), *Marriage and marital therapy: Psychoanalytic, behavioral and systems theory perspectives.* New York: Brunner/Mazel, 1978, pp. 25-88.

Minuchin, S. *Families and family therapy.* Cambridge, Mass.: Harvard University Press, 1974.

Minuchin, S., Montalvo, B., Guerney, B. G., Rosman, B. L., & Schumer, F. *Families of the slums.* New York: Basic, 1967.

Mittelmann, B. Analysis of reciprocal neurotic patterns in family relationships. In V. W. Eisenstein (Ed.), *Neurotic interaction in marriage.* New York: Basic, 1956.

Mowrer, O. H. "Sin," the lesser of two evils. *American Psychologist,* 1960, **15**, 301-304.

Murray, J. Narcissism and the ego ideal. *Journal of the American Psychoanalytic Association,* 1964, **12**, 477-511.

Nadelson, C. C. Marital therapy from a psychoanalytic perspective. In T. J. Paolino & B. S. McCrady (Eds.), *Marriage and marital therapy: Psychoanalytic, behavioral and systems theory perspectives.* New York: Brunner/Mazel, 1978, pp. 101-164.

Napier, A. Y. The rejection-intrusion pattern: A central family dynamic. *Journal of Marriage and Family Counseling,* 1978, **4**(1), 5-12.

O'Leary, K. D., & Turkewitz, H. Marital therapy from a behavioral perspective. In T. J. Paolino & B. S. McCrady (Eds.), *Marriage and marital therapy: Psychoanalytic, behavioral and systems theory perspectives.* New York: Brunner/Mazel, 1978, pp. 240-297.

Olson, D. H., Sprenkle, D. H., Russell, C. Circumplex model of marital and family systems: I. Cohesion and adaptability dimensions, family types, and clinical applications, *Family Process,* 1979, **18,** 3-28.

Palazzoli, M. S., Cecchin, G. F., Prata, G., & Boscola, L. *Paradox and counterparadox.* New York: Jason Aronson, 1978.

Paolino, T. J., & McCrady, B. S. (Eds.), *Marriage and marital therapy: Psychoanalytic, behavioral and systems theory perspectives.* New York: Brunner/Mazel, 1978.

Patterson, G. R. Foreword. In N. S. Jacobson & G. Margolin, *Marital therapy: Strategies based on social learning and behavior exchange principles.* New York: Brunner/Mazel, 1979, pp. v-vii.

Plum, A. Communication as skill: A critique and alternative approach. *Journal of Humanistic Psychology,* in press.

Ransom, D. C. Love, love problems, and family therapy. In K. S. Pope (Ed.), *On love and loving: Psychological perspectives on the nature and experience of romantic love.* San Francisco: Jossey-Bass, 1980, pp. 244-265.

Rappaport, A. F., & Harrell, J. A behavioral-exchange model for marital counseling. *Family Coordinator,* 1972, **21,** 203-212.

Rubenstein, D., & Timmins, J. F. Depressive dyadic and triadic relationship. *Journal of Marriage and Family Counseling,* 1978. 4(1), 13-24.

Sager, C. J. Transference in conjoint treatment for married couples. *Archives of General Psychiatry,* 1967, **16,** 185-193.

Sager, C. J. *Marriage contracts and couple therapy: Hidden forces in intimate relationships.* New York: Brunner/Mazel, 1976.

Sager, C. J., Kaplan, H. S., Gundlach, R. H., Kremer, M., Lenz, R., & Royce, J. R. The marriage contract. *Family Process,* 1971, **10,** 311-326.

Satir, V. *Conjoint family therapy,* rev. ed. Palo Alto: Science & Behavior Books, 1967.

Satir, V. A humanistic approach. *International Journal of Psychiatry,* 1971, **9,** 245-246.

Satir, V. *Peoplemaking.* Palo Alto: Science & Behavior Books, 1972.

Scheflen, A. E. Regressive one-to-one relationships. *Psychiatric Quarterly,* 1960, **34,** 692-709.

Shostrum, E. *Man, the manipulator: The inner journey from manipulation to actualization.* Nashville: Abingdon, 1967.

Sluzki, C. E. Marital therapy from a systems theory perspective. In T. J. Paolino & B. S. McCrady (Eds.), *Marriage and marital therapy: Psychoanalytic, behavioral and systems theory perspectives.* New York: Brunner/Mazel, 1978, pp. 366-394.

Sluzki, C. E., Beavin, J., Tarnopolsky, A., & Veron, E. Transactional disqualification. *Archives of General Psychiatry,* 1967, **16,** 494-504.

Speck, R. V. Some specific therapeutic techniques with schizophrenic families. In A. Friedman et al., *Psychotherapy for the whole family.* New York: Springer, 1965, pp. 197-205.

Speer, D. C. Family systems: Morphostasis and morphogenesis, or "Is homeostasis enough?" *Family Process,* 1970, **9,** 259-278.

Steinglass, P. The conceptualization of marriage from a systems theory perspective. In T. J. Paolino & B. S. McCrady (Eds.), *Marriage and marital therapy: Psychoanalytic, behavioral and systems theory perspectives.* New York: Brunner/Mazel, 1978, pp. 298-365.

Strayhorn, J. M. Social-exchange theory: Cognitive restructuring in marital therapy. *Family Process,* 1978, **17,** 437-448.

Stuart, R. B. Operant-interpersonal treatment for marital discord. *Journal of Consulting and Clinical Psychology,* 1969, **33**, 675-682.

Stuart, R. B. Behavioral remedies for marital ills: A guide to the use of operant-interpersonal techniques. In A. S. Gurman & D. G. Rice (Eds.), *Couples in conflict: New directions in marital therapy.* New York: Jason Aronson, 1975, pp. 241-257.

Stuart, R. B. An operant interpersonal program for couples. In D. H. Olson (Ed.), *Treating relationships.* Lake Mills, Iowa: Graphic Publishing, 1976, pp. 119-132.

Taggart, M. Abstracts. *Journal of Marital and Family Therapy.* 1979, **5**(2), 97-100.

Wachtel, P. L. An interpersonal alternative. *In psychoanalysis and behavior therapy: Toward an integration.* New York: Basic, 1977, pp. 41-63.

Watzlawick, P., Beavin, J. H., and Jackson, D. D. *Pragmatics of human communication: A study of interactional patterns, pathologies, and paradoxes.* New York: Norton, 1967.

Watzlawick, P., Weakland, J. H., & Fisch, R. *Change: Principles of problem formation and problem resolution.* New York: Norton, 1974.

Weiss, R. L. Contracts, cognition, and change: A behavioral approach to marriage therapy. *The Counseling Psychologist,* 1975, **5**(3), 15-26.

Weiss, R. L. The conceptualization of marriage from a behavioral perspective. In T. J. Paolino & B. S. McCrady (Eds.), *Marriage and marital therapy: Psychoanalytic, behavioral and systems theory perspectives.* New York: Brunner/Mazel, 1978, pp. 165-239.

Weiss, R. L. Resistance in behavioral marriage therapy. *American Journal of Family Therapy,* 1979, **7**(2), 3-6.

Weiss, R. L., & Margolin, G. Marital conflict and accord. In A. R. Ciminero, K. S. Calhoun, & H. E. Adams (Eds.), *Handbook for behavioral assessment.* New York: Wiley, 1977, pp. 555-602.

Weiss, R. L., Birchler, G. R., & Vincent, J. P. Contractual models for negotiation training in marital dyads. *Journal of Marriage and the Family,* 1974, **36**, 321-330.

Weiss, R. L., Hops, H., & Patterson, G. R. A framework for conceptualizing marital conflict: A technology for altering it, some data for evaluating it. In L. A. Hamerlynch, L. C. Handy, & J. Mash (Eds.), *Behavior change: Methodology, concepts and practice.* Champaign, Ill.: Research Press, 1973, pp. 309-343.

Wertheim, E. S. Family unit therapy and the science and typology of family systems. *Family Process,* 1973, **12**, 361-376.

Whitaker, C. A. Comment to presentation by anonymous. In J. L. Framo (Ed.), *Family interaction: A dialogue between family researchers and family therapists.* New York: Springer, 1972, p. 169.

Whitaker, C. A. A family therapist looks at marital therapy. In A. S. Gurman & D. G. Rice (Eds.), *Couples in conflict: New directions in marital therapy.* New York: Jason Aronson, 1975, pp. 165-174.

Wile, D. B. Is a confrontational tone necessary in conjoint therapy? *Journal of Marriage and Family Counseling,* 1978, **4**(3), 11-18.

Wile, D. B. An insight approach to marital therapy. *Journal of Marital and Family Therapy,* 1979, **5**(4), 43-52.

Zuk, G. H. Family therapy: Formulation of a technique and its theory. *International Journal of Group Psychotherapy,* 1968, **18**, 42-58.

Index

Ables, B., 18, 24-25, 67, 70, 72, 86, 89-90, 98, 102, 105-107, 114-116, 161-163, 172, 194, 205-206
Ackerman, B. L., 124
Ackerman, N. W., 29, 41
Adversary relationship:
  between partners, 4, 179
  between therapist and partners, vi-vii, ix, 28-30, 35-36, 64, 97-102
Alberti, R. E., 12, 155, 170
Alexander, F., 97
Anger:
  encouraging suppression of, 60-61, 169-172
  hidden desperation behind, 180
  incorporating, ix, 4, 61, 171-181, 211
  intrapsychic vs. interpersonal, 167
  recovery from, 138, 142-143, 171, 176-179, 208
Apfelbaum, B., 2, 4, 5, 9, 15, 25, 46, 55, 69, 70, 75-77, 94, 108, 110, 140, 145, 151, 164, 194, 200, 202, 207
Apfelbaum, C., 4, 7, 55, 70, 110
Arenas of comfort, 95
Assertion training, 12-13, 155, 157, 170
Assignments, 102, 107-108

Bach, G. R., 65-67, 155, 168, 170-172, 174-175, 177
Barnett, J., 66
Bateson, G., 27, 30, 32-34
Beavin, J. H., 30
Beels, C. C., 29

Behavioral exchange, see Contingency contracting
Behavior therapy approach:
  and change vs. understanding, 47-52, 54-59, 96, 99-100, 177-178, 184
  and cognitive restructuring, 46, 50-57, 96, 102
  and communication skills training, 57-61
  and contingency contracting, 3, 46-51, 57, 72-73, 183-184
  contribution and elegance of, 47, 64, 72
  disqualification in, 48-60, 102
  and forced solutions, vi, 46, 48-61, 64
  and inadequate behavioral analysis, 46-61, 64
  and moralizing, 46, 50, 52-53, 55, 59, 64, 102
  and positive reinforcement, 3, 46-50, 59-61, 72, 107
  and resistance, 50, 58-59, 102, 107-108
  and skills deficits and faulty habits, 56-57, 59
  and suppressing anger, 60-61, 102, 169
  and transforming insight into imperative, 54-56, 59
Benedek, T., 97-98
Berne, E., 8-9, 11, 29
Birchler, G. R., 46
Blanck, G., 5
Blanck, R., 5
Boszormenji-Nagy, I., 29
Bowen, M., 18, 27, 38-45, 89, 96, 107, 114-115